Wakefield Press

Derek Pedley is a journalist with more than 25 years' experience at Australian newspapers. He is now engaged in the dark art of daily news production at *The Advertiser* and adelaidenow.com.au. His second book, *Australian Outlaw – The True Story of Postcard Bandit Brenden Abbott*, was shortlisted for the 2007 Ned Kelly Award for Best True Crime. Pedley lives in Adelaide's far northern suburbs, on the wrong side of the Mullet-Proof Fence.

Praise for *Dead by Friday*

"A masterpiece of true crime … this unputdownable book has galvanised me into sleepless, haunted nights."
– Peter Goers, *Sunday Mail*

"Unprecedented insight into a case that captivated Adelaide."
– Sean Fewster, author of *City of Evil*

"An amazing read, a phenomenal story."
– Ali Clarke, Triple M Hot Breakfast, Adelaide

"Pedley looks behind the headlines and tells a disturbing but unfortunately all-too-true story … compelling and all too real."
– Chris Herde, *Daily Telegraph*

By the same author

No Fixed Address – The Hunt for Brenden James Abbott
(HarperCollins, 1999)

Australian Outlaw – The True Story of Postcard Bandit Brenden Abbott
(Sly Ink, 2006)

HOW LUST AND GREED LED TO MURDER IN THE SUBURBS

DEREK PEDLEY

Wakefield Press

Wakefield Press
16 Rose Street
Mile End
South Australia 5031
www.wakefieldpress.com.au

First published 2012 by Derek Pedley
Wakefield Press edition first published 2013
This edition published 2020

Copyright © Derek Pedley, 2012, 2013, 2020

All rights reserved. This book is copyright. Apart from any fair dealing for the purposes of private study, research, criticism or review, as permitted under the Copyright Act, no part may be reproduced without written permission. Enquiries should be addressed to the publisher.

Cover design by Paul Harnett
Cover photograph by Michael Milnes, *Advertiser*
Typeset in ITC Giovanni

ISBN 978 1 74305 781 0

 Wakefield Press thanks Coriole Vineyards for continued support

Contents

PROLOGUE
Public meeting: January 2001 — x

CHAPTER 1
Missy: July 25, 1963 – 2000 — 1

CHAPTER 2
Darren and Michelle: February 1989 – June 2000 — 10

CHAPTER 3
Suspicion, sex and room service: 2000 – July 2001 — 21

CHAPTER 4
Contracts to kill: February 2001 — 45

CHAPTER 5
David William Edgar Key, hitman: July 1, 2001 – July 11, 2001 — 51

CHAPTER 6
Carolyn's last day, Part I: July 12, 2001 — 66

CHAPTER 7
Carolyn's last day, Part II: July 12, 2001 — 84

CHAPTER 8
The hunt begins: July 13, 2001 – July 19, 2001 — 103

CHAPTER 9
The funeral: July 19, 2001 – July 20, 2001 — 117

CHAPTER 10
　　You're going to go down for it: July 21, 2001 – July 26, 2001   127

CHAPTER 11
　　Interrogations: July 27, 2001 – August 2, 2001   143

CHAPTER 12
　　Forever: August 3, 2001 – August 6, 2001   158

CHAPTER 13
　　Kev and Jase: August 7, 2001 – August 29, 2001   181

CHAPTER 14
　　The third offender: September 1, 2001 – September 26, 2001   203

CHAPTER 15
　　Payback's a bitch: December 7, 2001 – August 10, 2002   217

CHAPTER 16
　　On trial: August 13, 2003 – October 9, 2003   231

CHAPTER 17
　　Screwing the screws: 2003 – 2004   242

CHAPTER 18
　　Justice   248

CHAPTER 19
　　Profile of a killer   264

Acknowledgements

I AM GRATEFUL to the many people and organisations whose co-operation and assistance allowed this story to be told.

Yvonne Tidswell and her grandsons, Kenny, Shane and Daniel, agreed to relive the most painful chapter of their lives, in the hope that their daughter and mother Carolyn would receive the recognition she deserved. Their extended family also provided crucial information.

Michelle Burgess's ex-husband Darren Burgess spoke at length for the first time about his ordeal, motivated only by his need for the truth to be told.

I am particularly thankful to Arts SA for the significant funding they provided when the book was in its early research stage, through their Independent Makers and Presenters program.

The book was produced with the kind co-operation of South Australia Police. Sergeant Nicole Lycett, from SAPOL's Corporate Communications Branch, and the officers of the Major Crime Investigation Section, including Detective Sergeant (retired) Mick Standing, Detective Sergeant John Keane and Detective Senior Sergeant Michael Eichner, all made significant contributions.

My colleagues at *The Advertiser* played an integral role in the research, writing and editing of this book. News Ltd State Editorial Director Melvin Mansell provided crucial support. Amy Noonan was an invaluable adviser, editor and counsellor and Kate Kyriacou provided insight and advice. The book also draws on the reporting of many other respected colleagues, including Simonne Reid, Nigel Hunt, Sean Fewster and Michael Owen-Brown. Graphic designer Paul Harnett produced a fantastic cover design and current and former *Advertiser* photographers kindly granted permission to republish their photographs. Many of the images were taken by courts photographer Michael Milnes.

Andrew Rule generously provided sage advice and incisive editing.

Special thanks to Wakefield Press publisher Michael Bollen, for supporting this book and so many other South Australian stories and writers, and to Gunta Groves, for applying her razor-sharp editing skills to the final manuscript.

Thanks also to Minter Ellison partner Andrew Short for his crucial legal advice. South Australian Attorney-General John Rau kindly granted permission for the reproduction of material from the murder trial transcripts.

Forensic psychologist Dr Jack White committed many hours to analysing Michelle Burgess, enabling him to create the extraordinary "profile of a killer" that forms the final chapter of this book.

Some names have been changed for legal reasons. Conversations are based on police recordings, court transcripts and the memories of people involved. No payments were made to any people interviewed for this book.

And most importantly, thank you to my wonderful family – wife Belinda, our children and my mother Phyllis – for their love, patience and loyalty, which allowed me to spend so much time pursuing this story.

Derek Pedley
Adelaide, South Australia

*"Hell has three gates –
lust, anger and greed."*

Bhagavad Gita

Prologue
Public meeting
January 2001

COREY BAYLISS stopped in his tracks. The young mechanic had been about to pluck mail from the letterbox at the front of the home he shared with his mother in Oakden, in Adelaide's north-eastern suburbs, when the car parked across the road caught his eye; he immediately recognised it as the company car of his former boss, Beaurepaires regional manager Kevin Matthews.

Matthews had recruited Corey, who was 25, as assistant manager at City Discount Tyres in Norwood. But just a few weeks earlier, in December 2000, Corey had been forced to quit because of injuries he had suffered in a car crash. Corey assumed Matthews, whose office was only a few streets away in Windsor Gardens, must be looking for him, but had no idea why.

"Kevin?" he called out.

The metallic-grey Ford Falcon, with a distinctive blue and white JMJ sticker on the back window, was empty and no one was nearby. Curious, he went back inside and up to his mother's bedroom, to peer out the window to the expansive view of Roy Amer Reserve, where the car was parked. Between the path and the park's artificial lake, he caught the unforgettable sight of Kevin Matthews, regional manager of Beaurepaires, a former Semaphore Surf Life Saving Club president and married father of three, sprawled on the grass with a blonde woman riding him like the favourite in the home straight at Morphettville racecourse.

Looking away only to key in the numbers, Corey called Troy Cook, the manager of Beaurepaires at Edwardstown, and sat on the floor of his mother's room, mesmerised, watching the blonde jockey approach the finishing post while he talked.

"G'day, how are ya, Troy? Kevin Matthews is out the front of my place having cuddles with this woman. Do you know what his wife looks like?"

"Why? What's going on? What's happening? Why do you need to know?" Cook replied, immediately cautious.

"I live near Kevin's office at Windsor Gardens. Across from my place there's a park with parking bays and a lake. Kevin's car is there and he's having cuddles with some chick."

Cook, who was friendly with Kevin, was initially evasive. Corey knew he was on to something, so he pressed him: "What does Kevin's wife look like? Is she a bit younger than him? Is she a bit chubby with shoulder-length, blondish hair?"

"No, she's not really young and she's not really chubby," Cook admitted.

"They're having pretty decent cuddles. She's sitting on top of him and the way that they're cuddling, they don't look like husband and wife."

Cook was well aware of Kevin's extra-curricular activities. He was at Kevin's 40th birthday party in November 2000 and had noted just how "cuddly" Kevin had been with his "new best friend" Michelle Burgess. But he still very much doubted that Kevin was having public sex with her; a quick phone call would sort it all out.

"Hey, hang on a minute – he should be in the office. He'll have his mobile with him. I'll ring him."

Bayliss listened in, intrigued, as Cook placed the call on the other line, watching as the man in the park scrambled around for his phone.

"G'day Kev, it's Troy. Where are you at the moment? Have you got a moment to have a chat?"

Cook says Matthews told him: "I'm at a service station, just stopped to get some gas. I'm only five minutes from the office. Why?"

"Oh, no worries, I'll see you later. Somebody I know thought they'd seen you."

They ended the call and Cook relayed their conversation to Bayliss. But Cook felt uncomfortable about deceiving Kevin so, a short while later, he called him back and told him the truth. Matthews reacted badly and hung up but, a few minutes later, his curiosity got the better of him and he called back to admit that he had been in the park. He claimed the woman with him was Michelle's sister and they had been discussing solutions to Michelle's marital problems with husband Darren. He demanded to know who had seen him in the park but Cook stood firm, refusing to reveal his source. Later, Cook confronted him about his relationship with Michelle but he denied there was one.

Bayliss, who had no doubts about where Kevin Matthews was that day, continued watching the couple in the park. The phone call extinguished their passion and soon they both headed for their cars. Bayliss mentioned the incident to his mother, explaining that he'd seen his former boss in the park carrying on with a woman who wasn't his wife. Sandra Bayliss had also noticed them on other occasions. She later told police that over a two to three month period in early 2001, she saw the same couple on five to six occasions: "I don't know who they were, they just looked like two people secretly meeting."

She particularly recalled three "clandestine, unusual" lunchtime meetings. The first time, they parked their cars and the woman approached the man, standing on tiptoes to give him a kiss. On the second occasion, Ms Bayliss saw them seated at a table in the park leaning towards each other. On the third occasion, as she was driving home from the shops, she saw them hugging.

Later that year, a picture in *The Advertiser* newspaper caught her eye. She showed it to her son and told him he was the man from the park. It confirmed what her son had seen that day – the man in the picture was Kevin Matthews.

Chapter 1

Missy
July 25, 1963 – 2000

THE BROCHURE made it sound perfect – a new estate in a "very convenient location", just three miles from Adelaide, a ten-minute drive to the beach and only 100 yards from the local school. And the blocks were priced from just £1250.

It was 1963 and Doug and Yvonne Tidswell were a young married couple with a five-year-old son and a baby on the way; for them, it *was* perfect.

Doug, who was working as a mechanic at a garage on nearby Marion Rd, had heard about it through his boss. Yvonne immediately warmed to the idea; there were several variations of the brick and tile homes, but she liked the colonial best.

Like most Adelaide suburbs, Netley is small, no more than a handful of streets. Kangaroo Island resident Thomas Hudson Bear acquired the area in 1838, naming it after Netley Abbey in Hampshire, his home county on England's southern coast. Despite its proximity to the city, it remained virtually rural up until the 1950s, with orchards, dairies, poultry farms, piggeries and market gardens dotted across the landscape.

The brochure trumpeting the suburb's many qualities failed to mention one other important fact – to the west, Netley was bounded by Adelaide Airport. But like the Kerrigans, of cult Australian film *The Castle*, the Tidswells could see only the positives, the serenity.

Doug and Yvonne had met at a dance and hit it off instantly; he was at trade school, on his way to being a motor mechanic. They married in 1955, both aged 18, and son Geoffrey arrived 18 months later.

They moved out of a rental in Camden Park and into their new home at Netley, a £4500 house and land package, on Armistice Day, 1962. Yvonne was pregnant with her beloved first and only daughter, Carolyn Wendy Tidswell, who was born on July 25, 1963, the tail end of the baby boom.

She entered the world a week before Kaylene Kenyon, who lived across the road. The girls and their friends would be part of a mini-boom within the boom. Nine children were born from June to November 1963 across a handful of homes in the street.

"She was a good baby; I always wanted another girl," Yvonne remembers, more than 45 years later. "Geoff called her Miss Muffet from when she was very young and the name stuck; she was always Missy to the family."

In the next six years, three more boys followed – Glenn, Peter and Christopher, known as Charlie.

Charlie says: "I can remember all the things Missy used to get up to. She copped a bit of shit, being the only girl with four brothers. She'd always be arguing with us boys."

But she soon found allies; Carolyn, Kaylene and a third girl, Christine Nixon, became inseparable. Christine lived on the corner, Kaylene lived across the road and Carolyn lived two doors down. Christine, with three brothers, and Carolyn, with four, had much in common.

Christine says: "She would come to my grandparents' every Sunday, because every Sunday she'd automatically end up at our place. Either I'd be sleeping at her house or she'd be at mine. We got up to all sorts of mischief."

The three girls did calisthenics together from the age of three for about 10 years, followed by a year of netball. Kaylene stuck with netball, but Christine chose basketball and Carolyn focused on life saving. At school they found new friends, but their special connection remained rock-solid.

Kaylene remembers countless hours at Carolyn's home, fossicking around with clips and brushes in her bedroom, and being outside and running around with her younger brothers. Carolyn accompanied the Kenyon family on a holiday at Beachport in the South-East, and there were a couple of combined family holidays to the Coorong, where the dads would go off fishing together, while the kids would swim and play and get into mischief.

Once a year in January, the entire street would head off to Belair National Park for a street picnic, where the dads would play tennis and the kids would go adventuring, finding caves, following paths and climbing trees. On one occasion, the girls got stuck in a tree and the Tidswell boys had to come to their rescue.

Kaylene remembers a street that became a cricket pitch, where cars would always stop if an over was in progress. She says: "We had a ball growing up in that neighbourhood. It was a very different time to grow up."

Christine says they dressed as penguins for their first calisthenics concert and were leaving the stage after their performance when the trio spotted their dads. "We stopped on stage together and were yelling out 'dad dad dad' to the audience," she says.

Around the age of four, Christine and Carolyn decided to do some "cooking" with Yvonne's best gold tea set, using flour, milk and baby powder on a black goat-skin rug. Christine says: "Our mums didn't know whether to laugh or cry. So they took some photos. I don't think we were yelled at. In one of the photos, Carolyn has a mischievous look on her face, as if to say: 'Oh I'm busted, but it's been fun.'"

The girls would delight in tormenting Carolyn's younger brother Glenn. On one occasion, as Christine and Carolyn were fleeing his retribution, they closed the glass-panel door to the kitchen as he pursued them with the garden hose. As they stood on the other side pulling faces, safe from the water, he sprayed the door and soaked the laundry full of clean clothes. "We were terrors … such good memories," Christine smiles.

The girls remained close until their mid-teens. Before she took up basketball, Christine tagged along with Carolyn when she became a Nipper at the Glenelg Surf Life Saving Club.

They would walk to Netley Demonstration School together each day. At the end of Year 7, they all got new bikes and would ride to Plympton High School. When it rained, they would pile into the Kenyon family's car and Kaylene's mum would drop them off. Christine remembers playing cricket and chasey in the street until dusk, until her dad whistled and it was time to go home. Everyone knew everyone. She says: "It was such a free time. The childhood we had together was full of fun, laughter and love, it's something I will cherish forever."

Yvonne Tidswell says her daughter didn't like sewing, but found herself sewing curtains because a friend who lived three doors down had a curtain business and planned to offer her an apprenticeship. But the friend moved to Perth, so Carolyn continued working with her mother. Yvonne says: "The first job she got was out at Kent Town and then she came to work with me at Martine's after about 12 months. She was there until she went and started her own business with Judith (Roberts)."

Charlie Tidswell says: "Missy had been hanging around the beach for a few years. (Eldest sibling) Geoffrey was the first to join up. Geoff came down and started rowing boats at Glenelg and then I think Glenn joined the Nippers and maybe Peter. I was too young, 4 or 5. So she would have been 10, 11, 12. Mum and dad got involved with the Nippers a few years later, making tents and caps. She certainly had that beach life. (But) she wasn't a gun swimmer or athlete looking to win every meet."

Carolyn would sometimes spend a weekend with her cousins at their home in Salisbury, in Adelaide's far northern suburbs. She was invited to a party there one night, on August 16, 1977, to mark the one-year anniversary of Elvis Presley's death. Carolyn's uncle, Robert – her father's brother – worked at Beaurepaires and he had invited one of his junior employees, Kevin Matthews, to the party. Young Kevin was good looking, with an easy smile, and he was into life saving. He made an impression on Carolyn, and when they both travelled to Perth in March 1979 for the Australian Surf Life Saving Championships, they were again drawn to each other.

It was around this time that the surf life saving fraternity was debating whether to allow women to become members – a decision that was made on a club-by-club basis. Carolyn and another girl had wanted to join the Glenelg club, but when it was finally approved, her brother Charlie says: "I think Missy got the shits on. And she said: 'No, I'm going down to Semaphore', because she knew Kevin, and she went and joined up down there."

Initially, Carolyn wasn't a strong swimmer, but she embraced life saving and its culture. Yvonne and Doug were deeply proud of their girl when she became one of the first women in the state to earn an award previously restricted to the men. At the age of 17, she received the Surf Life Saving Association of Australia's Bronze Medal No. SA3472 on January 18, 1981. Kevin and Carolyn went on to become an integral part of the club's Rescue and Resuscitation section, and she was also involved in the march-past, as well as becoming a popular and respected coach.

Kaylene says: "I know Carolyn was only 14 when she met Kevin, and that it was through life saving. He was there a lot. Looking back, Christine says he took her away at 14, then he took her away from everyone later. And that's actually very true – she went down to Semaphore and basically never came back. He had a fair bit of say over who and where and what she actually did, he was quite manipulative. They were together from 14 to 18."

Charlie says: "(When Kevin came into Carolyn's life) I thought he was a top bloke. He'd do anything for you. He'd sit back after a carnival and have a beer, very cruisey, no worries. He was just one of the lads."

Kaylene met her future husband, Rodney Kenyon, at the age of 16. Later, after they became engaged, they made plans to move in together and decided to invite Carolyn to join them. She was now 18 and had split from Kevin because he'd been cheating on her. But she refused to talk about it with her friends.

Kaylene says: "Carolyn was always very loyal and kept things very close to her chest. All I know is there were some issues with another bird, and she wasn't going out with him anymore. We were encouraging her to come down south with us and hang out with us. But she would always go back to coach her Nippers at Semaphore. And obviously Kevin as well. But she wouldn't let anyone down, that was the kind of person she was. If she was the Nipper trainer, she would be there for them."

Carolyn agreed to move into a house in Richmond, adjacent to Netley, with Rodney, Kaylene, their two-year-old daughter, and one of Rodney's friends. Kaylene says: "I did quite a few things in my life and I always asked Carolyn to come. She usually said no but sometimes said yes. When I said we were going to move out and get a house together, she said she'd come. We had talked about it for a while and it was all very organised."

On moving day, Kaylene arrived at the Tidswells' home and reversed her mum's station wagon down the driveway, ready to be loaded up. She went inside, said hello to Yvonne, and found her friend in her bedroom. Carolyn hadn't yet found a way to tell her parents she was leaving.

Yvonne and Doug were as upset as she had feared, believing she was moving in with Kevin, but both Kaylene and Carolyn reassured them he was not part of the plan. Soon after the move, Kaylene suggested they invite Carolyn's parents to dinner to help smooth things over. Carolyn was working in the city with her mother each day, but Yvonne was yet to be convinced her daughter had made the right move. Kaylene's parents came as well and the night was a big success.

Kaylene says: "We ended up having two very drunk dads and Rodney playing darts and hanging off the clothesline. It was a lovely evening. It was a good opportunity for her parents to come and see how Carolyn was and see that no, Kevin wasn't living there, it was just us and we were all going OK. It worked really well. Everyone went off to work in the morning and we all got along really well at night, it was a really good house."

But soon after, Carolyn and Kevin got back together and he became a regular visitor. First he started staying the night and was initially pleasant enough to her friends. Before long, he had moved in. Kaylene remembers that Kevin would come home filthy after a day of tyre changing, but was fastidious about his appearance and would head straight for the shower. He was raised in Port Adelaide with a foster brother and sisters and there wasn't a lot of money. His tough upbringing had made him determined to better himself and he would buy classical music CDs from *Reader's Digest* and play them on Rodney's stereo.

But once he felt at home, there was nothing refined about Kevin's language or general behaviour. When Kaylene made dinner one night, he flung it back across the table and announced: "I'm not eating this fucking shit". And Carolyn's friends were appalled at the way he would speak to her. Rodney remembers him as a "rude pig". Within two months of Kevin's arrival, the happy little share house fell apart. Kevin and Carolyn moved into a unit together at Semaphore, the same suburb that was home to the surf club. Rodney and Kaylene, meanwhile, built their own house and got married.

Christine Nixon had taken an instant dislike to her friend's boyfriend when he first entered her life – and the feeling was mutual. Christine thought Kevin was arrogant and controlling and that her friend's fun-loving, easygoing nature was never the same after she met him. Around the time Carolyn met Kevin, she had a crush on one of Christine's brothers. Christine suspects Kevin felt threatened, and it was the beginning of the end of their friendship. They still saw each other when Carolyn was at the Richmond share house – but only when Kevin wasn't there – and later, when Carolyn would come home to mum seeking solace after a fight with Kevin, she would stop in to see Christine. But Christine believes she allowed the friendship to drift apart to keep the peace with Kevin. When Kevin and Carolyn were married in 1984, Christine was not on the guest list, but it did not prevent her from turning up to the ceremony.

Christine recalls: "She did look happy, but she didn't, looking deep inside. But that's what she wanted at the time. I saw in the wedding video that she looked at the camera at one stage. It was almost like she was looking for a way out. Of course she did love him, but I don't know if it was a matter of: 'I'm pregnant so I've got to get married, it's the way it's got to be.' She didn't want to upset her dad, who she loved heaps. I felt she was doing what Kevin wanted instead of doing what she'd always done, which was be mischievous Missy."

Kevin Matthews married Carolyn Tidswell at the Church of the Good Shepherd, Plympton, on November 17, 1984. Their oldest son, Kenny, was born on May 11, 1985, followed by Shane on September 21, 1987 and Daniel on January 18, 1989.

Carolyn's boys became her life. Following her mother's lead, she committed herself completely to her children and her husband. The rest of her time was dedicated to the surf club and her job. Christine says: "Carolyn would do anything for her kids. And she worked so hard to get what they had. She worked long hours and she was very good at what she did and she took pride in what she did."

Kaylene remained in touch with Carolyn, and always got in touch for her birthday and Christmas. When Kevin and Carolyn bought their first home, at Taperoo, two suburbs north of Semaphore, Kaylene would also visit for children's parties. But Kevin was always there and she rarely got to talk to Carolyn alone. Kaylene saw two different sides to Kevin, the smooth-talking, big-noting "good guy" at the surf club who would do anything for anyone. He could remain coherent after putting away two bottles of Scotch on a Saturday night and, come Monday morning, he would be making sales and working his way up the ladder at Beaurepaires. But at home, he was "just horrible" to his wife. Kaylene says she was "so disappointed" for her friend. When the family was able to buy a home in the upwardly mobile suburb of West Lakes Shore, Kevin thought he'd "made it" because he got out of Taperoo.

JUDITH ROBERTS, who declined to be interviewed for this book, established her business, Bedspreads Plus, in 1989. She had known Carolyn for many years, since she was still living at home in Netley and dating Kevin. Judith joined forces with Carolyn in 1994 and they both became directors of the soft furnishings company, which operated from a room attached to Judith's home.

A colleague of Kevin, whom we will call Robert, worked with him throughout their Beaurepaires careers. They started in the same week in 1977, Kevin a petrol pump attendant who moved into tyre fitting and Robert a factory worker.

Five years later, Robert was a counter salesman at the Beaurepaires store at Angle Park, while Kevin was a tyre fitter in the truck bay. Carolyn would drop off Kevin at work each morning and pick him up in the evening. Robert and his future wife got along well with Kevin and Carolyn, whom he described as "a nice lady, very polite and always friendly".

Robert recalls: "Kevin was rough, he was a man's man. He was rough as guts, but that didn't worry me, we just worked together. He struck me as ambitious and money-hungry. He was the one who was always organising everyone to chip in for the Lotto syndicate. He was always dreaming about becoming a millionaire and telling the boss to get stuffed when he won. He was driven by money. Even later on, when he was regional manager, he would send emails out to people to be in syndicates."

BY 2000, Kevin Matthews was a respected member of his community. While his wife's childhood friends had a poor opinion of him, it seemed that few others did. As he approached his 40th birthday, he was a man with a solid reputation and proud record of achievement in his chosen field.

As well as his happy 15-year marriage to a deeply loyal and loving woman, and three boys of whom he could be proud, there was a good home in a comfortable middle-class suburb, an easily managed mortgage and the surf club lifestyle he loved so much.

His son, Shane Matthews, now Shane Tidswell, says: "Who's your hero when you're a kid? Your dad is, if he's around. Up until (2000), he was the best dad ever. He was always a boys' dad, and we were Bodgie's boys. Kevin was always the person who would help everybody out with everything. He had his head screwed on. He was president of the surf club for three or four years. He headed up the Rescue & Resus division in our surf club. We were kicking arse, we were winning everything. Everybody respected him. *Everybody* respected him. He was state (regional) manager of Beaurepaires."

Shane recalls that when he was younger, his father would move from store to store as manager, winning sales awards and reaping the benefits of bonuses and prizes such as new TVs.

But in 2000, something changed in this son of a Broken Hill miner. The man who emerged was nothing like the "Bodgie" that his family and friends knew. Many would struggle to accept the truth, which was so hard to believe that it was easier to reject it outright. Had this "new" Kevin always been there, lurking beneath the surface? Almost certainly. His friends and colleagues already knew a man who believed that crudity equalled hilarity. He was fond of talking about sex publicly, long before he was having sex in public. He was also well-known for whipping out his penis at bars and putting it into his Scotch to ensure no one else touched it while he was in the toilet.

Detectives later gathered evidence of sexual behaviour, both earlier in his life and during his marriage, that did not fit the picture of a man who was respectful towards women. That evidence, while perverse and allegedly criminal in nature, was uncorroborated and not directly linked to the crime he was accused of, so it was never presented in court. Now, virtually all the people who were close to him remain silent. They have renounced their friendship and no longer want to be associated with Kevin Matthews, or are family members who have no wish to attract further attention to his appalling crime. He has been erased from photographs, honour boards and memories.

But Kevin's life throughout 2000 and 2001 was later dissected in minute detail by the South Australia Police Major Crime Investigation Section, and it is their extraordinary investigation which forms the basis of this book.

The facts they gathered stripped away Kevin Matthews's mask of decency; behind it lay a selfish, lecherous coward, utterly devoid of morality and driven entirely by lust and greed. He'd just been waiting for the right woman.

Chapter 2
Darren and Michelle
February 1989 – June 2000

THE FIRST MOMENT he laid eyes on Michelle Goldup, Darren Burgess was smitten.

Even as a 15-year-old blonde schoolgirl, Michelle wore a sly smile and knowing eyes. She had just been dropped off in the car park of Tea Tree Gully's Civic Park, on North East Rd, in Adelaide's far north-eastern suburbs. Darren was captivated as she emerged from her father's car with a friend – unfortunately he was standing in the middle of busy North East Rd as he stared at her, and was very nearly run over.

It was a warm Thursday night in February, 1989. Eighteen-year-old Darren and a mate had decided to head down to the local shopping complex, Tea Tree Plaza, and en route had noticed there was a concert in the adjacent park. They stopped in at the Modbury Hotel to pick up a few drinks, but quickly decided the Christian-themed concert wasn't for them; after finishing their drinks, they pressed on with their original plan of heading to TTP, leading to Darren's near-death experience.

But their mall adventure was short lived; Darren wanted to go back to the concert and see if he could find that blonde. He did, and Michelle immediately invited the two boys to sit with them because they were "Nigels" (Nigel No-friends). Darren and Michelle hit it off; at the end of the night he made the fateful decision to ask for her phone number. They were soon a couple.

Darren Wayne Burgess was born on September 14, 1970 at Glenelg Community Hospital, to Lindsay and Rosemary Burgess. He was the youngest of three children and grew up in the Pooraka home where his parents still live 40 years later.

Like Yvonne Tidswell, Rosemary Burgess was a dedicated mother who lived for her family. Lindsay Burgess was a man of black and white, known to his colleagues at Beaurepaires as straight down the line and hard but fair.

Darren attended Pooraka Primary School and graduated from Enfield High School in 1987, where his favourite subjects were maths, economics and accounting. He was a keen sportsman, playing football, basketball, baseball, volleyball and was also building a handy little coin collection.

He was a shy kid who had only a handful of friends. At school, he hated English, but was good with numbers and enjoyed accounting, economics and physics. But he was an ordinary student – his ambition was to become a policeman.

Even before he'd finished school, his father had found him a job as a tyre fitter at McLeod Tyres in Salisbury. Ambitions to join the police force were fine, but Lindsay Burgess's boy would not be lounging around the house when there was work to be done. Darren had one girlfriend in high school, another one named Michelle when he was 18 – and then there was Michelle Elizabeth Goldup.

She was born on August 7, 1973, in Queen Victoria Hospital at Rose Park in Adelaide and grew up in the Holden Hill home where her mother Angela still lives, after splitting with her father, Keith. Michelle has two older brothers and two older sisters, all of whom were born in England. (Michelle, her parents and her siblings were asked to co-operate with this book, but all declined.)

Michelle attended Holden Hill Primary School, Modbury High School and Modbury Heights High School. She played with GTs netball club and was one of the first girls to play soccer with the boys. She left school before she completed Year 10 and was asked to leave both high schools because of her poor attendance record. Aside from working a couple of days a week at her father's air-conditioning business, Michelle's first – and last – job was as a checkout operator at Big W at Tea Tree Plaza.

Darren got along well with his girlfriend's father – he and Keith Goldup would play golf and go to the soccer. But later, when Darren and Michelle split up, he instantly turned against Darren.

One of the reasons Michelle and Darren hit it off so well was their mutual love of football. She was a Glenelg Football Club supporter while Darren was part of the cheer squad at the West Torrens Football Club. They would go to footy games together and also to social events after the game.

More than 20 years later, asked to recall what it was that first attracted him to Michelle, Darren says: "Back then, she was reasonably attractive and a blonde. We had a bit in common with the footy. In hindsight, we didn't really have much else in common. Was it love? At the time it was. I still ask myself what it is that I saw in her."

And he soon discovered that he had much to learn about his girlfriend's personality. They would go to the West Torrens disco on Saturday nights and Darren was stunned when Michelle and one of her friends would "almost throw themselves" at football players. They had many fights over her behaviour but Michelle did not perceive that she was doing anything wrong.

Darren's first job at McLeod Tyres was followed by a factory position at Bridgestone in Edwardstown. But he wanted more and was still determined to pursue his dream of joining the police force. He passed all the written and physical tests, but the interview process was not so successful. He says: "When I asked them why, they said: 'What do you think?' and I said: 'Too soft, too shy?' And they said: 'yep'."

Michelle wasn't supportive of his aspirations and he felt she was "quite happy" when his hopes of a police career were dashed. Undeterred, Darren looked for a different escape route from the factory. In January 1990, his father, a veteran Beaurepaires manager who was in charge of the Richmond store, encouraged his son to apply for a trainee manager's position at Beaurepaires in Walkerville. He got the job and started almost immediately, striking up a good friendship with one of his co-workers, Brad Creten. Through that friendship, Brad would be introduced to one of Michelle's school friends, Sarah, his future wife. During this period, Darren says Michelle's flirting "settled down". They had formed a regular social circle and went to the same pub on weekends. Darren's traineeship was a success and in 1991, he was appointed assistant manager at Beaurepaires in Enfield.

Shortly before Darren's 21st birthday, in September 1991, Darren and Michelle decided to take a big step in their relationship, applying for a loan to buy a block of land at Salisbury Downs. Darren's grandfather had just passed away and he was visiting his brother's home with other family members. The block of land was nearby, so he took his mother and grandmother there, and they also visited the display home that they wanted to build.

Michelle, meanwhile, was staying at the home of a friend she worked with at Big W while her friend's parents were overseas. It was a Saturday and she was due to finish work at Tea Tree Plaza, so when he'd finished at his brother's home, Darren decided to head around to the friend's home, in Para Hills, to see Michelle. As his car turned into her street, Darren saw Keith Goldup's distinctive yellow Ford Falcon parked out the front of another house in the street.

Darren slowed and pulled up behind the car, noticing that Michelle was in the driver's seat and Brendan, a neighbour of Michelle's friend, was in the passenger seat. Brendan made a hasty exit on foot, while Darren and Michelle had a brief confrontation in the street before Darren followed her back to her parents' home. Michelle locked herself in her room and a screaming match ensued.

Darren was distraught. In the following days, he couldn't sleep or eat. Her behaviour was incomprehensible to him – she was cheating on him at the same time they were buying a block of land together? The incident brought their relationship to an instant halt. Darren decided to go it alone on the land purchase, but he still had to have some communication with Michelle to have her name removed from the loan. Then, the manipulation began.

He recalls: "She was just playing me, using me, she would borrow my car and ask for money. I don't know what was going through my head."

His anger boiled over on a visit to her home to pick up some of his belongings. New boyfriend Brendan was also there and a furious Darren grabbed Michelle and refused to let go. Fortunately, he had taken a friend with him who helped restore calm. Darren began considering a move to Melbourne, a fresh start. He was confused and hurt, but incapable of making tough decisions.

In January 1992, Michelle's mother called Darren to complain that her daughter's new boyfriend had assaulted her. Michelle was upset and wanted to see Darren. He felt sorry for her and they re-established contact. Soon after, they went to Melbourne for the Australia Day weekend – but Michelle spent the weekend ringing Brendan from public phone boxes.

As Darren and Michelle's reconciliation took more tentative steps forward, they agreed not to see each other every night of the week, and gave each other permission to go out socialising. During her relationship with Brendan, Michelle had become good friends with his sister, Jackie.

The two young women would go out together to Kelly's Room Disco at the Clovercrest Hotel in Modbury North. On one occasion, when Darren was with them, he met up with a former neighbour and good friend named Mark; Darren gained the impression his friend was interested in Jackie.

One Friday night soon after, Michelle and Jackie again spent a night out together. When Darren went to her home the next day, her mother told her she hadn't come home. Darren rang Jackie, who told him that Mark and Michelle had dropped her at home; Mark was supposed to take Michelle home. Darren correctly surmised that Michelle had ended up at Mark's home. He called Mark's place and after briefly speaking to Michelle, Mark dropped her off at home. Later, Darren had an altercation with Mark at Jackie's home but left before it got out of hand. But he still did not leave Michelle.

It was in the midst all of this drama that Michelle announced she was pregnant.

Michelle "swore black and blue" that the child was his, but Darren had doubts which would never be dispelled. He believed Michelle was simply trying to trap him and secure herself an income and security. "I provided her with stability, a home and money. That's all I was to her," he says.

He could have chosen to walk away, but did not even consider it. Loyalty and responsibility were two traits long ingrained by his father. He instead chose to move in with Michelle, into a rumpus room at the rear of her parents' home in Holden Hill.

At their first appointment at the hospital, the midwife asked Michelle if she had previously had any miscarriages. Michelle looked straight at Darren and said: "No – sort of." The midwife said: "There is no sort of, it is either yes or no." She eventually said no. "More lies," Darren thought to himself – Michelle had claimed to have had a miscarriage on more than one occasion.

During the pregnancy, Darren was still working at Beaurepaires Enfield. But just a couple of months before the baby was due, the company decided to close the store. Things were looking bleak for Darren Burgess – his unfaithful and deceitful de facto wife was pregnant; he was living in her parents' back yard; and his job was under threat.

Michelle endured a difficult 24-hour labour and their son, who is not named to protect his identity, was born on November 15, 1992. Darren says it made no difference to him – then or now – whether he was his son's biological father. "He's in here," he says with utter conviction, his hand over his heart. "I was excited to have a son and happy that he was healthy. I had someone to kick the footy with – although he ended up playing soccer."

Darren immediately started four weeks' leave and, during this time, was summoned to Beaurepaires head office to discuss his future. If he wanted to remain an employee, the only job they had available at the time was as second-in-charge at their Mildura store, a rural city on the River Murray, about 400km away, across the border in Victoria. Darren says he was told that if he took the position he could expect to be made manager.

But when he arrived in Mildura in mid-December 1992, Darren discovered the store already had an assistant manager, whom we will call Larry. He was demoted to make way for Darren's arrival. On their first journey to Mildura, Darren proposed to Michelle.

"I thought it was the right thing to do," Darren says. She accepted and they set the date for late the following year – November 20, 1993, which would be just after their son's first birthday. By then, hopefully, their lives would have settled down after the forced move. Michelle was even less enthusiastic about the move than Darren but, as new parents, the need for a steady income over-rode their desire to remain in Adelaide.

From the moment they arrived, their aim was to find a way back home – especially once they had both met Darren's new boss. He invited Darren and Michelle into his office, where they also met Larry. The boss looked Michelle up and down and said: "In the country, we share everything – and I like blondes."

Michelle instantly hated him; Darren took only slightly longer. But for all the manager's personal faults, Darren admits: "In the end, he was actually the one who taught me the most about the business and how to manage a store."

Darren wanted to quit and move back to Adelaide to find a new job, but his father talked him out of it. He says: "Dad said to me: 'Why are you worrying about your boss? What are *you* doing wrong? Go in there on Monday with a new attitude and looking the part'."

The young family had moved into a two-bedroom detached unit on 12th St, but Michelle would visit Adelaide at every opportunity – a habit which Darren says was "fair enough being a young first-time mother".

With Michelle away, Darren would often enjoy a night out and a drink with Larry, who lived with two of his cousins, both women. They also befriended Michelle, inviting her to play netball with them. On the surface, the family was settling in well. But new evidence soon emerged to arouse Darren's suspicions – Michelle was constantly buying pregnancy tests.

One weekend, Michelle's parents came up on a Friday night for a weekend visit. Larry joined the family for dinner, followed by a few drinks and a game of footy on TV. It was late when Michelle drove him home. When she did not return, both Darren and her father tried repeatedly to call her, but there was no answer. Almost two hours after she left, Michelle finally returned home and explained that she had stayed at Larry's place to watch a movie with him and his cousins. Darren was highly suspicious, but had no proof. Soon after, Larry transferred to another store.

In October 1993, just short of a year after they had arrived, Darren secured a transfer back to Adelaide. Surprisingly, he found he was almost reluctant to leave. He'd actually enjoyed his time in Mildura and was feeling more independent. Being away from his parents had been good for him. And, if he was honest with himself, Michelle embarrassed him and he preferred that friends and family weren't able to drop into their home. "She wasn't big on cleanliness. She was disgusting," he says.

Darren had heard two positions were about to become vacant at Beaurepaires Elizabeth and applied for both of them. Another staff member, Robert – the man who had started out with Kevin Matthews – got the manager's job. Robert had also worked with Darren's father and had known Darren since he was a little boy, riding his bike around the store in the early 1980s. When he was older, Darren would come to work with Lindsay on Saturday mornings and help out.

After he got the job, Robert immediately asked for Darren to be his assistant manager. Robert says: "And that's how we started working together. He was a good friend and hard worker and I needed a 2IC. So I said: 'Let's bring him back'."

Darren and Michelle moved back to Adelaide, this time into a unit at the rear of Darren's parents' home in Pooraka, while they tried to save for a house. But within weeks of arriving back, Darren, now 23, was faced with undeniable evidence that his 20-year-old fiancée was cheating on him.

About two weeks before their wedding, they were due to visit a minister for the usual pre-marriage counselling. Before they left, Darren was cleaning out their car and found a letter that Michelle had written to morning TV host Denise Drysdale, seeking advice. The letter said she'd fallen in love and had had an affair with Larry, confirming Darren's suspicions. He says he was outraged: "Here I am waiting to see the priest about our upcoming marriage and I found these letters."

But when the wedding day arrived, so did Darren. Neither family could be described as wealthy, but they made every effort to make it a big day for the young couple. On November 20, 1993, the bride arrived at the Wesley Uniting Church at Kent Town in one of two red Ford Falcon GTs hired to carry the bridal party.

As much as he wanted to, Darren couldn't find it in himself to call it all off. He felt too much pressure. His parents had spent so much money. He recalls: "I would've looked so stupid calling it off, but really I was stupid not to. I remember going into the toilet at the church with all the groomsmen and thinking: 'What the hell am I doing here?' But it was too late to pull out. We got married."

THE STRONG social culture at Beaurepaires involved traditional Christmas functions; Darren and Michelle attended the 1993 gathering at the Bridgeway Hotel in Pooraka. It was the first time that Michelle had met Kevin and Carolyn Matthews, and she took an instant dislike to both.

Darren recalls: "Michelle and another friend would call them feral, and pigdog or bushpig. One reason was that at one show, Kevin was leaving and he was intoxicated and he stood up and said ..."

The comment he made was of a sexual nature and involved his wife. It is so appalling and graphic that it cannot be repeated. The same applies to a second shocking "story" that Darren says Kevin would often tell in public. It was no surprise that Michelle was repelled by Kevin and his idea of humour. But her attitude towards Carolyn was less easily understood, since Carolyn's public behaviour was the polar opposite of her husband's vulgarity.

Robert quickly formed an opinion about his assistant manager's wife. She was a manipulator who knew what she wanted and would do whatever it took to get it. She was driven by money and material possessions and spent Darren's salary as quickly as he earned it.

He says: "She made Darren's life hard. She could have got out and got a job, but she didn't want to do that. She wanted a life with all the trimmings but didn't want to work. She would go out to lunch, go shopping, but when there wasn't enough money, she would take it out on Darren. It wasn't his fault – he was working hard and he wasn't spending any money and doing all the right things, but she wasn't helping."

Robert remembers the morning ritual – Michelle would drop off Darren at work and Darren would cheerfully begin his duties. By 8.30am, Michelle would be on the phone haranguing him. It was always something different, but their lack of money was usually a part of it.

In 1994, Darren joined a volleyball team with a mate, and they eventually decided to start their own team. Darren Bland, a man Darren had previously met through a mutual friend, was among the players. He worked at Peter Page Holden, just down the road from Elizabeth Beaurepaires, and then went to work with his father at an Elizabeth car yard.

Darren recalls that Bland would often stop by to complain about his job and ask if there was a position open as a wheel aligner. When the position became vacant, Darren gave him the job. Bland lived at Semaphore and would drive to the Burgess home in Pooraka each morning. He would take it in turns with Darren to drive the further 15km to Elizabeth. But Darren soon discovered his friend had another side.

He says: "He was really horrible to work with. He was just so moody, like a spoilt kid. Some days, the drive out to Elizabeth with him was terrifying because of his aggressive driving."

Sometimes Michelle would pick them up and drop them off. Bland became a good family friend – or at least so Darren thought.

"I don't know when things changed between them but I have my suspicions it was around the time of Michelle's 21st, on August 7, 1994. Darren was invited and I remember there was a photo of him and another guest and I later found that photo cut in half and Darren's photo missing. This raised my suspicions that maybe something was going on."

Despite this, the affair continued for close to three years, as did the increasingly strained friendship between the two Darrens. In mid-1996, Bland transferred to the tyre chain's Port Adelaide store. Bland later told police: "The situation working with Michelle's husband was getting a little bit painful and I eventually moved to Melbourne to resolve the situation."

Darren Burgess is, understandably, less diplomatic.

"I am guessing that his betrayal – his dog act of having an affair with my wife – was playing on his conscience and the only way for him to move on was to ask for a transfer to Beaurepaires Port Adelaide and continue his affair with Michelle."

In September 1996, Darren Burgess was appointed manager at the Beaurepaires Ridgehaven store, also in the northern suburbs. His regional manager – Kevin Matthews's predecessor – subsequently tried to move him back to Elizabeth as manager, but Darren resisted; he wanted a change.

Darren and Michelle were building a house in Evanston Park, and during this time their daughter was born. Bland and another friend of Darren helped celebrate the good news – although Darren was less than comfortable about having the man he suspected his wife was sleeping with in his home. Shortly after they moved into their new home, Michelle again fell pregnant.

Darren says: "I didn't know whose it was but it certainly wasn't mine. Michelle and I discussed the financial drain another baby would have on us. I gave her no choice but to have an abortion. In my eyes there was no other choice, as hard as that sounds, because of the financial burden and knowing that the child was not mine. I believe Michelle agreed to have the abortion because her lover wanted nothing to do with her and the pregnancy."

Interviewed by detectives in August 2001, Darren Bland admitted that he had a long-running affair with his friend's wife. He coyly described it as a "supporting friend" relationship. They would speak on the phone three to four times a week, sometimes meeting at St Clair Recreation Park in suburban Woodville while he was on a break from work. On two or three occasions, they had sex there.

The affair had continued after his 1996 move to the Port Adelaide store, where Kevin Matthews was the manager. He finally ended the relationship with Michelle in September 1997, and went to Melbourne for a three-month course, then spent another three months in the city working for Beaurepaires.

Later, asked by Detective Senior Constable Scott Duval what he had told Michelle prior to his departure, Bland explained: "That the relationship had to come to an end, as it was affecting my life more than I wanted it to and it was probably one of the reasons I wanted to leave and go to Melbourne. She didn't take it too well."

Duval: "Did she behave in an emotional way?"

Bland: "We probably both were at that point."

Duval: "At that point, did she make any reference to committing suicide?"

Bland: "I don't specifically remember at that point, but during the course of the relationship there had been mention of it, yes."

Duval: "Mentioned by whom?"

Bland: "Michelle."

Duval: "Was there ever an occasion where she raised the issue of pregnancy with you?"

Bland: "Yes, just before we broke up. She told me she was pregnant at that stage and going to have, or had had, an abortion, which I had no say or anything to do with."

Duval: "Do you know whether in fact she was pregnant or had an abortion?"

Bland: "I had no proof to substantiate them, no."

On the night of his mother's 60th birthday, in August 1997, the emotional toll overwhelmed Darren Burgess. With a new baby, a new mortgage and his wife pregnant with another man's child, the pressure was intense. He drank heavily and "apparently I got a bit mouthy". So much so that his brother sent him an anonymous letter advising him to keep his mouth shut. The next day, Darren sought refuge on the bank of the creek at the back of his parents' home, a favourite haunt from his childhood that always brought him a sense of peace. He reflected on the current state of his life and asked himself some hard questions.

He remembers: "This was the year that *Titanic* the movie was released. I remember seeing the scene where Rose risked her life to save the life of Jack. I asked myself: 'Would you do this for Michelle, the mother of my children?' And the answer was a steadfast NO'. At this point I knew my marriage was over, but I couldn't make the hard decision to end it there and then."

Chapter 3

Suspicion, sex and room service

2000 – July 2001

DARREN BURGESS was in despair. Unable to bring himself to end his marriage, he turned to alcohol. Through 1998 and 1999, he drank heavily "just to numb the pain of living with Michelle".

He started taking risks. On March 1, 2000, after a Beaurepaires meeting, he was caught drink driving and immediately feared he would lose his job and his home. The following day, Darren approached Kevin Matthews – who by now had risen to the position of regional manager – and told him: "I've been booked for drink driving."

Kevin replied: "You realise that's obviously a sackable offence?"

The decision was referred to head office, which asked Kevin for his opinion; Darren kept his job. His six-month licence disqualification began on May 16. Darren believes that it was in this period that Michelle and Kevin began communicating via text messages.

He says: "I think it was an open communication in the beginning where I was aware and involved in some of the texts but this soon changed. Michelle would become very secretive with her phone. She would always be in the toilet with her phone, so again my suspicions were raised."

It will never be known exactly what it was that so radically altered Michelle's opinion of Kevin. But she was soon exchanging dozens and dozens of text messages with the man she had once contemptuously dismissed as a "pigdog". She wanted to be wanted again, desired and coveted, just as she had been by the other men with whom she had had affairs; illicit meetings in parks and hotels for exciting, forbidden sex thrilled her like nothing else had in her life.

In August 2000, Darren had bought his own mobile phone and also updated Michelle's, putting both in his name. But Michelle chose not to use the new phone, instead going out the same day and buying her own and opening an account with Vodafone. Now she was free to flirt with whomever she chose.

MICHELLE'S THEN FRIEND, Cassandra Hutchinson, recalls that about two weeks prior to Darren's birthday, in September 2000, Michelle told her she was exchanging text messages with Kevin Matthews and that he had asked her to be his mistress. She made it clear their relationship had become intimate. On at least three occasions, Cassandra saw a grey Ford Falcon parked at Michelle's home, usually around lunchtime or late morning. When Darren and Michelle had a Beaurepaires Christmas party at their house in December 2000, Cassandra saw the Matthews family arrive in the same car.

Cassandra's friend, Jaylene Thompson, recalls similar incidents around mid-2000 after being introduced to Cassandra's friend and neighbour, who lived two doors away. She saw Michelle at Cassandra's home two or three times up until September 2000. On one occasion they were having a barbecue. A few weeks prior to this, Cassandra had told Jaylene that Michelle was having an affair with a man named Kevin, who was Darren's boss at Beaurepaires. At the barbecue, Jaylene recalls standing with Cassandra and Michelle under the pergola when the subject of Darren's boss came up. Michelle told them she was having an affair with Kevin. On another evening, Jaylene joined Michelle and Cassandra at the Village Tavern in Golden Grove. Within minutes of arriving, Michelle started a text-messaging marathon, telling them Kevin was in his lounge room and his wife was sitting nearby. She loved that it was happening under Carolyn's nose. While the other women danced, Michelle kept texting, at one stage having a conversation with Kevin while he hid in his toilet.

Darren says that in the lead-up to his 30th birthday in September 2000, he recalls that Michelle went out with Cassandra and a couple of her girlfriends one night. The next day, he noticed what looked like a love bite on Michelle's chest. He questioned her about it and she insisted someone had pinched her the night before in the nightclub. He says: "Absolute bullshit. She honestly thought I was stupid. Yes, I was stupid for everything I put up with but not stupid enough that I didn't know what was going on."

In another incident shortly before his birthday, Michelle told Darren she had to stay at the Hindley Park Royal in the city because she had some sort of training for a job she claimed to have been given at their son's school and it required an overnight stay. But Michelle dropped by at Beaurepaires before mid-morning the next day. Darren questioned her about why she was there so early, and she claimed some of the other people on the course had "misbehaved" so the training had been called off for the day.

Police later established that the first known phone call between Matthews and Michelle was on September 4, 2000, when he used his work mobile to call her mobile. A few days later, Darren and Michelle had a discussion about the guest list for his birthday party on Saturday, September 16, which was two days after his birthday. Darren was firm: "I don't want Kevin here," he told her.

"Well it's too late – I've already mentioned it to him. I've invited him and his wife," Michelle replied.

"Why?" he asked her.

"Well, he's at all the Christmas parties and he's your boss, so it would be good for you if he's here," she said.

The Burgesses hosted the Beaurepaires Elizabeth Christmas parties at their home each year. Because Kevin was regional manager, Darren would invite him and Carolyn to the parties. He recalls that at their first party, in 1997, he showed Kevin around his home. In the master bedroom, Kevin commented: "So this is where all the work gets done." Because Michelle disliked both Kevin and Carolyn, she didn't want them in her house. Now their attitudes to Kevin had reversed.

Darren says: "I couldn't believe what I was hearing. Here was a woman who hated Kevin and Carolyn immensely, didn't want them at our house at Christmas time and all of a sudden she's inviting them to my birthday party. I asked her why and she said that her opinion of Kevin and Carolyn had changed. I asked why and she told me that she and Kevin had talked and that they had some things in common with the troubles they had in their marriages."

Michelle later confided to another woman that on her husband's birthday she had gone to Matthews's office and had sex with him there. Matthews had never experienced anything like it; he was terrified they would be caught, but that also made it even more arousing. She'd arrived at his office with hungry eyes, wandering hands and a titillating proposition – *I want to be your mistress*. Matthews did not require thinking music – he was instantly besotted.

There were four more calls between Kevin and Michelle in the following days. On the Saturday morning before his 30th birthday party at their home, a suspicious Darren began browsing the messages on his wife's phone. When he discovered a message containing directions to Beaurepaires head office, sent from Kevin's phone, he confronted his wife. She lamely explained: "I had a feeling you were going through my phone and I put that in there myself."

That morning, she told Darren she was going to buy his birthday present, but was gone all morning. When she finally returned, she explained her extended absence by saying she had caught the train around the corner from where she bought the present, which was a Port Adelaide Football Club tracksuit. That evening, Kevin and Carolyn presented Darren with a Beaurepaires jacket. A decade later, Darren theorises that the jacket was probably the excuse Kevin used to go to his office that morning to have sex with his wife.

The guests at the party that night included the Burgess's close friends, Brad and Sarah Creten. Sarah later told police that she was very surprised to see Kevin and Carolyn there. Michelle told her Darren had invited them and gave the impression that she was only tolerating them for Darren's sake. But Sarah immediately picked up on Michelle's new attitude towards Kevin, talking and laughing with him like they were old friends. She also noticed that Michelle seemed to avoid Carolyn and she didn't see them speak at all during the evening. Days after the party, Sarah and a friend had coffee with Michelle and Kevin's name came up. But Michelle had little to say and Sarah was left to wonder about Michelle's odd changes in attitude towards him.

Shortly after the affair is suspected to have started, Michelle created a ruse to give herself more time outside the home. She told Darren she had a job at Evanston Primary School, which their son attended, which involved canvassing local businesses to sponsor the school. This would require Michelle to do some training and even overnight stays in Adelaide hotels, such as her visit to the Hindley Park Royal. She would drop off her daughter at her mother's home in Holden Hill while she went off to her "job".

Darren says: "I guess having experienced this before, I suspected there was an affair happening. I would question Michelle all the time and she would constantly deny it. At lunch times, I would ring both Kevin and Michelle and, as luck would have it, both their phones were off and I would leave messages for them both to ring me. Surprise, surprise, they would both ring simultaneously as soon as they switched their phones back on."

Also in September, Kevin Matthews rewarded himself with an extravagant gift for his approaching 40th birthday – ignoring the fact that the family's finances were already stretched – by taking out a $17,500 loan to buy a speedboat which he immediately dubbed *Bodgie*.

Kaylene and Rodney Kenyon thought it was odd that they weren't invited to Kevin's 40th birthday party, on October 18, 2000. It was only later that Kaylene found out that it was actually Carolyn who insisted that they not be included; she had feared that her husband would humiliate her that night – and she was right.

Michelle and a reluctant Darren were among the party guests. Kevin had called Darren earlier that day and said they were welcome to stay the night. Darren was incredulous – was Kevin serious? He still didn't have his driver's licence, so he'd already booked a room at the nearby Lakes Resort Hotel, correctly guessing that Michelle would end the night in no shape to drive. They took a bottle of Scotch for the birthday boy. For Kevin Matthews, there was no such thing as too much Scotch – indeed, his party "decorations" included a bottle of Scotch hooked up to a drip.

He was ecstatic that his birthday gifts – including those from colleagues and business acquaintances – included no less than 52 bottles of Scotch of varying shapes and sizes. He spent most of the evening squiring Michelle, his arm around her waist, as he introduced her to bemused guests as his "new best friend".

Darren Burgess noticed Kevin's friendly arm around his wife about five or six times that evening, but chose to keep the peace. He also noticed Michelle was drinking Scotch and Coke, rather than her usual Strongbow.

As she got steadily more drunk and her affection for Kevin became obvious to everyone at the party, Darren decided it was best if he stopped drinking because it looked like things were about to get out of hand. Later in the evening, Michelle spent an extended period on her knees in the toilet – although she was alone on this occasion.

While this was happening, there was an altercation between Kevin, some of Kevin's family members and several Beaurepaires managers. One of Kevin's family members started targeting Darren, but Kevin interjected, saying: "Leave him alone, he is one of my best managers". Darren eventually extracted Michelle from the toilet, but with the state she was in, no taxi would give them a ride.

Darren says: "I went against everything I believed in. I had sworn that while I didn't have my licence I wouldn't drive but desperate times called for desperate measures. I bundled Michelle into our car and drove around to the Lakes Resort Hotel. I put Michelle to bed. She was so intoxicated that by the morning when I woke her, she had soiled herself."

On Tuesday, October 24, 2000, Kevin Matthews booked a standard room with queen-size bed at the Novotel Adelaide in Hindley St. He checked in at 10.04am, and hotel records show that he watched *The Patriot* on the in-house movie system, ate a lunch that included two chicken burgers, wedges and orange juice, and checked out at 4.11pm, paying the $163.75 bill.

On November 8, 2000, there was a booking in the name of Burgess for a spa room at the Airport Motel, on Burbridge Rd, Brooklyn Park. On the same day, the White Horse Inn at Bolivar charged $76.90 to Kevin Matthews's credit card, indicating he was stocking up on drinks ahead of another night in a hotel. The following day, Kevin caught an Ansett flight to Melbourne and returned on November 11.

Leading up to Christmas 2000, Michelle told Darren she wanted a tattoo as a memorial for the baby they had aborted – it was of a rose, in the small of her back. At the regular Christmas party at the Burgess's home that month, a grim Carolyn Matthews walked in from the back yard to speak to Darren.

He recalls: "Michelle was so proud of her tattoo, she was parading it around to everyone who wanted to look. I remember Carolyn coming up to me in my kitchen and saying: 'Your wife is out there showing her arse to my husband'.

Another guest at the party says: "(Michelle) came out with the tramp stamp on her back and Darren said 'she didn't get it for me,' and she was saying 'oh no, I got it for Darren' but we knew ... It was a weird party. Darren Bland was there that night, too."

Darren recalls that the night ended strangely. Carolyn and her boys wanted to leave but Kevin did not. They did leave, but returned to convince Kevin that he needed to come home. One of the boys took his father's drink off the table and managed to coax him out to the car with it.

In mid-December, there was another Beaurepaires Christmas party, at the home of Robert, Darren's former boss at Elizabeth. Sarah Creten recalls that Michelle and Kevin were together for most of the evening, laughing and chatting. Michelle steered clear of Carolyn and was again drinking Scotch and Coke rather than Strongbow – despite her previous bad experience. During the evening, there was an awkward moment when Robert asked Michelle what she did. She told him she worked on Mondays and did a course on Fridays. Robert said: "What, intercourse?" Few people laughed – but Kevin and Michelle thought it was hilarious. When Kevin and Carolyn left the party early, about 10pm, Michelle's good mood immediately soured. Sarah had agreed to drive home Darren and Michelle because they had arrived in a taxi, but now Michelle didn't want to wait for the party to end – she wanted to go straight home.

Robert says his wife and Sarah had been sitting back from the crowd that evening and observing everything that was happening. After Michelle left, his wife told him: "There's something going on there." But Robert was dismissive: "That's bullshit, you don't know what you're talking about."

The intensity of the relationship was quickly making it very public. Already, a lot of people knew or suspected something was going on, but neither Kevin nor Michelle seemed to care. On December 19, they returned to the Novotel in Hindley St, checking in at 10.39am, ordering room service throughout the day and checking out at 5.47pm. The next day, it was the South Park Adelaide on South Tce in the city. Kevin checked in at 9.13am and paid a food and drinks bill of $35 when he checked out at 4.53pm.

The long days of sex and room service were serving a purpose; Michelle was making her move, giving Kevin a taste of what he would miss out on unless he left his wife. Michelle's friend Cassandra Hutchinson says she told her that at Christmas, she had given Kevin an ultimatum to leave Carolyn by mid-January. If he didn't leave, she would stop the sex. Michelle said Kevin had agreed and when the Matthews family returned from a Christmas holiday, he was going to leave. Cassandra was appalled at the situation, and resolved to try to stop the affair. She sent an anonymous letter to Kevin at his work address, explaining that people knew about the affair and if they didn't stop, Carolyn would be told about it.

Cassandra later told police: "I didn't intend it to be an ultimatum. I thought it would scare them both into realising what they were doing, that there were two families at risk here. I think I said in the letter that they were acting like children and that they were to halt the affair before Christmas."

On December 22, Rodney and Kaylene Kenyon and their two sons made the trek from their Hills property to the Matthews home at West Lakes

Shore. The two couples were relaxing in the outdoor entertaining area while the kids jumped in and out of the pool. It was a languid summer evening between friends, but Carolyn was preoccupied. Her father, Doug, was gravely ill and she had been spending a lot of time with him. He wasn't expected to see out the year. They talked about Doug, and each other's work, and the Matthews life saving activities. At 8pm, Kevin's phone started receiving text messages – lots of them. Kevin passed his phone around to show his guests the messages, which said the unidentified sender needed Kevin to come out. Carolyn told Kevin he wasn't going anywhere.

The messages stopped, but an hour later, they started flowing again. Kevin again passed his phone around. A woman was claiming to have slashed her wrists and was demanding that Kevin visit her in an unidentified hospital. Kevin and Carolyn started discussing some "problems" he was having with one of his managers. Kevin said he'd been to speak to the manager about not letting his marital troubles interfere with his work performance.

Kaylene says: "Kevin seemed quite open about showing the messages around. While these messages were coming in, Kevin and Carolyn spoke about calls they had received at the house, both threatening calls as well as calls that hung up. I asked Carolyn who had made the calls and she told me that it was people from Kevin's work and that the calls had been coming for a while."

Kaylene was not about to have her evening with her close friend ruined by Kevin's shenanigans.

"Well, if we ring the hospitals and no one by that name has been admitted, then he doesn't have to go anywhere," she told Carolyn, who nodded in agreement.

"That's right, that's right Kevin," she said, warming to the idea. After the women went inside to make the calls, Rodney spoke quietly to Kevin.

"Look Kevin, if you're doing anything wrong, come clean and get it out in the open," he told him. But Kevin was adamant: "No, there's nothing going on."

Kaylene recalls: "We made the calls – but I remember the name as Michelle Green, not Burgess. I remember feeling a sense of satisfaction – you can just stay here with your guests. So he stayed and the messages continued and he got quite … well, he was pacing around all the time, he hardly sat down. He made it uncomfortable, but that's Kevin's style. I decided I was just going to ignore him and enjoy my visit with my girlfriend."

In addition to Kevin's suspected philandering, Carolyn was coping with the imminent loss of her father. His emphysema, diagnosed 18 months earlier, had led to lung cancer. Yvonne had retired and they packed up the camper van, determined to spend every remaining minute together. Originally given six months to live, Doug defied the prognosis and was still alive 18 months later. But by December 2000, his condition was deteriorating rapidly. The Tidswells' strong, proud husband and father was reduced to drinking thickshakes through a straw. He came home from hospital that month, to be surrounded by his family.

Charlie Tidswell recalls that his sister would often visit and was deeply upset by her father's decline. Doug passed away on Christmas Eve and his funeral was on Boxing Day. Carolyn was devastated at the loss of her beloved father. But there was no support or comfort from her husband. Kaylene remembers that Doug and Carolyn had become very close during his illness. Kaylene went to the funeral with Rodney, Kevin, Carolyn and their children, returning to Yvonne's home in Netley for the wake. Watching on the back verandah, Christine and Kaylene saw that Carolyn was running around trying to do everything. Each time they went into the lounge room, they found Kevin watching TV and drinking. The only time he came out the back to where the guests were was to refill his drink. When the wake ended, Carolyn rushed home and packed up their van with everything the family would need before driving off for their holiday at the Morgan Riverside Caravan Park, in the Riverland.

Kaylene says: "Kevin was really, really arrogant and didn't lift a finger. He drank and Carolyn ran around and did all of it, as well as being there for her mum. What an arsehole. But that's Kevin."

Christine was equally appalled. "He sat on his arse and drank Scotch. Not a care about what she was feeling. Her dad meant a great deal to her, she was daddy's girl. He didn't care."

Without Michelle around to cajole him, Kevin backed out of the plan to tell Carolyn he was leaving her. With Doug's passing, he may have worried about how bad it would look if he walked out on his wife while she was grieving.

On Christmas Day, Darren Burgess noticed Michelle wearing a gold necklace. When he asked where it came from, she said she bought it from Zamels jewellers for $10. Darren recalls: "That was bullshit – it looked a lot more expensive than that. In the next couple of days, I looked in Zamels and saw a similar necklace that cost hundreds."

Darren also overheard a conversation that day between Michelle and her brother's wife. Michelle said she was thinking about getting another tattoo on her backside, this time of Daffy Duck. Darren asked: "Why would you do that?" Michelle replied: "Because Daffy Duck is my favourite cartoon character."

Darren was out the front of his home playing soccer with his kids on Boxing Day when Michelle took a call from a woman calling herself Julie, who asked to speak to him. She didn't recognise the voice of her neighbour, Cassandra Hutchinson. Michelle called Darren to the phone. "Your wife's having an affair with Kevin Matthews," Cassandra told him, and immediately hung up. Darren's anger was reaching a crescendo.

He says: "I rang Kevin and told him what I had been told and that I would beat the living fuck out of him. I think this was around the time Carolyn's father died and Kevin was not happy with what he was hearing. He just hung up on me."

Darren began arguing with Michelle, leading to him searching her car for more evidence of the affair. He soon found a Zamel's jewellery box and a Christmas card that read "Chook loves Daffy – this is just enough to tide you over for Christmas, don't spend it on Scotch".

Again, Darren confronted Michelle. She said it was from "one of the guys on one of the courses" she claimed to have completed. He fancied her but she had rejected him, she insisted. The next day, Darren again called Kevin, who was on holiday in the Riverland and in the car with his family. As Darren launched into a tirade about the affair, Kevin quickly took the phone off hands-free and told him to wait until he got out of the car. Darren says: "He swore on his kids' lives that he was not having an affair with Michelle. But … the conversation didn't last long."

Darren went to stay with a friend on December 27, in turmoil over what he should do. But instead of making divorce his New Year's resolution, he asked Michelle to spend New Year's Eve with him. He had tickets to an Adelaide 36ers basketball game and, afterwards, he returned home with Michelle – but slept on the lounge and returned to his friend's home the next night. Darren says Carolyn and Kevin wanted to hold a meeting to "clear the air" on January 3, but Michelle wasn't interested. On January 5, Kevin Matthews checked in to a room at the South Park on South Tce in

Adelaide at 9.29am, departing at 4.15pm after yet another day of sex with Michelle. Carolyn called Darren on January 7. He remembers: "She wanted to ask me what I thought of the rumours of Kevin and Michelle having an affair. She also asked me if Michelle was OK.

"I said: 'OK, why do you ask?'

"(Carolyn) said: 'With the stabbing'.

"'What stabbing?' I asked.

"Carolyn said: 'Just before Christmas, you walked in and found Michelle on the floor stabbed, sitting alongside your son.'

"I couldn't believe what I was hearing. But I remember the night Carolyn was talking about. It was just before Christmas and Michelle went to the servo for cigarettes but was gone for over an hour. She told me she ran into one of our friend's husbands and she was talking to him.

"Carolyn said: 'Well, Kevin rang you the following day to find out how she was.'

"And I said: 'Well, no, he didn't.'

"I told Carolyn that I believed that Kevin and Michelle were having an affair, but I don't think she wanted to believe it."

Around the time of this call – possibly shortly after – Carolyn also called Michelle and told her to stay away from her husband. Michelle ignored her plea. After his conversation with Carolyn, Darren called his wife and told her it was time for them to talk. They met at Civic Park in Tea Tree Gully, where they had first met. Michelle maintained her policy of blanket denials. Darren told her: "This is where it all began – maybe this is where it all should finish."

Darren suggested they needed to be alone to talk and work out a solution to the situation. Michelle agreed and organised for the children to stay at her mother's and they drove home. Darren wasn't comfortable at their home and booked a room at the Lakes Resort Hotel at West Lakes. Even while they were packing, Michelle was texting Kevin. She also sent a message to Carolyn from Darren's phone and immediately deleted it so he couldn't read it. Carolyn later told Darren that the text, which she naturally assumed was from him, said that she was not to contact him or Michelle again. The hotel stay was a failure. Michelle locked herself in the bathroom and stayed in the spa for the evening, again engaging in a text-message marathon. Nothing was discussed.

The next day, January 8, a 28-page itemised phone bill for $1200 for a single month arrived in the Burgess's letterbox. The bill also showed a previous account for $1600. And page after page was filled with calls and text messages to Kevin Matthews's mobile phone. Darren had continued staying with his friend, but on the day the bill arrived, he was back at home looking after the children. Michelle had returned to her fantasy job at Evanston Primary School that day – despite the fact that school did not return for three weeks.

Michelle had already told Darren about the big bills, but she'd claimed they were in relation to her "job" and the school had paid them. But there was no denying the hard evidence. Darren, as usual, was furious.

That afternoon, one of Michelle's friends, Kathy Cowled, called the house. She wanted Michelle to pick her up from the train station with her kids and take them home. Darren told her Michelle was not home and he was happy to do it. On the drive to her home, she asked him how his job was going. Darren told her he was still at Beaurepaires. Kathy, who as we will learn later is not one of the world's great thinkers, said she was surprised.

"Why's that?" Darren asked, curious.

"Well, you know Michelle's having an affair with your boss Kevin," she replied, and proceeded to tell Darren everything Michelle had told her.

After dropping off Kathy, Darren rang Michelle and got the usual denials and then called Kevin, who did the same.

He told Kevin: "I just want to thank you."

"Thank me? What for?" Kevin asked.

"For taking that stupid bitch off my hands."

"You can't say that!"

"No really, it's the best thing that could have happened to me."

Darren says: "Before Michelle got home, I decided this was it, I was leaving her. Once she was home, I confronted her with the bill and what Kathy Cowled had told me. She just denied it all and told me to pack my bags and get out – I was already going. It was really quite difficult and emotional to leave my children behind. With hindsight, on many different levels, it was one of the biggest mistakes to leave and not take the kids with me. I should have stayed and told Michelle to leave by herself."

Darren went to stay with his parents and made an appointment with Kevin to discuss his future with Beaurepaires. He couldn't handle Kevin as his boss any longer but the only job he offered him was as manager at Goodyear Modbury – a store still under his control. Another manager offered him a position as a storeman at Wingfield (on the same pay, until something more suitable came up) and, while Darren was grateful for the offer, he decided he would have to remain at Elizabeth until he could find something else that suited him. He immediately began applying for other jobs outside Beaurepaires.

Michelle celebrated Darren's departure by arranging another rendezvous with Kevin, booking into a room at the South Park Hotel under her maiden name at 8.50am on January 12. After a day of room service, sex and Scotch, they checked out at 4.18pm. There was another tryst on January 25 at the Novotel Adelaide, in Hindley St, where the couple also enjoyed two chicken schnitzel specials. But the regular hotel sex was expensive and wasn't enough to satisfy their need for thrills. Mechanic Corey Bayliss says it was around January 2001 that he witnessed Michelle and Kevin's public sex show at Roy Amer Reserve in Oakden.

They were also enjoying many long lunches at the Hampstead Hotel, in the inner north-eastern suburb of Collinswood. Barmaid Fiona Hughes later told police that a tall, fat bald man with a moustache and a stocky blonde woman frequented the hotel three or four days a week from December 2000 to July 2001, sometimes staying as long as four hours. Kevin would arrive first, and order two drinks, and Michelle would join him soon after, each time in the same booth in the saloon bar. They rarely ate, and if they did it was only a basket of chips. They would each drink eight full Scotches and Coke and Kevin would pay the bill of $60–$70 with a credit card. There was nothing discreet about their behaviour.

Ms Hughes told police: "They were very friendly and affectionate to each other. They would kiss and touch under the table. They would be half laying and half sitting on the seats. Sometimes it was embarrassing to the staff and patrons. Patrons would often move and sit at a different table away from them and make comments. I once heard him say that he loved her. On a couple of occasions, they had minor arguments. She would either sit there in tears or walk out."

A lawyer would later try to suggest that Ms Hughes "exaggerated the conduct she saw in the hotel". But she was having none of that: "I probably took a little bit of the gloss off, actually."

CAROLYN MATTHEWS was a very private woman by nature, and had done a remarkable job of keeping her feelings about Kevin's behaviour under wraps. But the cost of hotel rooms, Scotch and gold chains was quickly adding up and, while she had no proof of where the money was going, she feared Kevin's profligate behaviour was pushing their family to the brink of financial ruin. In July, 2000, their Property Power account had a debit balance of $126,000. By July 2001, it was $150,000. Kevin had been using their mortgage account to pay off his reckless spending on their MasterCard.

Bob Brooks, a life member of the Semaphore Surf Life Saving Club who considered the Matthews family to be close friends, received a phone call from Carolyn at 10pm on Saturday, February 3, 2001. He later told police that Carolyn was upset and said that "things were not very good" between her and Kevin. She had no idea where Kevin was and he was sending her text messages telling her he "wanted out, he wasn't coming back". Bob reassured her that Kevin was probably drunk somewhere and that things would probably sort themselves out the next day. He sent Kevin a text asking him to call him, but he didn't. The next day, Bob went to the Matthews home and drove a tired and upset Carolyn, and her boys, to a surf life saving carnival at Goolwa.

After leaving the boys at the beach, he returned to the car park to talk to Carolyn, who was initially hesitant. But she admitted Kevin had maxxed out their credit card and there was no money in their bank account. She had no money and feared they would be unable to make their mortgage payment, due on Friday. Kevin had also been threatening suicide. She explained that Kevin had put a lock on his phone so she couldn't use it or see any of his messages. Bob was astounded. He gave Carolyn $50 so she could buy lunch for the boys, who knew nothing of the situation. Yvonne was on the beach that day but Carolyn, who couldn't bear to see her, remained in the car park.

The carnival finished early due to bad weather and they drove back to Adelaide. Kevin still wasn't home when they arrived. Bob told Carolyn he would try to get some money for her from the surf life saving club. He drove to the club to see the president, Peter Campaign, about the money. Kevin and Carolyn had lent the club $1000 a few years previously towards a building fund and, with interest, the club actually owed them about $1300. Campaign, who was also a longstanding friend of the Matthews family, agreed to repay the loan so that Carolyn could meet her mortgage payment. That evening, Carolyn made an excuse to leave the house and drove to the club, where the money was removed from the club's bar safe and handed over to her. Carolyn begged Bob not to tell Kevin about the money. She was hoping Kevin would sort out their finances and she wouldn't need to use it.

She later told him that Kevin had paid the home loan and that she had told him about the money from the club.

Bob Brooks later told police: "Subsequently, Carolyn rang me at home and confided that someone had told her that Kevin was having an affair. I believe she said the person who told her was a sacked Beaurepaires employee and that this person's wife was having the affair with Kevin."

The loan to the club was indicative of how important surf life saving was to the Matthews family. It was this passion for surf, sun and sand that united them like nothing else in their lives.

Shane Tidswell recalls: "Kevin once explained it to me when he saw (country singer) John Williamson on TV, he said: 'Do you know how much I love the surf club? That's how much this bloke loves Australia'. Kevin loved the surf club a lot, he grew up with it.

"The Tidswells have been heavily involved in Glenelg SLSC and my old man was involved in Semaphore. We were born into it. All of my best mates are from the surf club. All my parents' friends' kids are my friends. After you've been on the beach all day together, everybody hangs around for the family functions. Life saving takes up so much of your time that if you're involved as much as we were, it's more of a lifestyle than sport. It's not part-time. I was doing 11–14 hours a week in the pool. Mum would get up at 5.20am to take us, then every Saturday and Sunday on the beach."

DARREN BURGESS immediately hit hurdles in his bid to continue being a father after leaving Michelle. She would make arrangements to drop the kids off to see him, but then cancel or postpone. It soon had an impact.

"About two weeks after I left, I went back to speak to Michelle. I was missing the kids badly. Some might say I went to reconcile but I really went to satisfy myself that I had made a tough but correct decision to leave Michelle. In my mind, I knew there would be dire consequences for my children. Michelle was a selfish person and she would not look after them properly. With what was going on, I knew she would risk their safety for her pleasure. After seeing her and speaking with her, I was satisfied it was all over and now I could move on with my life. In one way, I was devastated for the sake of the kids but happy to escape life with Michelle."

On February 25, in another conversation, Michelle concocted yet another fantasy, claiming she had cervical cancer and wanted to get back together. Darren says: "She told me she had cancer, she had about six to 12 months to live, and she wanted to get back together so that (their two young children) could have a family. She said she'd spent the last three days at a health farm."

The following day, Darren's father, Lindsay, decided it was time he intervened in the situation. He later told police that a month after Darren came to stay, he had confided to his parents that Michelle had been having an affair with Kevin while they had still been together. He told them about the mobile phone account with dozens of calls to Kevin and the call from "Julie" warning him of the affair. Lindsay was furious and decided he needed to get to the bottom of all this; he would interrogate Kevin.

On Sunday, February 25, 2001, he went to the Matthews home and spoke to Kevin in the front yard. Predictably, he denied the affair and explained to Lindsay about the night Michelle had claimed to have been stabbed. While he was recounting this story, Carolyn came out and stood next to Kevin. Lindsay asked her what she thought of the situation. She shrugged. "I don't know ... I think we have a perfect marriage."

Lindsay later told police: "Kevin said he wanted all four of them – himself, Carolyn, Darren and Michelle – to sit down and talk this affair thing over. Carolyn also confirmed this and did not seem shocked to hear this information about Kevin, but I always thought she was a calm sort of person. The only thing she was doing was pacing up and down a bit. I spoke to them for about half an hour. Early in the conversation, I felt that Kevin was lying because he wouldn't look at me. I left, telling Kevin I'd make up my mind later about whether or not he was involved with Michelle. But I did tell him I thought he was having an affair. I shook his hand when I left and said goodbye to Carolyn."

In February, after ending the worst relationship of his life, Darren Burgess's luck finally changed. After watching a Port Adelaide game and enjoying a few beers with some mates, he was feeling better than he had in a long time. When one of his friends received a couple of text messages from a female work colleague, Darren got adventurous: "Give me her number, I'll send her a message." It was a message that flashed "masturbation can disturb your vision."

The woman was bemused, replying: "Who is this?" More messages were exchanged. The next day, Darren rang to apologise, fearing he may have disturbed her. He had not.

More than 10 years later, Kathy Morton remains Darren's loyal and loving partner and they plan to marry. Michelle was oblivious to the fact that the man she had trapped was a good one. But Kathy, who instantly recognised Darren's qualities, soon fell in love. In its first tentative months, their relationship was forged in fire, put to the ultimate test time and again as the situation with Michelle spun out of control and ultimately put both their lives in danger. And from the moment Darren informed Michelle of his new relationship, her jealousy was venomous.

He informed her that Kathy would be attending their son's soccer match and asked that she be polite when he introduced them. Michelle wanted no part in it and made sure it was an awkward and uncomfortable meeting for Kathy.

On March 5, Darren made a diary note stating: "Told Michelle I hate her." followed two days later by: "I need to sort out Kevin otherwise I will quit my job."

Darren says: "I did quit. But (his relevant superior) refused to accept it. She said to have a think about it. She rang Kevin to question him.

"When I rang her back, I said: 'I'm not going to leave.'

"She said: 'I don't think you told me the full story, you didn't mention that you've got a new girlfriend.'

"I said: 'That's irrelevant to the situation. This wasn't about what I was doing when I was no longer with Michelle. This was about me working for Kevin after he had an affair with my wife.'"

She told Darren he no longer had to communicate with Kevin and he should instead contact her for work matters; but a week later, she lost her job. Soon after, a new national retail sales manager, Stephen Gower, was appointed and he undertook a tour of the stores. Darren found himself standing in the front of his store with the new boss and Kevin. Kevin left as soon as he could. Darren was upfront and explained the situation to Gower, but had doubts that his story was believed. He had a point to prove, so he gave Michelle's phone number to Gower and suggested he cross-reference Kevin's phone records. Darren says Gower rang him days later and said: "Well, I can tell you that I know your wife's number very well and I believe you."

Darren says: "There were more and more stories going around Beaurepaires about Kevin and Michelle. One that she was caught giving him a head job in the car. I think Stephen rang around a few of the managers, including me, and asked what we thought about Kevin's performance. I was a bit biased of course, but I told him we didn't have any sales meetings. We hardly hear from him or see him."

Gower, who was now Kevin Matthews's immediate supervisor, reprimanded him in an email dated March 26 over the use of his corporate American Express card. He later told police he had advised Kevin that he'd signed off on his expenses for the month, but Kevin needed to be more specific with details in the future. He also noted that Kevin's entertainment expenses were excessive and needed to be kept to a minimum.

Meanwhile, Darren also discovered that Michelle had yet another new man in her life. She'd met Jason, from Perth, on the internet, and he came to stay with her for a couple of weeks. Darren once saw him at his son's soccer match.

Michelle visited Rebel Ford Elizabeth on March 12 and told the manager she wanted to buy another car. But Michael Whellans, who had a working relationship with Darren and occasionally socialised with him, was a reluctant salesman on this occasion. Michelle told him she'd split up with Darren and needed to trade in her Nissan Pintara so she could get her own car. Whellans knew that Darren was a co-owner of the Pintara and he rang him later in the day to confirm that he would need to sort things out with Michelle before she could take delivery of another car. Michelle looked around the yard and found a red 1990 Toyota Seca. After a test drive, she agreed to buy it for $9888, plus costs. Once Darren had given permission for her to trade in the Pintara, Michelle made an application to a finance company which was approved – despite the fact she had no job – and arrangements were made for her to pick up the vehicle.

In April, Darren and Michelle's estrangement took a turn for the worse. Darren says he and Michelle were getting on "relatively well" and, up until just before Easter 2001, she had been allowing him regular access to the children. He recalls: "I made the point to her when we broke up that, for the sake of (the children), we had to be on friendly terms. I didn't want them stuck in the middle of two parents fighting. That changed when I met Kathy."

Up to this point, the custody arrangement with the children was informal. They would stay with Darren every second weekend and he took them out to dinner every second Tuesday. But now, he was forced to take court action to see them. He was granted fortnightly visits and allowed to have dinner with them on Tuesday nights. Michelle believed Darren shouldn't have the kids when Kathy had her boys with her because she didn't want them mixing. Darren, in turn, wasn't comfortable with having her boyfriends – particularly "Jason", the man from Perth – around the children.

One Tuesday night in late March, as Darren was dropping the children home and saying goodbye out the front, his estranged wife snatched his mobile phone from his hand, ran inside and locked the door. After extracting Kathy's phone number, she returned the phone. Darren recalls: "I quickly rang Kathy to tell her what had happened and to expect a call."

On April 9, Darren made a diary note stating: "Michelle rang. Asked what me and my bitch were doing in the street on Sunday. She said that I was dead and that Kathy was dead, and that was a promise, not a threat."

Kathy Morton later gave police a detailed account of the incident, which occurred on a Sunday prior to Easter 2001. She was with Darren and they were driving home after checking on the Burgess's house at Evanston Gardens. Darren's mobile rang and when he answered it, Kathy could hear Michelle screaming at him: "She's dead. You're dead. I'll kill you both." Darren hung up and shortly after, he received a text message which read: "Please call, no more fighting." A second, less conciliatory message read: "I know where she lives, it's a promise, not a threat."

The next day, Kathy was on the train on her way home from work when Michelle called her mobile. Kathy tried to discuss the children, because she was hoping Darren could have them for Easter so they could meet her children. But Michelle began screaming abuse at her, calling her a slut, a whore and a troll. Kathy snapped back: "If you're going to call me abusive names, at least get it right. It's a trollop, not a troll. I don't live under a bridge." And then she hung up. The woman sitting next to her on the train had heard the exchange and looked at her with disgust.

Darren says: "Kathy is a very strong and brave person who stands up for herself. But this was disturbing even for her."

Michelle immediately sent Kathy a text message saying: "You tell Darren he will not be getting sex this Tuesday night when he drops the children off. I am really pissed off and angry." Kathy rang Darren's parents to check the status of Darren and Michelle's relationship. They assured her there was nothing going on and the relationship was over. His father told her that she was the best thing that had happened to him. That evening, Darren and Kathy went to the Christies Beach police station and requested the paperwork for a restraining order against Michelle.

Darren says: "The officer laughed at us and made us feel insignificant. He said to me: 'You want a restraining order against your ex-wife?' In hindsight, we should have gone ahead with it. I was genuinely concerned for my safety after what Michelle had threatened."

Another separate, nasty spat broke out over a recurrent health issue one of the children was suffering. The situation culminated in a meeting between Michelle and an officer from Family and Community Services, who commented that: "Michelle presented as a loving mother who was sensitive to the needs of the children."

In a related incident, on April 15, an anonymous female complainant – almost certainly Michelle – rang FACS and reported Darren. The woman told FACS he was deliberately not administering a prescribed medication to the child to make it look as though the mother was not caring for her. The caller also said Darren had his driver's licence suspended for drink-driving, had been regularly drinking and driving with the children in the car and made them refer to their mother as "bitch". The person who took the call had serious doubts about the veracity of the complaint and accurately marked "notifier concern" on the report.

On April 12, 2001, Darren's father Lindsay decided the situation again required his firm hand. He went to Beaurepaires head office to confront Kevin again. He told him the verdict was in and he was guilty of having an affair. Kevin denied it. Lindsay warned him of the impact it was having on the children involved, but Kevin was having none of it. Frustrated, Lindsay left.

He says: "I know at that time a lot of things were happening between Darren and Michelle and Michelle's parents. In the next few days, Darren told me that Michelle's father, Keith Goldup, had said to him that I want to be careful about what I say to Kevin. I thought it was strange that what I had said to Kevin was coming back through Michelle's parents."

Lindsay called Carolyn a couple of days after Easter, and immediately assured her that he wasn't ringing to create hassles. He says: "I told her I believed that Michelle and Kevin were still communicating and I said she could do whatever she liked with that information. She just said 'thankyou' and we hung up. Shortly after this, Darren moved out of our house."

Also over Easter, the Matthews family went to stay at a shack on the River Murray, at Scott Creek, near Morgan, which belonged to Valerie Rismondo, a close friend of Carolyn whom she met through their boys attending the same school. Valerie later told police that she talked to Carolyn throughout the weekend, but the focus was mostly on the children. She mentioned that she was worried about Kevin's drinking and that they'd received a series of odd phone calls between October and Christmas. She also briefly mentioned that she had asked Kevin if he was having an affair and he'd told her "not to be so stupid".

On April 20, a petty criminal named David William Edgar Key was released from a South Australian prison. Key had no connection whatsoever to Michelle Burgess or Kevin Matthews. But within just a few weeks, a series of bizarre circumstances would make him the lightning rod for Michelle's dark fantasies.

Michelle Burgess booked into cabin 24 at the Adelaide Beachfront Tourist Park from April 25–27, under her maiden name. Notably, she had her children with her on this occasion and it is not known if Kevin Matthews joined her. On the morning she checked out, Kevin Matthews checked into Room 103 at the South Park on South Tce in Adelaide at 9.42am, checking out at 1.27pm.

One man, it seemed, was rarely enough for Michelle. Jason from Perth was no longer around, and she had been scanning the personal ads in the local *Messenger* newspaper. In early June, 2001, a man we will call Steven placed two separate ads, several weeks apart, in the Talking Friends section of the *Messenger*. About 15 women left messages, including a woman who described herself as 26, with blonde hair, blue eyes, children and recently separated, who was looking for friendship, view relationship.

Steven called the woman, and they immediately hit it off. They spoke on the phone for a couple of hours on June 5 and he arranged to meet her at the Billy Baxter's café in the Munno Para Shopping Centre. Michelle explained to him that she had split up with her husband Darren earlier in the year and they were in the process of selling their house. The conversation flowed smoothly and while Steven explained he would be meeting other women, Michelle was happy to exchange phone numbers. Then Steven, who was quite the gentleman, walked her to her car.

He says: "We became friends. She seemed an intelligent girl, but I don't think we hit it off in the romance department. She would drink a lot and ring me and talk a lot, about her husband, the kids, driving her insane. How she would like to get rid of her husband. Not kill him, just get him out of her life somehow. I would just try to calm her down. She would generally call me early, around 6am or 7am, or after 4pm up to 8pm. We would talk on the phone for up to four hours at a time.

"She told me she had a couple of friends with benefits. I backed off from that sort of relationship, I'm not into that sort of stuff. But she didn't mention any names. She would say her life was shit, complaining. I'm told I'm a good listener. I would then give my two cents worth. She always tried to make herself look pretty with make-up. We went to dinner a couple of times and she came to dinner at my place once. We just spent time as friends. She made up stories about her husband beating her up, putting her up against the wall and strangling her in front of the kids."

THE CONSTANT RUMOURS, poor performance and excessive spending on his company credit card finally brought Kevin Matthews's corporate career to a screeching halt. Stephen Gower flew to Adelaide in June 2001 and met Kevin in Ansett's Golden Wing lounge. Gower told Kevin his performance was unsatisfactory. Branch managers had advised that he rarely visited them. They could not contact him at work or on his mobile and when they did, he was very aggressive. Kevin had left his boss with no other choice – he would be demoted to branch manager at Port Adelaide. Gower didn't mention that the other reason for the demotion was the irrefutable evidence of Kevin's affair with Michelle.

On June 10, Kevin started his new role at Port Adelaide. By coincidence, Darren Bland – with whom Michelle had previously had an affair – had been managing that store, but had quit. He started work at the Ultra Tune store, just across the driveway from Kevin's new workplace, in mid-June. They were both smokers and their paths would often cross outside the two businesses. Bland later told police he saw Kevin out the back or in the driveway using his mobile phone for up to a couple of hours spread across the day. He had heard the rumours about Kevin and Michelle and was concerned. He liked Kevin and didn't want to see him hurt, so he approached him on several occasions and questioned him about Michelle. Kevin insisted there was no affair, but Bland made his point – Michelle was nothing but trouble and Kevin would be better off steering clear.

Also that month, Kevin had to endure the ignominy of attending the Beaurepaires annual budget meeting as a store manager. Beaurepaires manager Robert says that at the start of the financial year, the managers would meet for store budgets to be handed out. In 2001, it was at Wirrina

Cove, a resort and conference centre on the Fleurieu Peninsula, south of Adelaide. Robert's wife recalls: "He was drinking triple Scotches at 10.30 in the morning. He was even reprimanded for his drinking."

Robert remembers that Kevin was clearly uneasy. He says: "He'd gone from being regional manager to being one of us. And you could see he wasn't comfortable. There were all these rumours and innuendo and then suddenly he's been demoted."

Kenny, Shane and Daniel Matthews also knew something was seriously amiss with their parents' marriage, but they were shielded from the truth.

Shane remembers that while the word was never mentioned, the spectre of divorce hung heavily over the Matthews household. He had noticed that his father was going on more interstate trips and he was staying at work later a lot more often.

"The first time I realised something was wrong was when I was at the footy one Saturday. My game was over and I went to sit in the car, my dad's work car. There was a tape player, Dictaphone-type thing in the car and I turned it on. It was dad's voice arguing with someone else. He was saying something about two kids and obviously Darren and Michelle Burgess have two kids. I really can't remember what was said, but it was something that didn't add up to me. It sounded a bit weird, but I had no idea what I was listening to. That would have been in the winter. It sounded like he was at work and somebody else was telling him to do something. I was confused by it and just put it out of my mind."

The strain was starting to show on the usually happy and carefree face of Carolyn Matthews. Anne McKenzie, a mother whose children went to the same swimming centre as the Matthews boys, noted Carolyn's distress when Carolyn came to pick up her kids from swimming in the second week of June 2001. She looked very tired, as if she hadn't slept and was visibly upset. Anne commented on her appearance and Carolyn told her she'd been up all night and was upset. Carolyn rang her a week later to let her know that she'd changed their phone number to a silent number. Anne asked if it had anything to do with what happened the week before and Carolyn said it did – they had been getting threatening phone calls and even a death threat. Anne was nonplussed. "Who could be doing this to you?" she asked. Carolyn didn't know, but whoever was making the calls knew details of their life, including when they went to the river. Anne asked if she had reported the calls to the police, but Carolyn told her the police had said there was nothing they could do unless there were three or more calls in a week.

While Carolyn was struggling to feed the family and begging for money to pay the home loan, Kevin's corporate American Express card remained valid, despite his demotion. On June 15, he used it to pay for $60 worth of flowers and chocolates delivered to "Liz" (Elizabeth was Michelle's middle name) at her Evanston Park home. The note read: "Liz, love you more."

In recent days, they'd been house hunting for Michelle, because the Burgess's home had finally been sold. A Century 21 property manager later told police that Michelle became a tenant at a villa in Bluebush Court, Craigmore, on June 18, 2001, with rent set at $330 a fortnight.

The manager met Michelle at the property for an inspection the week before she moved in. She was waiting at the house and saw Michelle arrive in one car, and Kevin arrive in another. They embraced and kissed before they came into the house. The manager asked if Kevin would also be living at the property, but he said he wouldn't.

Michelle would now have her own little love nest, and there would soon be a sizeable cheque coming her way from the sale of the house. But it was far from enough. Her hatred of Carolyn Matthews was growing; Carolyn's now-regular phone calls warning Michelle to keep away from her husband infuriated her. Michelle wanted what Carolyn had and was prepared to take drastic action to make it happen. She fantasised constantly about the life she and Kevin could have together – if only they could get rid of Darren and Carolyn. Mick Standing, a straight-talking, no-nonsense, veteran detective who is now retired, recalls: "Burgess saw that she was just a loose screw for him and so she forced the issue. I don't think Kevin Matthews was ever going to leave his wife. Look at what he had to lose – his house, half of everything he'd got. In a divorce, he would have lost a lot. He had three young sons. So he had a lot to lose to go running off with her. And for what? To put it bluntly, because she was good in bed."

Chapter 4

Contracts to kill

February 2001

FOR HOME MUMS like Kathy Cowled, school pick-up was a few minutes away from the daily grind, a chance to catch up with the neighbourhood's goings-on. While waiting, she often chatted to Michelle Burgess, the mother of a boy in her son's class who'd become her friend; Michelle's stories were never dull.

When the kids had returned to Evanston Primary School, in Gawler, 40km north of Adelaide, for the start of the school year in February 2001, Cowled had immediately noticed a difference in Michelle. She already knew about Michelle's affair with Kevin, but now Michelle told her that, since Kathy had seen Darren when he gave her a ride home from the train station, he had moved out. Michelle loved boasting about her affair and enjoyed seeing how it enthralled Kathy. She told her that she would go down to the beach at Semaphore to watch Kevin work out.

When the women compared photographs of their respective boyfriends, Kathy had to hide her shock. Kevin Matthews was once a handsome, well-groomed young lifeguard with a winning smile. But age, genes and alcohol abuse had not been kind to him. The man in Michelle's picture appeared to be in his early forties. He was fighting – and losing – a battle against baldness, wore glasses and a moustache, and his enormous gut was straining at the buttons of his Hawaiian shirt. Not the type of man who would usually attract a female audience at the beach.

"I've got some exciting news," Michelle confided one day. "I met up with Kevin at Fremont Park (in Elizabeth). And we did it on the tables and chairs."

Cowled blanched at the mental image of the man in the loud shirt grinding away on top of Michelle in public. Michelle also told her they went to Pioneer Park, in Gawler, for liaisons. Later asked by a lawyer why this information had stuck in her mind, she answered: "It's not every day that people do it in a park."

Michelle eagerly revealed more in her daily instalments. She was also meeting up with Kevin at hotels for long, boozy lunches during which they would be all over each other and she would often turn up to school with alcohol on her breath.

Cowled told police: "She told me Kevin was charming, he was a good father, a good provider who didn't want to be with his wife any more – they were constantly having arguments."

But in March, Michelle's mood had darkened along with her stories. Her fantasy life with Kevin was falling apart. She was turning up at school distressed and crying. She told Kathy there were problems with Darren, problems with family issues, and parents and in-laws ringing her up all the time and hassling her. Carolyn Matthews had found out about the affair and Michelle said she had been harassing her and abusing her. Kathy later told police she was present when Michelle received some of the calls. After one particularly heated exchange, in which Carolyn informed Michelle there was no way she was surrendering her husband, Michelle fumed: "I want her out of the way."

In May, Michelle had told Cowled she had had enough of the phone calls and she had been to the Gawler and Elizabeth police to report it. No such reports are on record with the police. Cowled later told police that about two weeks after Michelle claimed she'd reported the situation, she told her she wanted Carolyn Matthews "put six foot underground".

The phone calls from Carolyn and Darren's threats to take the children from her and sell the house were just all too much to cope with. She also said Kevin would do anything to get out of his marriage so he could be with her.

Michelle wrongly suspected that Carolyn had reported her to the Family and Community Services Department for child neglect. A report was made, but not by Carolyn. Finally, with her marriage over and her marital home about to be sold, Michelle's hatred of Carolyn Matthews had turned to pure malice.

She asked Cowled: "Do you know anyone who could get rid of her? I don't care how it's done ... maybe a car accident."

Cowled says: "It occurred to me then that Michelle wanted Carolyn dead, but I never thought it would come to (that). I only thought Michelle wanted to scare her. She repeated these threats over the next few days and weeks. I got sick and tired of hearing it.

"Around the same time, she also mentioned she wanted to get rid of her husband Darren, to be done a couple of days after Carolyn. She said something about it being an accident and the kids weren't to be with Darren at the time. She asked me if I knew anyone who would get rid of Carolyn."

It was an outrageous question to ask anyone, let alone another mother outside a primary school. Kathy Cowled could have said no, or she could have gone to the police. Inexplicably, she decided to help her friend. And the answer she gave would be the catalyst for a series of events plucked from the darkest corners of Michelle's twisted imagination: "I told Michelle that my brother David might know someone that could help her."

Cowled rang her brother the next day and explained Michelle's situation and how she wanted to solve it. David Key didn't even hesitate. He told his sister he knew someone who could help her and he asked for more information about Carolyn Matthews and Darren Burgess. Cowled said he sounded intrigued, even excited, by the proposition. That afternoon at school pick-up, she told Michelle that her brother knew someone who could help her.

David Key later told police: "I'd been out (of jail) about two months before I met Michelle through my sister. I had told my sister Kathy I was looking for work. You know, if someone wanted a lawn cut, go and get the brother-in-law's lawn mower, get a bit of quick cash. I do a bit of labouring work. My sister rang up and says she's got a job for me. I said: 'Yeah? Get me some more information'."

Key had no second thoughts in upgrading his job aspirations from labourer to contract killer. But David Key was not a man of great intellectual capacity. A forensic psychologist who later evaluated him found that Key was of low to average intelligence, virtually illiterate, vulnerable to stress, self-conscious and inclined to hostility and anger. He satisfied the relevant criteria for alcohol abuse, amphetamine dependence, cannabis dependence, chronic post-traumatic stress disorder, anti-social personality disorder and borderline personality disorder. He was a walking time-bomb.

Key is the man you cross the road to avoid; who revs his engine and tries to catch your eye at the traffic lights or aggressively tailgates other drivers without reason. In July 2001, he was wiry, almost skinny, after a couple of months out of prison, having reacquired his voracious appetite for drugs, particularly amphetamines. His shaved head, goatee and wraparound dark sunglasses completed the picture of a man angry at the world for the hand it had dealt him.

Cowled saw Michelle at school on the same day and relayed Key's request, along with her brother's mobile phone number. At school the following day, Michelle told Cowled she'd spoken to Key. Michelle handed Cowled an A4 piece of paper with a colour photo of Carolyn Matthews sticky-taped to it. Michelle explained to her friend: "I told Kevin we'd found someone to do the job but they need more information, so Kevin wrote this down and gave it to me."

Cowled studied the document. In blue biro, Kevin Matthews had listed his wife's personal details in neat cursive writing: her date of birth, home address, work address, the time she left home, the time she arrived home, her mobile phone number, home phone number and work phone number.

It was effectively a murder contract. Cowled put it in her handbag and rang her brother when she got home. He came around that evening to collect it. Key, who can barely read, says: "I walked in and she's got this paperwork. She gave me the paperwork and I opened it all up. I had a look and I knew straight out it was a contract. (Kathy) said: 'This chick's got to be knocked and fucking Michelle's getting sick of this chick, the abusive phone calls'. Kathy thinks that her and this Matthews were sleeping together and (Carolyn) rang children's welfare on her. And she started raving on ... I was like: 'All right Kathy, shut up, I got what I need.'"

A detective who later quizzed Key asked: "What did you understand she was doing by giving you that piece of paper?"

Key: "It was a job, to be murdered. This chick had to be shut up, to be shot."

"You had no doubt about that?"

"No mate, no doubt."

Key folded up the piece of paper, put it in his pocket and left his sister's house. He'd felt utterly aimless when he left prison, but Michelle Burgess and her murder contract intrigued him; now he had a purpose. Within days, Michelle visited Cowled to give her more details. Michelle was moving out of her home at the time, and, as we will learn later, she may well have already been considering killing her husband herself. On the back of an old envelope, Cowled watched her scrawl four dot points:

* look like a car accident (both)
* alone
* one done this week (by Friday)
* one next week

A smile of satisfaction spread over Michelle's face when she finished writing – if all went to plan, at least one of them would be dead by Friday. Cowled was supposed to pass it on to her brother, but forgot, and she would stumble across the envelope at home months later.

After the sale of the Burgess marital home at Evanston Park had settled, Michelle moved to Craigmore, but continued to drive her son 15km to Evanston Primary. A few days after the move, she brought a second murder contract to school, this time in her handwriting. Cowled, who at no stage expressed any constarnation about her role as agent for a hitman, again called her brother to arrange to pass it on. Key later claimed to police that he wasn't aware the second contract was coming, but his sister's statements contradict this. When he arrived at her home, she gave him a second A4 sheet, this time bearing the photo and personal details of Darren Burgess.

Key remembers: "It was Michelle's ex-husband, she wanted him dead. She wanted full custody of the kids. She was sick of his phone calls, sick of him threatening Kevin, sick of him fucking getting his own way in the court when it came to custody of the kids. She just wanted him out of the kids' lives and her life."

Within days of receiving the second contract, Key says he "popped up (to Evanston) one morning".

"I was off my nut, off my dial. I'd been out driving all night through the back country, just wasting time, bored shitless."

He pulled alongside his sister and nephew in his old Ford Falcon as they walked home from school.

"Jump in Kathy, we'll go for a drive, I'll drop you home," he told her. "Michelle's back at the school if you want to meet her," she responded as she and her son climbed in. He did.

He later told police: "I parked in front of (Michelle's) red Seca, I'm sitting in the car, you know, trying to be discreet. Fucking pulling cones and trying to be discreet and me sister's come up and she's … (said:) 'Oh Michelle wants to have a yarn with you'. Oh yeah, all right. Put everything away, grabbed my smokes and mobile phone, jumped out of the car, sat on the boot of my car and met Michelle. We just started talking about contracts and the paperwork Kathy's given me. We're talking about how she wanted Carolyn murdered, how she wants it to be done. Like she wants to have a car accident, to make it look like that. Started going through different scenarios. I said: 'Don't worry about it – I'll take care of it'."

"It's going to cost you 50 grand, 25 apiece," Key told her, suddenly business-like as he looked her up and down and idly mused to himself: "I wonder if I could get a screw out of this?"

Michelle nodded. "I'll let him know."

But she was vague on Matthews's exact involvement.

Key says: "She said that he's just a good friend, that fucking, he's got problems with his marriage and wants out. He's sick of it, sick of being accused of having an affair."

Key "can't remember" if he specifically asked why these people had to die. "I think I did, I'm not really sure. I remember Michelle saying that she was going to pay for Carolyn Matthews to be killed and Kevin Matthews was going to pay for Darren Burgess to be murdered."

Key waited for the school traffic to clear, then pulled out the contracts to double-check his targets: "Are you sure these are the people?"

"Yeah," Michelle answered, grabbing her husband's contract and writing extra details on it before handing it back. "Good fucking riddance to the lot of you."

Key seemed satisfied. "I've got some friends who'll do it, not a problem, I'll get back to you. Give me your phone number and I'll ring you back."

CHAPTER 5

David William Edgar Key, hitman

July 1, 2001 – July 11, 2001

WITH MURDER CONTRACTS in his wallet and big money on his mind, David Key felt like James Bond. He didn't have the intelligence, charisma, wit, charm, dress sense, discretion or morals, but none of that mattered. In his mind, he now had what he needed to become a professional hitman – a licence to kill.

He opened up the contracts and looked them over again. *Think. Focus. Concentrate.* He would have to use some serious brain power to pull off this hitman thing. It was way bigger than any crime he'd ever done. He needed a plan. First, he figured, he needed a gun. Hitmen used guns, usually big buggers with silencers. And now he had the cash to get one.

On July 3, 2001, Kevin Matthews withdrew $1500 from his already-strained mortgage account. Within days, Michelle handed Key a down-payment of $1500 in $100 notes. He wanted to keep a chunk of that for weed and speed, so he needed to find a cheap compromise; but this was a contract killing – he definitely needed a gun with a silencer.

Key had recently been associating with a man we will call "George", whose name is legally suppressed. He lived near Key's mother's home in Davoren Park, a far northern suburb of Adelaide not known for its high property values or median incomes. They would talk about cars and often shared a few pipes or bongs or a couple of bourbons. George thought Key seemed harmless enough. Full of shit, mostly, and he liked to big-note himself. But he would sometimes bring with him the kind of high-quality hydroponic cannabis for which Adelaide is famous – and that was never a bad thing.

"I got a job to do. Can you get me a pistol?" Key asked his new friend, trying to sound both casual and mysterious as they sat at George's kitchen table one afternoon. George was immediately cautious.

"Maybe. What kind? What you need it for?"

"Nine mil Beretta pistol with silencer. I got a little job to do. This chick's gotta be silenced."

George squinted through the bong haze at Key's earnest face. He thought Key was either joking or utterly mad. But a few days later he came back with more weed and more questions. And he still seemed serious, this time asking for three clips of ammunition as well.

"It's gotta be untraceable and it needs to keep the shells after they've been fired. I've got two to three grand put aside to cover costs," Key told him. He expected George to be impressed, but instead he seemed tense and doubtful.

"This is serious shit, Dave. Why would you want to do this?"

Key plucked Carolyn Matthews's murder contract from the top pocket of his flannelette shirt and unfolded it with a flourish.

"This is the lady that's got to be hushed. The chick who's paying for it is jealous of her."

"You're mad getting involved in women's problems, Dave."

"Nah. It'll be fine. This high-class sheila from Craigmore hired me to do some odd jobs, and then she's lined up this big job … And now I'm screwing her, too," he finished, both proud and embarrassed.

"You're a fucking idiot," George rebuked him. "You don't mix business with pleasure."

George didn't pay too much attention to the contract that Key was waving, but saw that it had a woman's picture attached to it.

"So, can you get me that price?" Key prodded. "I've got the cash."

David Key was no hitman – the idea was ludicrous. But he was definitely up to no good, George thought. He would see where Key's bullshit led to.

"All right, mate, I know some guys. I'll try to find out a price and get back to you."

Three days later, they were seated at George's kitchen table again. George told him the price for the pistol would be $1500–$2000. Key looked sheepish. Three days ago he still had most of the money, but money burns holes in drug addicts' pockets very quickly. He later admitted that "I drank it, smoked it, and bought a shitload of speed". He'd been off his head from virtually the moment he laid his hands on the cash.

It was just as George had suspected. "No cash, no gun," he told Key with finality. Key's visits did not stop, but the gun talk did. And a few days later, he brought Michelle to George's home to show her off, cuddling and kissing in between the obligatory bongs and bourbons.

George relaxed; these people weren't going to kill anyone. Dopey Dave was no master villain and Michelle was definitely no Bond girl.

BY HIS OWN ADMISSION, David William Edgar Key is not the sharpest tool in the shed. Intellectually, he is as dull and blunt as they come, a product of a dysfunctional childhood, a man of borderline intelligence, with a prodigious appetite for drugs and the propensity for angry, violent outbursts. Even his name is longer than his attention span. Asked to describe himself, he says: "I don't know, sometimes I can be a real arsehole. Sometimes I can be aggressive. Sometimes I'll be talking to someone and I'll just be staring at them. I'd rather be bent. When I'm bent, I can just sit back and I don't give a fuck about what anyone says."

Key was born at Queen Elizabeth Hospital, Adelaide, on August 17, 1974, to a father he says was a violent alcoholic and a mother he describes as his "counsellor, friend and mum". But he also says his mother had two sides. "On one side she was nice, polite and helpful and the sweetest, kindest person you could meet," he told forensic psychologist Dr Jack White in one of two assessments he would later undergo with mental health professionals. "On the other side, she was a vicious lady who could not stand for much."

In spite of this, he felt very close to his mother and believed that at least earlier in his life, he was her favourite over his three sisters, Kathleen, Samantha and Kerry. Key says his mother told him he was a twin, but the other child was stillborn. He had no known developmental issues as a child, but was afflicted with severe asthma as a toddler and recalls frequent hospital admissions. His childhood, he says, was "hard, up and down. In one way it was good, in another way it was shit." He says he was not an excessively rebellious child, but he did test the limits of his parents' authority. He would "run amok", and also harass his sisters.

The family moved frequently in his early childhood, around the northern suburbs of Adelaide and surrounding country areas. Key says his father moved regularly because he worked as a labourer in the farming and agriculture sector and as a truck driver.

Asked to describe his father, Key says: "It depends. If he's been drinking, he's a real arsehole. When he's not drinking, when he's actually working, when his head is actually clear, he's a good father. When he drinks, he is very boisterous and demanding. He is also a control freak. When I was a kid, he would kick the shit out of me every day." He says his father was also violent to his three sisters and would physically assault them before turning on their mother.

Key says his father assaulted him with belts, open hands and fists, whenever he came home drunk, which was three to four times a week. At age 15, Key started running away from home, usually when his father was drunk and violent. He would sleep under a local bridge and return home when his father was sober.

When he was younger, Key would stay in his bedroom when his father was drunk but things changed when he was physically large enough to defend himself and his mother. The most serious incident occurred when Key was 16. He says his father held a knife to his throat after he defended his mother from another beating. Key says this prompted him to "go ballistic" and he beat his father until he was unconscious. He was arrested and charged with assault, but his father later withdrew the complaint.

Key and his father fought regularly after their showdown. He says he would have left, but he feared his father would have further brutalised his sisters and mother. Key began to see himself as the family protector and "trained" his father not to be violent, or he would receive equal measure in return. His relationship with his father improved when he did leave home months later, he says, because he had "proved that he was stronger than his father".

Key says his parents' marriage fluctuated, depending on his father's alcoholism and violence. They separated when he was 25 but stayed in contact. He describes his childhood temperament as: "A bastard. Just a bastard. Because that's what mum used to call me every time I used to get out of the house. She used to say: 'You bastard, get back here'."

He says his sisters often warned him: "You keep going like that, Davo, and you'll get locked up. One day you'll get locked up for murder and no one will come and see you."

Key attended four schools, the last in the small town of Nuriootpa. His grades were poor and he attributes this to a learning disability and his intolerance of teachers. From Years 8–10, he was in a special-ed class and says he was deliberately unruly so he would be kicked out. By the age of 15, he was a frequent truant and would rather sit on an oval and smoke cigarettes than sit in a classroom he hated listening to crap he didn't understand.

In 1989, when he was 15, he called a teacher a "kid fucker" and was caned, but was never suspended from school. He was expelled the same year, in Year 10, over a schoolyard brawl in which a teacher intervened. He abused the teacher and was sent to the principal and subsequently expelled. He often fought with other students for no reason, but his stamina was poor because of his severe asthma. He insists he wasn't a bully and was in fact incessantly teased at school, although he does not understand why he was victimised by his peers. He had two close friends as a teenager and says he would take responsibility when they got in trouble. He and his mates were into drugs and alcohol; kicking the footy around was as close to sport as he came.

Key says the remainder of his teenage years were unstable. He travelled for short-term labouring jobs and otherwise survived on the dole. The rest of his time was spent building his own addiction to alcohol and drugs and "generally running amok in the community". Key estimated that since leaving school at 15, he had only worked for a total of 18 months. He blamed boredom and his issues with taking directions from authority figures for his inability to hold down a job.

He says he was slow to learn and constantly had to be told by others what to do when he started a new job. He says some employers were patient with his learning problems, but his work experience was limited to labouring in the agricultural sector and in a quarry. Key's longest period of employment was as a machine operator at Commet Farms in Virginia.

He described his recreational pursuits as drug and alcohol abuse, chasing women and listening to music. His hobbies were fishing, camping and rally driving, although the closest he ever came to the latter was driving a stolen car in a police chase.

But in spite of all his disadvantages and disabilities, both perceived and real, David Key had no doubts about his talents with the ladies. Forensic psychologist Dr Richard Balfour found that: "Key does not experience any difficulty socialising with women. He has a history of extensive sexual promiscuity. He has never been in a stable relationship. He has a history of being in relationships one to two months long."

Asked why he drank and used drugs, Key says: "It breaks the boredom and helps me socialise with people I'm unsure of. I can talk to women easier, a lot easier than I can normally do. It's more than just being off my face. When I'm using my drugs, I'm relaxed, I'm not aggressive. I'm not uptight."

In 1990, he moved to Darwin to escape his problems in Adelaide. He dated a woman for several years, and they had three children, but Key never lived with her. He left Darwin in 1993, when his mother retrieved him to prevent him ending up in jail in the Northern Territory. He "couldn't be bothered" having a relationship with his three children and it is not known if he ever saw them again. He claims to have occasionally sent money to their mother, who later married another man, but it was always returned.

Back in Adelaide, he was jailed after being convicted of armed robbery in 1993. His motive, he says, was unemployment, a house devoid of food and a raging drug habit. He was using amphetamines intravenously as well as smoking copious amounts of cannabis. His robbery target was his next-door neighbour. He held a knife to the terrified man's throat, which gained him $3000 and a six-year jail term, with a three-year non-parole period. After his release, he breached parole on three occasions for offences such as driving unregistered and uninsured and failing to report to his parole officer. As a result, he was returned to custody twice, each time for three months.

Before Michelle entered his life, Key says he had three significant past relationships. The first was between 1991 and 1993, with the mother of his three children. He described it as a relationship based almost entirely on sex. After his release from prison, he had a six-month fling with a woman named Linda, whose appetite for drugs was similar to his own. He described their relationship as "unreal", but her parents did not approve of him and that contributed to their break-up.

Then there was a relationship with a woman named Jodie in 1999–2000. They had met in a nightclub and Key described their relationship as "the best". He claims he supported her and her daughter and lived with them for about six months. The relationship ended when he found her in bed with one of his best friends, but he felt relieved that it was over. He said he'd been duped and had even asked her to marry him.

Key's last stint in jail, three months for his third parole breach – over "an incident at TAFE" – ended on April 20, 2001. He initially went to live with his mother in the far northern Adelaide suburb of Smithfield. Days after his release, he met Debbie Richards, a mother of five who lived in the same street as his sister, Kerry, in the adjacent suburb of Davoren Park, where many of his friends also lived. It was these streets, and the notorious neighbouring suburb of Elizabeth, that Key called home. Davoren Park is a magnet for the downtrodden – dysfunctional families caught in the vicious cycle of poverty, domestic violence, drug abuse and welfare dependence. They are often crammed into dilapidated Housing Trust homes, built on the rock-hard clay of the northern Adelaide Plains, and adorned with car bodies on dead front lawns. This is the enduring stereotype – and reality – that so many locals struggle to escape.

There are exceptions, of course – impeccably neat, modest homes, with well-maintained gardens, big fences regularly scrubbed clean of graffiti and discreet but essential security measures such as alarms, roller-shutters and large dogs. But these proud little fortresses are few and far between. The truth is that crime is high, income is low, and the mood is rarely anything but grim.

At night, when the streets are quiet and still, it feels ominous rather than peaceful. Because this is truly a dark place. As Adelaideans well know, only one of the notorious Snowtown serial killings actually occurred in the small Mid-North town where the bodies were dumped in a bank vault – many were committed in their own northern backyard. And when the producers of the internationally critically acclaimed *Snowtown* movie wanted authenticity, their open-call auditions were specifically aimed at the residents of Elizabeth, Salisbury, Smithfield Plains and Davoren Park.

It was here, in these northern suburbs, that Key felt most comfortable. He loved working on and talking about cars, plotting petty crimes, using drugs, drinking heavily and chasing women – and there was no shortage of kindred spirits in this neighbourhood.

Ever the ladies' man, he hit it off with Debbie immediately and within two weeks took up residence in her home. Debbie knew little about Key aside from the fact that he had only recently been released from prison. Key told her he was doing "work for the dole" building sheds, but there seemed to be no routine to when he worked. In mid to late June, Debbie was cleaning up her bedroom floor when she spotted folded pieces of paper near her bed. Key had left both the murder contracts lying around. Debbie went to the kitchen and confronted Key, asking what the documents were. He looked surprised.

"Don't worry about it, it's not mine, I've got to hand it on," he said dismissively, taking the contracts from her, refolding them and returning them to his wallet. Debbie says Key left her home for the last time in early July that year.

"I think David thought he was breaking up my family as two of my boys seemed jealous of him and were causing problems. I don't know where David went then. I heard rumours he was sleeping in his car and rumours that he was sleeping with someone called Michelle. A couple of weeks after he moved out, I heard David was living with this Michelle."

Key later told police that after their initial meeting, Michelle would ring him up to five times a day for up to 20 minutes at a time and they also met regularly, to the point where "I fuckin' wished she'd just shut up".

He recalls: "One particular night (around the last week of June), we were both drinking. I've rocked up at her house after she rang and asked me to come round. You know, I had a can in my hand, and she's sitting there talking and she just finished yelling at the kids to go to bed and we started talking and somehow I've ended up on the floor on my back with her sitting on top of me. From that minute onwards, that's when it started. Kissing, cuddling and bedroom activity on the lounge room floor. I wouldn't say I moved in, but I'd go there three or four days a week and then leave. It was unreal. It was the best. She didn't care where or when we had sex, in the house, the car. We had sex every second day and sometimes twice a day."

Key was also maintaining the charade of working for the dole. He arrived 75 minutes late for his first appointment at Para Worklinks. He was given a new appointment the following week and warned that if he didn't show up, he'd be reported to Centrelink. Key grinned at the Worklinks supervisor: "That's OK, I don't need their money. I'm a crim."

But he did keep his appointment on June 20, 2001 and was put into the Cambodian Community Support program, at Salisbury Highway, Parafield Gardens. He started there on June 25, but managed only two more days – June 26 and July 2. Key called in sick on every other day he was supposed to work.

WENDY FRASER, who also lived in the Elizabeth area, was home alone one afternoon in late June when David Key dropped by looking for his mate, her boyfriend Mark Duffy. Mark was out, but David was talkative, following Wendy down the side of her house as she put rubbish in a bin.

"So, what have you been up to, Dave?" she asked him. He didn't need to be asked twice. He immediately pulled out his wallet and plucked out the contract for Carolyn Matthews's life.

"I'm speeding off my face and I've got to go and do this," he announced proudly.

"Do what?"

He handed her the contract. She looked at the photo and handed it back.

"I've got to go and do her over."

"You're a fucking idiot if you're going to do something like that. What are you doing that for?"

"I need the money."

Wendy stared at him closely, turned her back and returned inside. Key shrugged at her contempt, then went back to his Falcon and left. Later the same day, which was in the weeks before Debbie Richards broke up with Key, Wendy went to Debbie's home in Rowe St, Davoren Park. Debbie made lunch for herself and Key and the three of them sat at the table. Key again pulled out the murder contract and laid it out in front of him, seemingly inviting comment.

"What's that for?" Debbie asked.

"A job," said Key mysteriously.

"What kind of job?"

"To do her over and get some money for us."

Debbie walked away. Wendy looked at Key and shook her head, pointing to the details on the contract.

"What's all this on the bottom?"

"Her name, age and where she lives. She's got kids. If I want the job, I've got to sign here," he said, pointing to the bottom of the page. He folded it up and put it back in his wallet. Wendy glared at him and left him in no doubt about her opinion.

"You're a fucking idiot if you do that."

Key shrugged, unperturbed, and began eating his lunch.

MARK DUFFY had known Key for a couple of years and he started dropping by regularly again after his release from prison. Duffy later told police that Key visited his home early in July, possibly on a Thursday. Also present were Duffy's girlfriend Wendy, Key's sister Kerry and his girlfriend Debbie. Without explanation, Key pulled out his wallet and opened it, displaying

Carolyn Matthews's picture from the contract, which was now tucked behind a plastic window. "This is the one," Key told them.

Duffy was dubious. He says: "I looked closer at the wallet because I thought he was knocking her off and he was bragging about it. I also thought he was bullshitting." Later, he realised he actually recognised the woman in the photo. He had lived in Semaphore Park between 1986 and 1991 and recalled seeing Carolyn regularly at the Franklins supermarket in Port Adelaide.

Later the same evening – without making the link to Carolyn's picture – Key asked Duffy if he wanted to "earn some good money". Duffy asked what he meant and Key said he would get back to him, but never did.

IN THE DAYS leading up to Friday, July 6, when the sale of the Burgess home in Evanston Park was due to settle, Darren Burgess stopped by with a colleague from work to pick up the few possessions of his that remained at the house. He recalls that Michelle was "going off her face", saying: "You need to be here tomorrow by yourself to help me clean it." But Darren was having none of it: "I haven't been here for over six months, it's your mess in there – you clean it."

Driving home, the real estate agent rang Darren, concerned that the home was in no state to be handed over to the new owners. At the same time, Michelle rang and left him a voicemail, telling him to come back the next day and insisting that he be alone. When Darren picked up Kathy from work, he replayed the message to her. Kathy told him: "We'll go out there now and do it. I'm not letting you go out there by yourself."

Darren says: "(Based on subsequent events) I'm glad she didn't. And Michelle had the audacity to ring the police on me because I was cleaning the house. The police came in and asked Kathy what was going on, and she said: 'Well we're not having a picnic. We're cleaning because it's got to be done.' Michelle had told the police I'd been bashing her, so they had to stand by while we did the cleaning."

On Friday, July 6, a cheque for $33,192 was issued to Michelle Burgess, the net proceeds of the divorce settlement, derived entirely from the profits from the sale of their home. Because he had a job and only part-time custody of the children, Darren Burgess received just $1800, most of which was used to pay outstanding bills associated with the house. Michelle now had sufficient funds to pay for at least one of the murder contracts she had issued to Key, who was still grappling with the details of his modus operandi.

Davoren Park resident Scott Rose later told police he met Key in late June at a mate's place, during a discussion about car parts. On Monday, July 9, 2001, Key approached Rose at the front of his home and asked if he would set fire to a vehicle at West Lakes Shore. He said it was a blue Nissan eight-seater van, parked in Nambucca Ave, which belonged to a mother of three children. Key told Rose that the woman who owned the van had "taken out a hit" against Key's girlfriend, so key wanted to scare her. He offered Rose $900 to set fire to the van, but Rose says he wasn't interested.

Meanwhile, while his wife worked at Judith Roberts's home from 6am–5pm that day, Kevin Matthews enjoyed another long, languid, liquid lunch at the Hampstead Hotel, cuddled up to Michelle. But if they were celebrating, it was premature.

That afternoon, Rose dropped off Key at the Elizabeth City Shopping Centre, where he stole an early model, cream-coloured Holden Commodore with a brown vinyl roof. Key claimed he was going to use the car to get to West Lakes so he could "do the job". Rose phoned him at 6pm to see how it had worked out. Key said his target had already left work, so he was instead going to her home address.

At 6.20pm, Key pulled up at the United service station on Tapleys Hill Rd, Seaton. He filled up the Commodore, but discovered his credit union card had expired. He produced his driver's licence, but the attendant was dubious – the picture didn't look like him. Key filled in a voucher with his personal details, promising to return with payment for the fuel. When Scott Rose called Key again, he couldn't bring himself to admit he'd failed to go through with it. Key plucked a 007-style tale from his limited imagination.

Rose says: "He told me he sent an SMS to someone in the street and that person had replied that there was a plain clothes police officer in the street, so he decided not to do it. The message was either to the woman (sic) of the husband or someone in that street who lived across the road or something."

Key later framed that afternoon's events as a reconnaissance mission. He told police: "I actually went down there (to the Matthews home at West Lakes Shore) with my car. Borrowed a street directory off me mum. I went down there to sus it all out just to see if Michelle was full of shit. If the street actually existed. I followed it all up, looked for every escape route, a way that I can slip in, slip out without being noticed."

The unfortunate owner of the stolen Commodore, who could ill-afford to lose their only method of transport, received a phone call from police at 2am the next day. Her car had been found burnt out on Short Rd, Penfield. Key's first outing as a hitman had been an abject failure. And his reckless boasting meant that half the northern suburbs now knew that dopey David Key was full of shit, dangerously stupid, or both.

CAROLYN GARLAND, another friend of Carolyn Matthews from the Semaphore Surf Life Saving Club, had picked up on the discord in her marriage. She'd driven her home from the club many times when Kevin insisted on remaining behind to continue drinking. And she was also aware that when the Matthews family was driving home from Darren Burgess's birthday party, Carolyn had stopped the car and kicked out Kevin before continuing home with the boys.

On a Sunday afternoon in early July, Ms Garland recalls that she was on the door at the Semaphore Surf Life Saving Club, checking off names as people arrived for a meeting. It had already started when Carolyn came up the stairs, late. At the back of the room, she sat next to her friend, who put her hand on hers and said: "Is everything all right?" Carolyn replied: "Yep, yep, I'm fine." Her friend said: "I know there's something, you can tell me if you want." But Carolyn, who was clearly troubled, insisted otherwise: "No, no – everything's fine."

On Sunday, July 8, 2001, Carolyn's brother Charlie and sister-in-law Amanda dropped by for a visit at the Matthews home. Charlie remembers sitting down with Kevin and the boys, who were watching TV, but noted that while Kevin offered him a drink, he was "a bit reserved".

Amanda sat down at the kitchen table with Carolyn, who had pulled out her wedding photo albums, which Amanda had never seen, even though they were a close family and regular visitors to the Matthews home.

Amanda recalls: "(Looking back on it) she was still thinking about her family and had some hope for Kevin and her. (At the time) I had no idea anything was wrong."

Carolyn told her that she wanted to lose some weight and Amanda, who was heavily pregnant with her son Matthew, promised that after the baby arrived she would go walking with Carolyn. Amanda also noted that Kevin was "very, very distant", and had been since Christmas. She says: "One of the hardest things is that she didn't reach out to anyone. And she would have been the first person I went to if I had trouble. It's distressing to think that she didn't want to burden anyone with her problems, or was maybe embarrassed about it."

Carolyn's business partner Judith Roberts later told police that they would usually close the business during school holidays, which in this case started on Monday, July 9. But they had some jobs to get out of the way on the Monday and Tuesday and Carolyn was at work from 6am–5pm on both days. On Tuesday, Carolyn also had her boys' needs to take care of. She dropped Daniel at the home of her close friend of 13 years, Sharon Cama, at 8am. Sharon's son Garry and Daniel went to school together and were good mates. Carolyn was running late to get Kenny to work experience. As Carolyn rushed down the driveway, she paused and turned to her friend.

"I've got something to tell you, can we meet?"

Sharon paused, thinking: "It'll have to be later in the week. What about Saturday afternoon?"

"That's fine, I'll catch up with you Saturday," Carolyn agreed.

Sharon later told police they were often at each other's homes, having coffee or dropping off their boys. The two mothers confided in each other and Sharon was well aware of Carolyn's problems with Kevin, as well as their growing financial troubles. She was baffled that the family could be short of money and Carolyn clearly didn't know where it was going. Her friend explained internet banking to her and what she needed to do to sign up for it. Sharon was also aware of Kevin's heavy drinking and the growing evidence of his affair.

Sharon later told police: "She told me she had found records of jewellery purchases in their bank records, a gold necklace and pendant. But she had not been given any new jewellery by Kevin. She said she had rung the husband of the woman she believed Kevin was having an affair with and asked him if he knew anything. Carolyn had put on considerable weight as a result of glandular fever and also giving up smoking. She said Kevin had apparently lost interest in her."

ON WEDNESDAY, July 11, 2001, David Key slipped back into 007 mode and drove to Beaurepaires in Elizabeth Way, Elizabeth, ostensibly to buy a battery for Michelle's Corolla, which he was driving. He had been driving past the business regularly, and often casually remarked to Michelle's son that if he had a gun, he would walk in and shoot his father. On this day, he was intent on reconnoitring Darren's movements and his work environment to help work out how he should kill him. Darren was shocked to see Key arrive in Michelle's car. He watched Key exit the car and walk into the store, immediately noticing his rough appearance and the strong smell of alcohol on his breath. This guy looked like trouble. Darren assumed he must have stolen the car because he'd seen Michelle in it at their son's soccer match the previous weekend. Key bought a battery as his cover story for being in the shop. He noticed that Darren appeared wary and suspicious and kept looking out at the car. He explained that he'd bought it for $9000. As soon as he left, Darren called Michelle, who instantly denied knowing Key.

Darren said: "Well, he seems to know you or your boyfriend."

"Well, I know of him," Michelle admitted.

Darren said: "I'm not very happy with the sort of people you're hanging around with, especially with regard to the children."

Key, a master of covert operations, had no hesitation in providing his real name and his mother's address for Beaurepaires' records when he bought the battery. He later told police that after buying the battery, he reported back to Michelle, telling her: "To get him, you've got to be fucking nuts, because he has too many people around him. You'd have to use a weapon, you'd have to use a gun to get him."

She replied: "No, no, no, get him while he's on the road, cut his fucking brakes on his car."

Key told police: "She came up with all these different ideas on how to murder him. I got fed up with it and went back to how she wanted Carolyn Matthews done. So I basically pushed his contract to one side and basically forgot about him. We went back on discussing how she wanted Carolyn Matthews murdered."

That afternoon, an apparently conciliatory Kevin Matthews called his wife and asked if she wanted to go away for a few days, just the two of them, without the boys. Earlier that day, between 11.30am and 12.45pm, Carolyn had confronted Kevin at work. The content of their conversation is not known, but it's likely that an envelope that arrived in the mail at their home that week was the centre of the discussion.

The previous Friday, Darren Burgess had posted the Telstra home phone bill to Carolyn, highlighting the huge number of calls between Michelle and Matthews for the March quarter. Darren says that a few days previously, while cleaning out the pantry of his former home he had discovered a letter from a credit agency that was pursuing him over the bill. He rang the phone company and asked for a fully itemised copy. As well as posting Carolyn a copy of the bill, he followed up with a phone call on the same day.

He says: "I rang Carolyn because, back in January, she'd asked if I had any proof of phone calls and could I please show her if I did. So I rang and told her I'd found a bill for $480 for January, February and March, 2001."

On Tuesday, July 10, Darren had also faxed a handwritten letter and a copy of the phone accounts to Kevin's office, to show Kevin that he knew he was lying when he said nothing was going on. He phoned Kevin, who angrily told him: "Your wife's a psycho bitch." Darren replied: "I don't want anything to do with it, that's it, see you later." So now Carolyn and Kevin both had copies of the phone bill – irrefutable evidence that the affair was not only continuing, its intensity was growing.

Beaurepaires employee Adrian Gaymer-Derham later told police that on Wednesday, July 11, he was in the workshop when he noticed Kevin and his wife in the corner near the office. He walked over and Kevin introduced his wife, explaining that Carolyn was having problems with her mobile phone. Gaymer-Derham thought the problem must have been sorted out, because Carolyn left shortly after. But the "mobile phone problems" were far from sorted out. And in one single, horrifying day, the lives of every person caught up in the fantasy world of Michelle Burgess and Kevin Matthews would change forever.

CHAPTER 6

Carolyn's last day, Part I
July 12, 2001

SHE WAS UP at 4.15am and hard at work before dawn, toiling non-stop all day, without complaint. But she couldn't concentrate, nor control the worry and fear consuming her mind and her life. For Carolyn Matthews, there was not a moment's peace during her last day on Earth.

At 6.35am, she arrived at the West Lakes home of her business partner, Judith Roberts, where a converted garage served as workshop and headquarters for Bedspreads Plus, their soft furnishings business.

Carolyn had joined the business about seven years earlier, and they were both directors. She worked between 8.45am and 3.15pm each weekday while the kids were at school, and usually took a break during school holidays. But during the first week of these July holidays, Carolyn had been working like a Trojan, helping get some difficult jobs out of the way. After her 12-hour days on Monday and Tuesday, she was back again at 9am on Wednesday. Not because she had to work, but because Kenny, 16, Shane, 13, and Daniel, 12, were "pissing her off", she confided to Judith, before setting about making some bed linen for the rambunctious trio. A decade later, an adult Shane confirms his mother's statement. "We were the devil's children," he admits.

Judith knew Kevin Matthews had been demoted at work recently, for "disciplinary reasons", Carolyn told her. It was a surprising admission. Despite working together closely, Carolyn was a private person and personal talk was rare. "I didn't pry into Carolyn's private life and she respected mine," Judith later told police. "This was one of the reasons our relationship worked so well. We never overstepped the mark with each other and our business was successful. We worked the hours we wanted and generated a respectable income."

But Judith had known her business partner for 20 years and she also knew Kevin's work dramas were just the tip of the iceberg; Carolyn was a deeply troubled woman. She'd told her she had been getting calls claiming that Kevin was having an affair; and Kevin claimed he was receiving calls saying Carolyn was doing the same. She also said there had been phone threats against Kevin. Carolyn said she didn't believe the affair claims, but sounded far from convinced. The demotion was also a financial blow for the family. Carolyn had no idea where all their money was going, but their finances were now in a dire situation, despite her hard work and the $1700 that she brought in each month from the business. Judith told police that her business partner was stressed, sleeping poorly and depressed about weight gain caused by the bout of glandular fever a couple of years previously.

On the morning of July 12, Judith and Carolyn worked quietly and conscientiously, pausing for lunch at 12.15pm. Carolyn sat eating her pumpkin soup, bread and leftover mince chow mein, pondering Kevin's offer of a short holiday – if two days at a West Beach caravan park qualified as a holiday. Did he think that a weekend away was going to convince her that it was over with this woman, after all the lies of the past 12 months? She didn't know what to think. She also didn't have time to. There was still much work to be done. Carolyn finished her lunch, and returned to her labours for the afternoon.

Judith says: "We had a little bit of stress about work, people ringing up about jobs for which fabric had only just arrived and we were scheduling the work as best we could."

Around 10.30am, a friend of the Matthews family, Anne McKenzie, was visiting a branch of her family's business on Port Rd in Woodville, to pick up a tool. She dropped into Beaurepaires in Port Adelaide to say hello to Kevin and found him subdued and monosyllabic. She later told police: "He didn't appear to be his usual self."

On the same morning, in Craigmore, David Key and Michelle Burgess were discussing how and when they would end Carolyn Matthews's life.

Key frightened Michelle's two children. Aged eight and four, they were in their bedrooms while their mother casually plotted murder with her lover.

Key says: "We were just sitting there talking, discussing how Carolyn Matthews is going to be killed. At one stage, Michelle's talking about cutting the brake lines on her van. I said: 'No, you've got to think of the kids as well'. And she's ... 'fair enough', we were just generally talking, going through scenarios of different things. How, you know, certain other murders, how people got the murder done, how they got away with it."

Shortly after, Key was rummaging in the car for cigarettes when he came across Michelle's divorce settlement cheque. Key says he'd been haranguing Michelle all week to put it in the bank. Security cameras at the Commonwealth Bank branch in Gawler recorded Michelle entering at 12.34pm that day.

Key later told police: "Michelle said: 'Just stay in the car with the kids while I put the money in the bank'. I got sick of sitting in the car waiting, so I grabbed the kids and locked the car up and went into the bank. I seen her sitting there talking to the bloke."

The security camera footage showed the two adults and two children leaving the bank at 1.01pm.

Over the next few hours, they criss-crossed the city, seemingly aimless, but Michelle already knew how she wanted the day to unfold. If she could feed Key enough drugs and bullshit, he would do as she told him – and Carolyn Matthews would end up dead. Michelle's mother Angela Goldup, who lived in Holden Hill, says her daughter rang her at 11am that day to ask if she could drop off the kids, but didn't say exactly when she would be around.

Key says: "We drove around to my mum's house in Davoren Park. I went and made coffee for me and Michelle, mum made a cup of tea. The kids were with us. We were there 15 minutes to 30 minutes. I drove them to see Sandra (Hendy, an acquaintance of Key) a couple of streets over in Charmouth St, Davoren Park. I introduced Michelle to Sandra. We had a yarn for about half an hour, also caught up with Jason Colenso (a friend of Key who would later become a willing participant in the unfolding drama) and a few other people. I drove around Davoren Park, Elizabeth, Smithfield, Elizabeth South, just generally driving around, looking for Mark English, to buy some pot, but couldn't find him."

Crown Prosecutor Steven Millsteed, QC, later queried Key on his priorities that afternoon: "Was this (buying cannabis) a big deal? You had a quarter of a bag and plenty of speed and plenty of ecstasy."

Key explained: "When you get low on one thing, you want to go around and top up so you've got plenty of everything. It's the same when you're getting low on milk. You instantly think to go down straight away and buy a litre of milk to top up, so you've got plenty there. It's the same thing."

Key, Michelle and the children drove out of Gawler in Michelle's red Toyota Seca. Nearing the outer suburbs, they stopped at the Smithfield Hotel drive-through to buy six UDL cans for Michelle and six Woodstock bourbons for Key. "Then we just went out driving around. Drinking and driving," says Key. But their apparently aimless day was about to take on a purpose. At 1.17pm, a call was placed from Kevin Matthews's mobile phone to Michelle Burgess's mobile phone. Phone records show another four calls were made from Matthews's phone to Burgess's phone between 2.29pm and 3.40pm that day. There were a total of 14 calls between Burgess's and Matthews's mobile phones, and her home phone, between 6am and 12.23pm.

Key says: "She wouldn't say what the calls and text messages were about. I called her everything under the sun. She still wouldn't let me in on what was going on. I kept telling her that two heads were better than one if you've got a problem. She kept telling me not to worry about it. Finally she admitted: 'I'm talking to Kevin, if you really want to know.'"

The only exact phrase that Key recalls her saying on the phone is: "Calm down. I'll get it sorted. Just calm down."

Then later, she says: "I've got to go down and see him."

Key: "See fucking who?"

Michelle: "I've got to go and see Kevin. He's losing the plot, I've got to go and talk to him."

Key says: "(She later admitted to me) Matthews was stressing out and sending messages saying he was going to knock himself. Being real pathetic and sending stupid messages."

Key: "What are we going to do with the kids?"

Michelle: "Just drop them off at my mum's."

Key: "All right, how do I get to your mum's?"

Michelle gave him directions and a short time later they arrived in Holden Hill. Key says she asked her mother if she could leave the children while she did some Christmas shopping. (It seemed a little early for Christmas shopping, and Mrs Goldup would later claim her daughter said she was going to buy tyres.) They were only there about 10 minutes. Both Michelle and Key used the toilet, with Key seizing the opportunity to inject amphetamines.

Quizzed later about his drug use on the day, Key explained: "I'd had dope, I'd had speed, I also dropped an ecstasy tablet. My daily routine, every morning I get up, that's what I have, just to get me going." He estimated he'd had four to five joints – two in the morning before leaving Michelle's home, and two outside the bank. He put the cost of his weekly drug habit at $1800.

He later told police: "I had speed when I was on the toilet earlier that day in a needle. I had a speed bomb in a Tallyho paper outside the bank. Four or five points, I had half an eight ball on me. About 1.30–2pm (at Michelle's parents' home), the ecstasy tablet went in with the speed. I was pretty hyped up."

After they left the Goldups' home in Holden Hill, Key says: "When we were driving, we were still arguing and stressing and still getting phone calls and messages. We stopped and Michelle said: 'We've got to find a phone box. We have to find out what his problem is.' So she rang him from a phone box." Key drove them to Beaurepaires on Port Rd, Port Adelaide, arriving shortly after 5pm. Frustrated by her lack of answers and pumped up by the drugs and alcohol, he drove aggressively and dangerously, screeching to a halt in the car park.

He says: "Michelle told me to stay in the car. I thought: 'Fuck that' and I got out of the car. I had a cigarette that had dope in it and leaned up against the car smoking it. She walked inside and started talking to Kevin."

Key watched them walking backwards and forwards, from the office to the tyre showroom, pushing each other aggressively. Their arrival had not gone unnoticed across the driveway at the Ultra Tune branch.

Manager Glenn Smith later gave a colourful account to police of what he saw that afternoon: "When that man got out and started hanging at the back of the car and eyeballing everybody ... I come out of Scotland where it's pretty tough and you get a bit of a radar. The hair on the back of my head went up, he started eyeballing me ... He looked like a vulture.

"He was standing up, kind of puffing his chest out, he had a bit of attitude about him. You know, he was kind of keen to stare everybody down, like he came there in a bad mood. My mate Darren went over there (to Beaurepaires). He was working on a car on a hoist and when he seen the red car come in, he got a bit excited. He got in a bit of a flap and started cursing."

Darren Bland couldn't believe what he was seeing. He'd heard the rumours at work that his former boss Kevin Matthews was having an affair with Michelle. Since Kevin had recently arrived as manager at the adjacent

Beaurepaires, Bland had seen him pacing and smoking outside, engrossed in conversation on his mobile phone for hours.

Bland had already had a word to Kevin about the rumours on several occasions, but Kevin insisted it wasn't true. And yet here was Michelle, turning up again like a bad penny. He needed to sort this out. He marched across to the Beaurepaires showroom, where Michelle appeared to be arguing with Kevin, and yelled threateningly: "I want to talk to you before you leave."

Michelle ignored him and he left, intending to give her a mouthful when she exited. Bland still had his own issues to sort out with her. A mutual friend of theirs was getting married soon and both Bland and Darren Burgess were in the bridal party. Bland was convinced that Michelle had told her ex-husband about their affair in an effort to start trouble between them at the wedding. Key eyed Bland belligerently as he stalked back to his own workshop, where his manager also watched him cautiously. He resumed work on a car, while continuing to keep tabs on the drama next door.

Key says: "This man turned around and walked back out and stared at me as if to say: 'Well, who are you and what are you doing here?' I followed him with my eyes, all the way back to his work. Michelle waved me in. 'It's got to be done tonight,' Michelle said to me."

A detective who later took a statement from Key seized on the importance of these words, halting Key's ramblings and insisting he repeat Michelle's exact declaration for the record. "What do you think she meant by that?" he asked.

"The murder of Carolyn Matthews. I was sitting back thinking about it. How we gonna, how can we do it without getting busted, without leaving any sort of trail? As soon as she said 'It's got to be done tonight,' I turned around to the bloke, which I now know is Kevin Matthews, and asked him if I could use his phone. He said: 'Yep not a problem'. He turned the phone around. I rang Scott Rose and said to him: "Hey buddy, can you come down tonight? Because it's on ... but he said: 'No I can't come down, I haven't got a car'. I said: 'All right then, sweet, not a problem' and that was the end of the call."

Key says his original plan was to "leave Carolyn Matthews – tie her up and put her in the van, and take off and leave it on some side road and make it look like a car accident. Cut the brakes, put her in the front seat, tie her hands to the steering wheel."

The detective asked: "When did you decide to do that?"

"That minute."

"Why did you ring Rose?"

"I wanted someone there, to be with me, to come down and give me a hand."

"To do what?"

"To get her to come out of the house so we can put her in the van and take the van and her away and do it away from everything."

"Are you talking about Carolyn Matthews?"

"Yes."

"So you wanted Scott Rose to come down and help you murder Carolyn Matthews, or assist you in some way?"

"Assist in some way. All I was going to do was grab her, put her in the car and burn the vehicle."

"Was there any further conversation after the phone call?"

"Yes. About the kids at the house. I turned around and I've said to Michelle, I've gone, 'What are you gonna do about the kids?'"

"(She said): 'Oh, Kevin will take them to the video store. By the time he gets back, it'll be done.' (She) didn't think much of it. It was 'yeah, not a problem'. After that, um, I think we left, I'm pretty sure we just left after that."

"Did Michelle give any instructions to Kevin?"

"Just to go and pick the kids up and take them to the video store."

"She said that to him?"

"Yes."

"Did he hear that?"

"Yes."

Kev's call to his friend was made at 5.21pm. The heated conversation at Beaurepaires between Matthews and Michelle lasted about 15 minutes and they left around 5.25pm. At the same time, Kevin Matthews picked up his office phone to call home.

KENNY MATTHEWS had woken that morning when his mother came into his room in the pre-dawn darkness. His brothers, Shane and Daniel, would usually rise around 4.30am, four days a week, to head off to the Seaton swimming centre. But Kenny wasn't that keen, especially during school holidays.

"I'm too tired," he sleepily told his mum.

She laughed.

"I just wanted you to know what it's like for your brothers when they have to get up," she told him, before letting him drift back off to sleep.

Daniel and Shane got up and Carolyn dropped them at the swimming centre at 4.50am, returning home for a shower before her long day at work. Kevin Matthews picked up the boys and dropped them back home around 7.30am, before he also left for work about 8am. Daniel watched a movie and played on the computer until about 9.15am, when Kenny got up. With swimming out of the way and both parents at work, the boys were left to a day of their own typically teenage devices – playing on the computer, watching movies, spaghetti on toast for lunch and, for Shane, a quick trip to the deli down on Military Rd for some hot chips. By the time their mum arrived home around 5pm, they had even ticked off the list of chores their father had left.

Daniel later told police: "Mum came in and said hello and started to unload the top tray of the dishwasher in the kitchen and asked me to put out the garbage. I was kind of busy because I was still watching a movie and didn't take too much notice. Mum was grouchy that the dog hadn't been let outside all day and asked us to let him out."

Kenny told police: "I was playing on the computer when mum came home. I remember her saying she had made an appointment for a haircut the next day. Everything seemed normal. At 5.30pm, I heard the phone ring and Shane answered it. He told me to get ready because dad was coming home to take us to the video store. I hadn't changed from my pyjamas so I went to my room and put on some shorts and a top. Shane and Daniel went out the front of the house and were mucking around. At about 5.40pm, when I'd gone back in the house, I heard one of the boys say 'Kenny, Dad's here' and I went straight out. I left the house without saying goodbye to mum."

An adult Shane remembers: "It was school holidays and our treat was we got to go to the video store and that didn't happen very often. If we were good during the day and didn't ring up mum at work and bother her all day, then we would get videos. Usually it was something that was set up before – if you can be good for the next few days, you can get videos and watch videos all day. But this time, I just got a phone call in the afternoon and it was dad and he's, like: 'Grab the boys and wait at the front gate, we're going to the video store'. And I said: 'No worries, cool'. I hung up the phone and mum was sitting at the computer. I said: 'We're driving to the video store'. And we went and waited out the front but we were waiting and waiting. I was expecting him to be five minutes."

AS KEVIN RUSHED to close up the Beaurepaires premises, Darren Bland crossed the driveway again, intent on grilling him about Michelle. Matthews, clearly distracted and in a hurry, reassured him that they weren't having an affair and said it "had been taken care of". It certainly had. He got into his company ute and drove away to set up his wife's murder. He arrived home at 5.40pm to find Shane and Daniel waiting patiently on the front lawn.

Shane remembers: "He finally rocked up and we jumped in. We were only small boys so we could fit in (the front of) the ute. I remember he was drinking a UDL. Just as we jumped in, he had just put his phone into the glovebox. We drove to the video store at West Lakes."

A few minutes earlier, David Key and Michelle Burgess had a screaming match as they drove to Nambucca Ave.

Key told police: "We were yelling at each other about how it's gonna happen, about how things were, about the consequences. (I told her) she should be thinking about our lives, you know, what's going to happen if we get busted, if we get caught. Spend the rest of your life in jail. Never be able to see your kids again."

Questioned later by detectives, Key was asked what he thought would happen when they arrived at the Matthews's home: "We left Beaurepaires to go down to Carolyn Matthews, down to her house, to kill Carolyn Matthews. I was pretty sure Michelle was going to do it because she was pretty arced up."

Detective: "Why did you think she was going to do it?"

Key: "Because I really didn't want to do it. I really didn't want to fucking, to kill a woman. It's not my style ... I got a sore arm though. (Michelle) hit me in the arm because I kept calling her names, I was stirring her up, tormenting her."

Detective: "Why?"

Key: "Because I didn't want to do it. Because I didn't want to kill Carolyn Matthews. I called her a bitch, a home wrecker, I tormented her about her own personal life. I said straight out: 'I wonder why Darren left you? Because you're so much of a bitch.'"

Detective: "Did Michelle say anything else on the way to West Lakes Shore?"

Key: "(She said): 'The sooner she's dead, the better.' All my plans flew out the window as soon as she took over."

Detective: "What was her plan?"

Key: "Kill her and just walk away."

Detective: "And how was she going to do that?"

Key: "Most probably stab her or fucking shoot her or something."

Detective: "Did she tell you?"

Key: "No."

Detective: "How did you think things were going to develop when you got to West Lakes?"

Key: "I was either going to strangle her or kill her, just stab her to death, one of the two. We had no gun. That was what I was looking for. I would rather fucking, if I was going to kill someone, I'd rather just get it done quicker, quick and painless. Michelle went there with the intention to kill her. I was basically just along for the ride, because I didn't want to kill her. I'd rather just scare the living shit out of her, not actually harm her."

Pressed again on exactly why he was going to kill Carolyn, he says: "Being under the influence of alcohol and drugs plus my past history, you tend to, you know, forget about a lot of things. I'm not sure if I was exactly told the reasons."

Michelle and Key drove down Military Rd and turned left into Nambucca Ave. As they passed No. 5, Michelle pointed it out. They drove to the end of the street and turned into Mooloola Way, doing a U-turn so the car faced back towards the entrance to Nambucca Ave. Michelle was relentless in her provocation, and insults and threats poured from her mouth.

Key: "She started threatening me. She started saying, fucking: 'You bail out now I will make sure you'll never be able to find, you'll never be able to get a female again'. She brought up about me being charged with rape. Brought up about the armed robbery that was done in the Barossa, the house break, the forgery. She was getting aggressive, calling me names like a coward and an idiot who would never come to anything. She said I was a soft cock, I needed to get myself out of the clouds and do a real crime, make a name for myself. An armed robbery, break and enter and forgery is nothing. Do something real, kill someone, prove your point, prove that you are a man, not a sook. If this doesn't happen tonight, it's over."

It was too much for Key. He got out and sat on the bonnet of the Corolla. The car's suspension creaked as Michelle joined him, still ranting. Key tried to ignore her as he watched Kevin Matthews's Beaurepaires ute drive down Nambucca Ave, then exit a couple of minutes later. Michelle immediately began walking towards the Matthews's home. Key says he followed, claiming he was stung by the rape-charge taunt. (The charge had been dropped.)

Key: "I'm not going to have this. She called me a dirty rapist. We walked in from the street on the left hand side, we walked about a quarter of the way up (Nambucca Ave) and we crossed the road, walked across the front lawn of the house and walked in (to the home's front courtyard)."

AFTER THE BOYS had left, Carolyn continued with the evening's rituals, changing into a tracksuit. She finished up some business invoices on the computer, then went into the kitchen, picking up the recycling tub and walking the short distance to the front door. Carolyn paused in the doorway, startled, as the woman she knew her husband was having an affair with strode across the courtyard towards her. There was also a scary-looking man in blue jeans, black boots and blue jacket. His face was screwed up in anger. He walked straight up to her.

"Is your name Carolyn Matthews?"

"Yes," she replied warily. Key showed her the murder contract written by her husband.

"Is this your picture and address?"

Carolyn took the piece of paper and read it. We will never know if she recognised her husband's handwriting.

"Yes," she answered again, handing the paper back to Key, wondering where this was leading. Key himself had little idea and in that moment of indecision, Michelle seized the opportunity. She lunged forward and punched Carolyn in the face, knocking her off balance. She stumbled back into the screen door, and Michelle hissed at Key: "Grab her, get her inside."

Carolyn reeled, her right cheek stinging from the punch. Key bundled her past the timber screen near the front door, which was filled with surf life saving photographs, medals and memorabilia. In the dining area, he roughly pushed her into a seat at the table.

"Sit," Key ordered. Carolyn complied, terrified and still utterly clueless as to what these people wanted. She knew it must have something to do with Kevin, but they weren't making any sense.

"Please, tell me what I've done wrong," she begged Key. But each time she tried to stand up, he shoved her back on to the chair.

"Shut the fuck up, don't say a fucking thing," he spat at her. Key could see Michelle ducking down and reaching around, clattering in the kitchen drawers.

"Dave, bring her here."

Key reached down and grabbed Carolyn's arm.

"Stand up."

Carolyn reluctantly allowed herself to be pushed into her tiny kitchen, where Key shoved her into the corner. He turned around and kicked one of the drawers shut. Michelle was standing next to it, brandishing a Wiltshire knife with a 20cm blade.

Key would later explain lamely to detectives: "I was under the influence of alcohol and drugs, you know. I didn't want to do it but that (the knife) put me in a situation … it reminded me of a situation with my grand … with my father, when he put a knife to my throat. I felt that I was under pressure."

Michelle ordered him: "Now kill her."

"You fucking do it."

"No, you do it. If you wanna be with me, you prove to me how much you love me. Kill her. If you don't kill her, you'll never see any sort of payment and you'll never see me, you'll never see anything. I'll have you knocked. Now kill her."

Carolyn was shaking. What must have gone through her mind as this surreal scene unfolded in front of her? In such a small room, with two people blocking her only exit, there was no way for her to escape. Exactly who did what over the next two minutes will never be known; but there is no doubt that at some point, Key took the knife from Michelle's hand and he lunged at Carolyn. Then his frenzied, brutal blows began.

"Please! No!" Carolyn begged.

But Key couldn't hear a word. He was consumed with anger, a lifetime's worth, and was unleashing it all on an innocent woman he did not know for reasons he did not understand.

"I started stabbing Carolyn. Twice in the chest. She started going down and I stabbed her once in the back, and the right-hand shoulder, pulled the knife out, threw her back up, pushed her against the wall and just went ballistic at her. I can't remember how many times I stabbed her or exactly what happened. I just went bloody ballistic. I'd already stabbed her five or six times when she went down."

But Carolyn Matthews was not out. She grabbed desperately for a frying pan on the stove top and waved it in front of her chest.

"That's how the knife actually got bent, because I stabbed the frying pan. I didn't hear a thing. I didn't even hear Carolyn Matthews fucking begging for her life. I just blanked out. I couldn't hear nothing."

Forensic pathologist Dr John Gilbert later found 41 separate injuries on Carolyn's body, some delivered with "moderate to severe" force. His report says they included abrasions to her forehead; a 22mm-long wound over her left cheek, 12mm deep; bruising and swelling to her left cheek; an abrasion to the right lower jaw; an abrasion over the lower lip; a 22mm stab wound to the left forearm, above the wrist; two 7cm wounds on the left wrist and palm; a 5cm stab wound to the left hand; stab wounds to the fingers; and stab wounds to the chest which penetrated the left lung, 18cm deep; a kink in one wound suggested a change of direction of the blade – the depth was 17cm.

The cause of Carolyn Matthews's death was multiple stab wounds to the chest, resulting in injuries to both lungs, leading to their partial collapse and bleeding into the chest cavity. The most significant wound involved the penetration of a large pulmonary artery in the right lung. One of the stab wounds also penetrated her heart. Death resulted from rapid blood loss from the heart and lung injuries. Dr Gilbert noted that injuries of this type cause faintness and dizziness within a matter of seconds. He also found that it was "very doubtful that rapid medical intervention could have prevented the death once the injuries were inflicted."

When it was over, when Carolyn Matthews lay covered in her own blood, slumped on the floor of her kitchen, the last of her life slipping away, Key finally stopped, standing over her with the bent knife clenched in his hand. Still emerging from his frenzy, he had no idea if this woman was alive or dead, but he knocked the frying pan away from her chest anyway.

He explained to police: "It had my prints on it, so I had to take it."

Key claimed Michelle had remained standing in the doorway, careful to avoid the blood spatter that covered the room like macabre graffiti. But serious doubts would later be cast on whether Michelle was a bystander or a participant in the physical act of robbing Carolyn Matthews of her life.

Key: "I turned around and looked at Michelle and she just stood there, pale, as if to say "fuuuck".

"Get the fuck out of the house," he spat at her.

Key: "And she ran as fast as her fat legs could take her. And I'm staring at Carolyn Matthews, in the corner bleeding like a stuffed (sic) pig, and I'm thinking to myself: 'What the fuck have you just done, you fucking idiot?'"

"Think quick," Key told himself. This was a daunting challenge at the best of times. Loaded with drugs, alcohol and adrenalin, and covered in his victim's blood, even he could dimly comprehend the seriousness of the crime he had just perpetrated.

Key: "You've got no gloves on, you're standing in her blood, do something. I kept telling myself I had to do something. I had to fucking get the fuck out of the house … You got to wipe the knives, got to get out of the house."

He grabbed a tea towel from the kitchen bench, mopped the blood from his face and hands and grabbed the knife. He stuffed the towel into his pocket, gathered up the frying pan, the murder weapon and two other knives he'd seen Michelle touch.

Key: "I grabbed all that because it all had fingerprints and everything over it, especially my fingerprints. That's when I walked outside. I must have got a little bit lost. I had to stop for two seconds and work out where I was going. I found the doorway and walked out, still sort of like in a daze."

He pulled a grey sock from a clothesline in the carport and wiped down all three knives, before discarding them near bushes next to the front courtyard's path. This would later cause detectives to consider – and discard – the theory that the arrangement of the knives was staged as some kind of serial killer signature.

Key continues: "I wiped the frying pan and threw that on the ground and put the sock in my pocket. I walked back out, scuffing my feet along the lawn trying to get the blood and shit off my boots. I walked to the end of the street. I was about to cross the street when I realised the car wasn't there. So I just turned straight around and it was on my left. I took my jacket off and turned it inside out. Jumped in the car, the driver's side. Michelle's … she's sitting there killing herself fucking laughing. She was fucking … she was killing herself laughing. It was a vicious, cackling laugh. 'Now you're under the thumb' sort of laugh. It's the sort of laugh you give someone when you can get them to do anything you choose. Then she said: 'Well done, about time someone had enough balls to kill her'."

"Shut the fuck up or you're next," Key growled, pausing to roll a cigarette between his bloodied, shaking fingers and trying to regain some kind of composure before driving off. They had been in the street barely 10 minutes. Michelle's laughter continued, further riling Key.

"What the fuck are you laughing at?"

She smiled malevolently, replying: "You stupid cunt. You're under the thumb, you're all mine."

"And then in the middle of her laughing, she said she had to go to the toilet. I've gone: 'Well, we'll go down to Grange (beach).' And she said: 'All right.'"

So Key drove away, Michelle still sniggering at the horror she had just orchestrated. Shock, fear and dread were about to consume the safe, middle-class suburb of West Lakes Shore – how and why had such evil been visited upon a happy and respected family?

KEVIN MATTHEWS collected his boys from outside their home at 5.40pm, then made a beeline for the drive-through at the Leg Trap Hotel in West Lakes. He paid for four cans of UDL Scotch and cola at exactly the same time that his wife was valiantly fighting for her life. Michelle's endless phone calls had already driven him to drink a couple of hours earlier, before the confrontation at Beaurepaires. He'd bought a bottle of Scotch at the Alberton Hotel's drive-through at 3.39pm, but figured he'd need a drink or two more before the afternoon was over. When they arrived at the nearby video store, Shane Tidswell remembers that he and his brothers bolted in, but their dad, a big movie buff, remained in the ute. He gave the boys $20 and told them to come and grab him if they needed permission for an M-rated movie.

Shane: "I guess that would have taken about 15 minutes, finding what we wanted to watch, paid for it and jumped back in the ute, and went home. It was a normal day. But there are the things that I look back on now – that he didn't jump out of the car and he put his phone in the glovebox."

At 5.58pm, the computer at the West Lakes Video Ezy recorded the boys' selections – *The Kid*, *Charlie's Angels* and *The X-Men*. At 5.59pm, just as they were leaving the shop, there was a three-second phone call from a public phone box at 489 The Esplanade, Grange, to Kevin's mobile – a signal to say the job was done.

What went through Kevin Matthews's mind as he drove home? He knew his wife was dead and they were about to walk into a murder scene. Whatever his thought processes, somewhere on that journey he came to the conclusion that the three boys crammed into the ute cab next to him would walk through the front door first. But the trio noticed nothing unusual about their father's behaviour.

KEY AND MICHELLE had arrived at Grange beach at about 5.55pm. Michelle was about to call Matthews on her mobile, but Key, who used to live in the area, pointed to the nearby phone box. He got out and headed for the beach, telling Michelle: "I've got to go down and wash my face, try and calm myself the fuck down." Michelle, meanwhile, went to the phone box to make the shortest but most important phone call of her life.

Key: "I followed the footpath down to the sand and walked down the side of the jetty on to the beach. I dug a bit of a hole in the sand so it could fill with water and I washed my face and my hands to get the blood off me."

Key was oblivious to the grim irony as he washed Carolyn's blood from his hands and face with water from the ocean she loved so much. The blood had already soaked into his clothes and he didn't bother trying to remove it.

"I walked back to the car and (Michelle) was sitting on the bonnet having a cigarette. She said she still had to go to the toilet, so I took her to the shopping centre on Grange Rd, heading back towards Adelaide."

A frustrated Angela Goldup, whose Thursday night shopping ritual at Tea Tree Plaza was being delayed, rang her daughter at 6pm. She later told police it was to find out if Michelle wanted her to give the children dinner, but it is more likely that she asked how much longer her daughter's "shopping trip" was going to take – was she coming back for her kids or not? She tried again at 6.37pm when there was still no sign of them. She had only met Key once, earlier that month, when Michelle had brought him to a family birthday party and introduced him as a "friend". Mrs Goldup would later admit: "I didn't like him, he scared me."

Key says: "We went and picked up her kids from her parents' place and went home. I think it was after 7pm when we got to her mother's place. I stayed in the car."

Michelle's father Keith would later quiz her about that night in a phone call: "I want to ask you this straight-out question – I want a straight answer."

Michelle: "Yep."

Keith: "I was very disturbed to hear that you were driving around with a whole heap of guys on that Thursday night."

Michelle: "I ... what?"

Keith: "You was driving around with a bunch of guys, wasn't ya?"

Michelle: "Yeah, Dave was with me, Jason (Colenso) was with us, there was a whole group of us."

Keith: "They're a bunch of no-hopers. I'm sorry Mish, but I got to tell you how I feel. And to me they're a bunch of no-hopers and I want to know how you got mixed up with them."

Michelle: "I just met Dave through his sister Kathy at school."

Keith: "I'll tell you what puzzles me. Now I keep going back to it. That night you flew back to our place at about 7 o'clock while we were waiting for you. You wouldn't let me see who was in the car and took off like a rocket with the kids. That concerned me because I know how long it takes to get from A to B. And that concerned me. You were not involved. If you were involved you're a stupid fucking bitch and that's all I will say."

Michelle: "Thank you."

When they arrived home at Michelle's villa in Bluebush Court, Craigmore with her children, Key grabbed his jacket and told Michelle to wash it. She threw all the clothes they'd been wearing that day into the washing machine and put his boots in the bathroom. She later took her Adelaide Crows football jacket, which rarely left her shoulders, to the dry cleaners.

Key says: "Halfway through the shower she came in, and said: 'What do we fucking do now?' And I said: 'I don't fucking know. You're the one with ideas.'

"She said again: 'What do we do now?'

(Key told her) 'You're the one that's taken over this little episode. If you'd let me figure out something it would have been clean, not so messy, you stupid bitch.'

"I wanted to have a go at her. I felt myself arcing back up inside."

Key worked out his frustration by cleaning the car interior, going through it with disinfectant. Michelle came out and followed his cue, emptying the car of McDonald's detritus and toys. After dinner, Key says he "tormented" Michelle's children – who would both be haunted by the brief period he was in their lives – until they went to bed.

Scott Rose later told police: "At 11pm on July 12, I rang Dave to see if he was coming around. He said he was busy, but had done the job and was cleaning up and was going to a party. I didn't ask him what he meant by the job and didn't take much notice. He said something about having used something of hers back on her, but I couldn't work out what he meant. I had been drinking all afternoon. The next morning, I heard about the murder on the radio and thought that Dave had something to do with it."

But Key was in no mood to go out that night. He set about demolishing half a carton of beer and a bottle of Scotch with Michelle's help and fell into a drunken, dreamless sleep. The nightmares would come later.

CHAPTER 7

Carolyn's last day, Part II
July 12, 2001

KEVIN MATTHEWS steered his work ute on to the front lawn of 5 Nambucca Ave at 6.05pm, willing himself to behave normally.

The boys were excited about watching the videos and were keen to get inside. What reason could he possibly give for stopping them from going in first? Anything he said now would only arouse suspicion later. So he calmly locked up the ute and ambled into the front courtyard behind his sons. There was no need to rush.

Shane recalls: "We jumped out with our videos and we headed through the gate, down towards the house and there was the recycling black bin – it was tipped out on the lawn, and we saw a frying pan out there as well. But that wasn't necessarily a completely unusual thing. At the time, I thought – because I knew mum and dad were on the rocks – I just thought that mum had spat the dummy and just gone: 'Bugger this!' when she was putting the recycling out.

"The front door was locked, but not the screen door. I grabbed up a few of the things and headed towards the front door. We must have been waiting there and dad unlocked it from behind us and we've gone in first. We were climbing over each other to get in and start watching these movies. As we came into the foyer, I headed straight to the lounge room and got out the DVDs and was sitting on the couch looking at what we had got."

Kenny told police: "I was the first one to walk in the kitchen. I saw mum laying on her back and her eyes were open. The dishwasher was open and there was blood all around her mouth. I thought she must have tripped over and bumped her head. Dad was crying or shouting something and he went down to help mum. I quickly grabbed the phone and gave it to Shane and I went down to help dad."

Shane remembers: "I heard my old man say: 'Oh no!'. But ... it was almost a fake 'oh no!'. I thought mum had made the kitchen a mess or something; that's what it sounded like. I just jumped up and ran into the kitchen, and saw my mum laying there, and just blood everywhere. You can't comprehend how much blood someone has in them until you see it not in them. It's incredible. In some movies, you just think, in murder scenes, you think it's a little bit overdone. But it's not, considering what I saw. There was blood on the roof (ceiling), blood on the walls, the whole floor was just blood, everything. I noticed that her wrist was cut. I'm pretty sure dad jumped down and started resuscitation and stuff."

"Call the police!" Kevin yelled at the boys.

Shane grabbed the phone and called triple zero; Kevin urged Kenny to assist him with the CPR.

Operator: "Ambulance emergency."

Shane: "Yeah, we need an ambulance, quick!"

Operator: "What's the address?"

Shane: "5 Nambucca Ave, West Lakes Shore."

Operator: "What's happened there?"

Throughout the call, there was chaos and Shane struggled to focus on the operator's questions; his father was yelling frantically and in front of him was the deeply disturbing sight of his mother on the floor covered in blood.

Shane: "Um, pardon?"

Operator: "What's happened?"

Shane: "What?"

Operator: "What's happened there? What do you need the ambulance for?"

Shane: "She's lying on the floor ... bleeding, quick!"

Operator: "What's happened there?"

Shane: "She's ... her wrist is slashed."

Operator: "OK, is there a lot of bleeding?"

Shane: "Yes, there is. Get them straight away!"

Operator: "You need to put something on the bleeding to try and stop it."

Shane: "Hurry up! Send them now!"

Operator: "Are you there?"

Shane: "Yes."

Operator: "OK, you need to put something on the bleeding, to stop the bleeding. Is she still awake and talking?"

Shane: "No, she's not."

Operator: "All right, put her on her side. While the ambulance is on the way, put her on her side."

Shane: "What?"

Operator: "You need to put her on her side."

Shane: "Put her on her side, dad."

Operator: "How old is she?"

Shane: "There's no pulse!"

Operator: "OK, you need to make sure there's nothing in her airway and then you need to breathe for her. Do you know how to do that?"

Shane: "Breathe for her, dad."

Operator: "Do a few quick breaths into her mouth."

Kevin (in the background): "I'm resuscitatin' her, I'm resuscitatin' her."

Shane: "He's resuscitating her."

Operator: "OK. How old is she?"

Shane: "Uh, Dad, how old is she? 37."

Operator: "What's your name?"

Shane: "Shane Matthews."

When the operator asked for their phone number, Kevin, who by now was hysterical, yelled: "Fuck, just get 'em here! Get 'em here, please!"

Operator: "They're on the way already."

As Shane gave the number, Kevin yelled: "There's no pulse, she's dead!"

Operator: "Put me on the phone to your father, can you take the phone to your father?"

Shane: "Yep. Dad, phone."

Kevin: "No, I can't stop!"

But when Shane handed it to him, he took it.

Operator: "Sir, do you want me to help you until the ambulance gets there?"

Kevin: "I'm a life saver, I'm a surf life saver, I know …"

Operator: "OK, all right …"

Kevin: "There's no pulse, she's dead."

Operator: "Are you doing some breathing for her? You need to do mouth-to-mouth."

Kevin: "Me and the boys are going to keep breathing until they get here."
Operator: "OK, do you know how to do compressions on her chest?"
Kevin: "Yes, yes I can do that. Gotta go. Gotta go. Bye."

Kevin later told police: "There was a lady on there and I think she told me to do something. I can't remember what she told me. It was just a basic resus thing. Recovery position. I think I was nasty to her on the phone. I was just screaming out for the ambulance. It seemed to take forever. We had to ring a second time. She had no pulse. There was blood everywhere. I couldn't see anything 'cause I was just ... all I wanted to do ... I just seen that there was blood all over her face. I just wanted to resus her but she wasn't moving. I think the first thing I checked was her pulse. There was no pulse. I didn't know what happened. I think Kenneth or somebody screamed out: 'She's cut herself'. Somebody screamed out something, but I couldn't see any cuts because I was working on the head area."

Shane remembers: "I knew from surf life saving training that if there is a casualty, that you go and wait for the ambulance, so they can respond as quickly as possible. I grabbed Daniel and led him out the front and we went out up the street to Military Rd and we were waiting there for the ambulance. I remember it seemed like it took a lifetime to come. I thought: 'This is horrible, standing out there waiting for this ambulance to come.'"

At 6.12pm, Constable Leonie Meyer and Senior Constable Mick Lorincz were tasked to attend a suspected suicide at 5 Nambucca Ave, West Lakes Shore. At 6.15pm, they found Shane waiting vigilantly for the ambulance on the corner of Military Rd. Below the adjacent Nambucca Ave street sign was the distinctive yellow triangle of the "Safety House" network. In the most tragic of ironies, it directed children in trouble to go to the Matthews home.

"Where are the ambos? Have they been and gone?" SC Lorincz asked them.

"No they haven't been yet. There's something wrong with mum. She's inside and she's bleeding," Shane replied. The officers continued on to No. 5.

SC Lorincz recalls: "With that, I ran towards the front of the house and put disposable rubber gloves on as I went. I ran through a gateway and along a paved path for about 10m and then through the front door. One of the sons was behind me and he told me to turn right as I went in through the front door and then turn left. I then turned right as instructed and rounded the end of the screen wall to the left.

"Matthews was on the kitchen floor area, almost lying on his left side and a lad in his late teens was on his knees. They were combining their efforts in administering CPR to a person lying on their back in the kitchen area. Kevin Matthews was face to face with the deceased, breathing into her mouth. He looked up as I came around the corner. His face was covered in blood, as were his hands and his son was performing chest compressions on the deceased.

"Matthews said words to the effect of: 'She's not breathing, she's not breathing, there's no pulse.' Matthews and his son continued CPR and I went back outside via the front door and requested, via the police radio, a hurry-up call for the ambulance."

Daniel made another call to 000, his voice frightened and hesitant.

Operator: "Ambulance emergency."

Daniel: "Um, we're waiting about … is the ambulance coming to 5 Nambucca Ave?"

Operator: "Yes, it was coming while you were on the phone but we got disconnected. What's happening now?"

Daniel: "The police have just got here. Will the ambulance be here?"

Operator: "They're coming with their lights and sirens. They've been coming since we were on the phone to you. What's happening now? I know the police are there, but what's happening with the lady?"

Daniel: "I think she slit her wrists or something, I don't know."

Operator: "Right, is she still … not awake and not able to talk to you?"

Daniel: "Yes."

Operator: "So she's still unconscious, is she?"

Daniel: "Yes."

Operator: "All right, I think the ambulance has just arrived there now."

Daniel: "Yes it's here."

Operator: "All right, OK, well you go out and show the ambulance where to come in."

Daniel: "Yeah, my brother is."

Operator: "OK. Is she bleeding at all? Have you tried to stop the bleeding?"

Daniel: "No, she's not bleeding from the wrist, she's bleeding from her mouth or something, I don't know."

Operator: "Oh, OK. Can you see the ambulance? Oh, you can hear them."

(Sirens in background)

Daniel: "Yeah, it's pretty loud. My brother's at the end of our street. He'll be able to see it."

Operator: "OK, all right. Bye bye."

SC Lorincz continues: "I was about to go back inside when I heard the sirens approaching, so I waited. The ambulance entered Nambucca Ave at 6.18pm and I directed the ambulance officers inside the house."

INTENSIVE CARE paramedics Amanda Lemmon and Stacey Solomou were tasked to attend a female suicide attempt (respiratory arrest) at 6.07pm, and were advised en route that the victim had lacerated wrists and that CPR was in progress. When they arrived, SC Lorincz led them inside, where Ms Lemmon observed: "Kevin Matthews was administering mouth-to-mouth. Stacey stepped over the patient, I went to the left side of the patient near where Kevin was positioned. Kevin was distressed and had blood on his face and hands and I asked him if he could move out of the kitchen and we asked for police assistance to remove Kevin."

Const. Meyer recalls: "Kevin was in a state of shock and could not move from the floor. Lorincz and myself were required to physically remove him from the kitchen because he was in the way of the ambulance officers. As we assisted him from the kitchen, I noticed two full cans of UDL mix on the breakfast bar. Kevin reached for and took hold of a third can which was partly consumed. Kevin went to have a drink and then decided he did not want any after all. We assisted him to a chair in the dining area directly next to the kitchen."

When the paramedics saw the brutal wounds on Carolyn's chest, the initial suicide call was immediately dismissed. There was no doubt this was a homicide. Ms Lemmon says: "I informed police we would probably cease resuscitation, that the patient had stab wounds to the chest and CIB were needed immediately, and to keep everyone out of the house."

Shane remembers: "We were just standing outside the front door. I remember my old man coming out the front door led by one of the ambulance officers and he just passed out, fell over the bin and he's a great big man, he just went down and wasn't moving. They put him into the recovery position. I think I was walking around the yard, just absolutely flabbergasted I guess, and I found three knives underneath the rose bushes. I remember asking the police officer, I said: 'There's some knives here, do you want me to pick them up?' He said: 'No, no just leave them.'

That's when they got us to go out the front of the house instead of in the front yard."

Const. Meyer recalls: "One of the children came into the house to say that their father had collapsed in the front yard. I exited the house to see if Kevin was all right. He had collapsed and on the way to the ground, had hit the wheelie bin just outside the front door. Lorincz had finished his radio call and we assisted Kevin into the coma position. I asked one of the boys for a blanket for their father and placed it over him. Shane pointed out to Lorincz the three kitchen knives lying under a bush, near the front door."

When one of the officers called 000 for a second ambulance for Kevin, he could be heard sobbing hysterically in the background. Paramedic Stacey Solomou examined Matthews and asked him some questions. After initially answering "Taperoo", when asked where he was, he gradually became more coherent.

Matthews: "Are you taking my wife to hospital, is she going to be OK?"

Solomou: "No, I'm sorry, your wife has passed away. Everything that we could have done was done – her injuries were quite extensive."

Matthews: "I was only gone five to 15 minutes. I took the boys to the video shop. I was doing CPR for 20 minutes."

Solomou: "He asked me for his cigarettes and I asked one of the police if I could go inside and get them and he said yes. I went into the kitchen and got a packet of blue and white cigarettes off the kitchen sink. I opened them and saw cigarettes and a lighter. There was blood on the packet. I brought them outside and gave them to a female police officer."

The second ambulance arrived at 6.30pm. Paramedic Kerry Dohnt and colleague Ian DeBono had learned en route that the first crew had ceased resuscitation but they would still be required for a second patient. Lemmon and Solomou updated them on developments and took them over to the porch to check on Kevin.

Dohnt later told police: "I spoke to another paramedic who said they'd stopped resus on a patient with multiple stab wounds to the chest and lacerations to her hands. She asked us to assist a man. We went to the front courtyard area of the house and saw a man aged 45–50 sitting on a concrete path with his back leaning against the house. He seemed upset and distressed and was crying a little. We asked him to walk to the ambulance with us, which he did. He sat on the rear step on the ambulance while his blood pressure was taken. I asked him if he knew what day it was and he said Thursday. A female police officer was present and he asked her what happened. There were also three boys present, I think they were his sons, and we put blankets around them. Detectives arrived and took a brief statement from him. He had bloodstained hands and blood on the front of his top. I asked if he had been drinking and he said he had had 1½ UDL cans."

At 6.55pm, Kevin asked Kenny to fetch his mobile phone from the ute's glovebox. His hands were shaking too much, so he asked Const. Meyer to dial the mobile number of Senior Constable Allan Dalgleish, a Port Adelaide plainclothes detective who was also a member of the Semaphore Surf Life Saving Club. Kevin and Allan had been good mates for 20 years; they called each other Bodgie and Doggy respectively.

"Doggy?"

"Yep."

"Bodgie."

"How you going?"

"Not good. Something's happened to Carolyn."

"What?"

"I need you; I fucking need you."

Kevin choked up and had trouble continuing. One of the other officers took the phone and told Dalgleish that Carolyn had passed away and it appeared to be a suicide. He immediately left home to drive to what was now West Lakes Command, the centre of the rapidly growing investigation into the murder of Carolyn Matthews. He soon learnt the suicide theory was a long way wide of the mark.

Shane remembers: "More and more cars kept arriving. More police. I remember seeing about 10 cars at one point. Police cordoning off the street and detectives. We were still waiting out the front and Kevin was in the ambulance. There were pictures of him on the news with a blanket around him, walking around the ambulance. I remember my two brothers were standing together and I was sitting down next to a light pole in the street. One of the ambulance officers got the boys together and I thought: 'I need to hear this' so I went over to them. They explained to us that mum had passed away. From there, we went to the police station."

Yvonne Tidswell remembers: "I'd tried to ring Carolyn lots of times ... and the police ... she was laying three foot from the phone. They could hear the messages I was leaving but they didn't get back to me. But you never rang Carolyn between seven and half past – that was *Home & Away*.

So I didn't ring then, I rang a bit later on and I said: 'You're not home still, I guess you're at the swimming with the boys'. Then when she didn't get back to me, I just thought she didn't get the message or something; it wasn't urgent or anything."

PORT ADELAIDE detectives Sergeant John Bradshaw and Senior Constable Garry Johnson were called to Nambucca Ave at 6.30pm and Dalgleish arrived a few minutes later. After advising the detectives he was there as a family friend, Kevin approached and hugged him, crying. They sat down in the gutter opposite the house. Kevin tried in vain to steady his hand as he lit a cigarette, so Dalgleish got a blanket from the ambulance to put around him.

He later said: "The media arrived, so we sat Kevin in a police vehicle and we talked. He spoke openly about things. He began talking about our history at the club and my friendship with him and Carolyn. He said he'd planned to go away next Monday with Carolyn to the West Beach caravan park and Yvonne was going to look after the kids. I just listened. He was rambling and it was hard for me to get words in. Kevin told me he thought he'd done something wrong while trying to resuscitate Carolyn and that he hadn't cleared the airway properly. I reassured him that he wouldn't be criticised about the way he performed the resuscitation and that he would have done the best he could have. He said the boys had done a good job and he was concerned as to where they were. He was also concerned about Carolyn's mother finding out and I reassured him I would contact her as well as (his brothers-in-law) Charlie and Peter. Kevin said he was told by ambulance officers that Carolyn might have had a heart attack. He couldn't understand why there was so much blood."

At 9.04pm, Dalgleish and SC Johnson took Matthews to Port Adelaide police station, where he was led to an interview room. The interview started at 9.28pm. Senior Constable Ashley Sermon from the crime scene examiners' office at Port Adelaide took photos of and forensic samples from Matthews, before they paused for a break at 9.50pm. Dalgleish recalls: "Johnson explained the procedure to Kevin and that I was accompanying him as a friend rather than as a police officer. We sat together while Johnson took a video statement from Kevin."

In the interview room, Johnson explained: "Kevin, we've got a change of clothes here for you from your house. If you'd like to come with us, we'll get you some facilities to get you cleaned up, change your clothes. We'll come back and have a chat and a coffee and get through as quick as we possibly can so you can catch up with your sons and do things that way. Now, while we have a break, do you want Allan to make some sort of arrangements to have someone go and speak with Carolyn's family?"

Matthews recoiled at the thought of having to face Yvonne and Carolyn's brothers himself.

"If you don't mind, please."

Dalgleish replied: "No that's all right, mate."

Dalgleish recalls: "After that, I took Kevin to the toilet to wash his face. Kevin looked into the mirror and saw blood on his face and collapsed on the floor crying. I helped him up and managed to wash his face and hands. I took Kevin out to his boys in the police station and bought them some drinks."

Shane remembers: "I had to do an interview and they kept us all separate. I came out of my interview and dad must have just come out of his. I remember seeing him in the passageway and he still had blood all over him. He hugged me and was crying and stuff. I wasn't crying, I just patted him on the back and said: 'It's going to be OK, it's going to be OK.'"

Shane also remembers the surreal quality of the night's events: "I remember everything happening, but I had no thought process. I was unsure about what was going on. Nothing made sense."

He and his brothers had been excited about watching *Charlie's Angels*. He knew mum and dad had problems, but that evening, everything seemed fine. His mum should have been bustling around the kitchen, organising dinner when they got home; they had only been gone a few minutes. Instead she was lying on the floor, stabbed to death. Then his dad collapsed. And now they were at the Port Adelaide police station.

"The first time I cried, aside from when I first went out the front of the house, was when I actually walked into the foyer of the police station in Port Adelaide. My nanna was there, (Kevin's mother) Irene, and as soon as she hugged me, I lost it, just bawled my eyes out. My interview must have taken longer because my brothers were already sitting there. I ended up falling asleep in the foyer. Then we went to my nanna's place. I remember sleeping for over a day. Not wanting to move or see anybody."

In the interview room, the detectives resumed their first interview with Kevin at 10.28pm.

SC Johnson: "Kevin has washed himself and changed his clothes and spoken with his children and made some general family arrangements. Kevin, as I said, you are well aware that your wife has died tonight and from initial investigations made at the scene at your house, it appears she may have possibly been murdered. And that's what the forensic people and all the detectives are doing there at the moment. And because of that, it's very important that we get as much detail as possible about family relationships, lifestyle, movements and habits and what have you. It could have some bearing on the way this investigation goes if it does turn out to be a murder investigation. At this stage, I believe the likelihood of it being a murder is fairly high. First, can you tell me how long you and Carolyn have been married?"

"Seventeen years."

Matthews went on to explain that he'd worked at Beaurepaires for almost 25 years. They'd lived at Nambucca Ave for almost 10 years. His wife worked at Bedspreads Plus and had a good working relationship with her business partner.

"Do you share the same bed with your wife?"

"Yes, we do."

"Had any periods of separation?"

"No, there was one night where I walked out but we haven't been separated. It was six, seven months ago. It might have been five months. A long time ago."

"How would you rate your general day-to-day relationship?"

"Good."

"Pressing issues?"

"Stress with the kids. Shane at the moment is going through a difficult period. Kenneth went through it and came out of it and Shane is going through it at the moment, rebellious."

"Any problems in your relationship with regards to finances or sex or behaviour?"

"We've always had disputes about finances, about trying to get back on top ... I am on holidays next week. We were trying to work it so she had next week off so we could all be together."

He claimed he had told the boys earlier that day that if they didn't call either him or Carolyn at work that day, then they could each pick out a video. He had tried ringing but the phone was engaged and he assumed they were using the line for the internet. He told the detectives he eventually spoke to Daniel, the youngest. (In fact it was Shane.)

"I said: 'I'm on my way home, have you rung mum?'"

"They said: 'No, we didn't want to bother her'. I said: 'Have you done your chores?' which was to hang up their wetsuits and stuff from board training last night. I said: 'I'll meet you out the front' and they could go and pick a video each."

"What happened when you got home?"

"I just pulled up at the front. The boys were out the front on the lawn. Daniel came out and said something like: 'I told you I heard dad pull up'."

"Just as I was about to get out, they came out the gate. We drove to the Leg Trap where I got some cans of UDL and then we went to the video shop."

He said he sat there and drank 1½ cans of UDL while he waited for the boys. After they piled back into the ute, Matthews drove straight down West Lakes Bvd, turned right into Bartley Tce and into the second or third street on the left – both led to home.

"When we arrived home, I pulled up out the front. The kids jumped out. I asked Daniel to get my cans of UDL from the glovebox. The kids ran through the gate, which was wide open. The kids normally leave it open anyway. I locked the door on the car. One of the kids, I'm not sure which one, it might have been Kenny, said: 'Oh, mum's spat the dummy' because the recycling, like the cardboard boxes and the milk cartons that we keep under the sink that the kids are supposed to put outside each day and they didn't do it and they were spread out all over the lawn. I think they had a go at Daniel about it because I think he must have been told to do it. So they think their mother has spat the dummy.

"As I was walking in, I seen the frying pan out the front, so I thought: 'What's a frying pan doing out the front', you know? I thought, well the kids obviously pissed Carolyn off. Maybe Daniel didn't do the dishes or something, I don't know.

"I went in the house last because I went back to pick up the frying pan and then walked in, and then when I walked in, I think two of the boys went into the lounge room to put a video in. We don't normally watch videos until after *Home & Away* finishes.

"I thought Carolyn was in the lounge room or something. Kenny was, I reckon, at the encyclopaedias in the hallway, to put me wallet and smokes on top. Kenny screamed out 'fuck' and then I thought the way he said it, as though there was a mess in the kitchen as well.

"I figured Carolyn was pissed off with the kids so I just walked in to see what it was. I figured 'oh well, keep the peace and just clean it up' or something. But then I seen Carolyn laying on the floor and Kenny was just standing there so I pushed through. I grabbed her and tried to speak to her. She didn't answer. Um Um … I started to do the um, resus. Kenny um, Kenny said to me: 'You should clear her throat.' So I tried to clear her throat. Then he wanted me to do cardi. Somebody said something about ring the ambulance, dial triple zero or something. I'm really not sure who done that, I think Shane might have.

"I still don't know how she died. The ambulance people came in or the police … there was somebody there. But they were standing back, they weren't helping, so I figured it would have been the police, not the ambulance, because when the ambulance people came in, they virtually pulled me off. And then I had to get out and then it was the police lady or something tried to help me out. It feels to me as though I was resuscitating Carolyn for at least 20 minutes."

SC Johnson asked: "This is a difficult question but it is asked for a reason. Have you had any reason to suspect your wife may have been having an affair?"

"No, I haven't."

"To your knowledge, have you ever known your wife to be having an affair?"

"No, to my knowledge she never has."

"Have you ever had an affair?"

Kevin Matthews paused and took a deep breath. In the coming years, he would stubbornly stand by his next three words, despite overwhelming evidence to the contrary.

"No, I haven't. But I've been accused."

"How long ago?"

"Six months ago."

"And who accused you?"

"Um, one of my store managers."

"Did he accuse you of anyone in particular that you were having an affair with?"

"Ah, yes – his wife."

"What was his name?"

"Darren Burgess."

"Can you tell me the circumstances or the reasoning behind Darren Burgess accusing you of having an affair with his wife?"

This was one of the difficult questions the detective had warned of. Kevin fumbled around for an explanation.

"His wife was a model ... actually, both of us were all family friends and he was ... based it on the fact that ... I think it was all over a phone call that she was making to me and making to Carolyn. And she's actually a friend of Carolyn's and a friend of ours and Darren no longer wants to be a friend of ours and ..."

"Is it wholly and solely as a result of the allegation about an affair? Is that what broke the friendship off between you two?"

"Only between Darren and I but his wife still remained a family friend."

"How serious was that allegation? Was it a throwaway line?"

"I think it was. I don't know if it was a throwaway line but he tried to tell as many people as he could. Carolyn was aware of it and it didn't bother her. She knew the truth."

"Can you categorically say you did not have an affair with her?"

"I can categorically say I did not have an affair with her."

"Did he threaten you as a result of that allegation?"

"No, he wouldn't do that."

"Have you had threats from anybody recently, whether it be in your private life or your business life?"

"I've had a couple of ... two death threats about ... before Christmas. Would have been November or something. They weren't to me personally. Well, just, somebody just rang up and said, sort of said, you know, we're going to get youse or whatever, I can't remember the exact words. I rang the police at one stage. They said it's a nuisance call if it happens more than three times in a week, then it becomes a nuisance. At the moment, it's inconvenient but not a nuisance. Once was at work and Carolyn got a phone call one night and got a hang-up as well about seven or eight months ago. This was prior to the affair allegation. We've just changed our phone number to a silent number about a month ago."

"What's your understanding of how Carolyn died?"

"Numerous people told me she had a cardiac arrest but there was blood everywhere and Kenny said she cut herself but I didn't see any cuts. I think

Shane or Daniel found some knives in the front garden. The police told them not to touch them."

The detectives asked him about whether the kids had ever been violent towards their mother and if he knew anyone who used speed or magic mushrooms or drugs of any kind: "No."

"Did you have any part whatsoever in killing your wife?"

"No."

"Do you have any questions, Kevin?"

"Um, what goes on now? I don't know if I can go back to the house. I've got pets to feed."

No questions about his wife. No questions about her killer. No questions about the police investigation, which now involved the Major Crime Investigation Section. Matthews simply wanted to return to the blood-soaked scene of her murder to feed Max, the family dog. Fortunately for David Key, the dog was in the backyard when the murder occurred and unable to protect Carolyn.

The interview concluded at 11.25pm, five minutes after Major Crime's Detective Sergeant Michael Eichner, Detective Sergeant Mick Standing and Detective Senior Constable John Keane entered Nambucca Ave with an officer from the Physical Evidence Section. Standing, an enormous bear of a man, was a veteran with more than 35 years on the job. He was well known for his inability to suffer fools, particularly those who ended up sitting opposite him in a police interview room.

After the first briefing at the scene from the local detectives, he felt an immediate sense of apprehension. This murder contained none of the usual elements of the typical Australian homicide. Statistically, they are most likely to involve a victim and offender aged in their thirties and they are often known to each other. Alcohol or drugs will usually be factors and so is a dispute of some kind. In this case, the victim was a middle-class wife and mother, in a safe, respectable neighbourhood, found murdered in her home on a week night.

Sgt Standing recalls that his first and most pressing question at the crime scene was: "Is there some crazed person out there wandering around? Is he going to strike again tonight? If so, where?"

Recalling the events of the night, Sgt Standing says: "When I was briefed on what had happened, my initial reaction was that we were going to be in trouble with this murder. For someone to be found dead in their home on a Thursday night, a week night, everyone's at home cooking their tea. Who walks into someone's house at that hour of the night and brutally stabs someone to death? Where do you start? It was the middle of winter. Everyone's inside, so what witnesses are you going to have? Was this a random attack? Are we going to be in for more? A lot of things went through my mind that night. Unless this comes down to a very personal issue, then we're going to be in bother."

SC Keane recalls: "When we arrived at the scene, what struck us was the time factor. Kevin's come home and picked up his three boys and gone to the video store for 20 minutes, and in that 20 minutes, Carolyn's been murdered. It was either someone, a stranger, who was very lucky, who was able to get in and out of there. Was it pure luck or was he watching the place? Or was that 20-minute window orchestrated by somebody in the family?"

The crime scene is always among a detective's greatest assets, and Sgt Standing immediately realised it was never more so than in this case. This house had a story to tell and he needed to read it carefully. The officers had to wait several hours for the crime scene investigation team to complete their work before they could enter. Sgt Standing started at the front gate, moving slowly and methodically through the front yard, observing and absorbing every detail, from the knives to the recycling bin, before moving into the house. His description of the scene itself consumed dozens of pages in his notebook. He noted shoe prints in the blood. The horrific injuries inflicted upon Carolyn Matthews took many pages to fully summarise. What could have provoked such a frenzied attack?

He recalls: "I walked inside and there was a wall that had all sorts of memorabilia on it. It looked as though it had been bumped. Some of the photographs were off-centre. Some of the medals were on the floor. So it looked as though there had been some pushing and shoving.

"When I got into the family room, you could see into the kitchen and could see there was blood everywhere. I could see Carolyn Matthews's foot. Once you got into the kitchen and had a look and could see what had gone on, it was obvious there had been quite a savage and brutal stabbing.

"With the crime scene blokes, you go looking to see different things. Open drawers, blood in drawers. Blood on the refrigerator. You could see there had been a violent struggle. And blood everywhere. I don't think she died easy, that's for sure. It would have been tough. She would have had a bad time. I think the post mortem showed that as well. Whoever did this, really wanted this lady dead. Once I had seen that, it removed from my mind the thought that this was done by a stranger that had walked in off the street. It looked to me that it was quite personal. It looked to me as if this was a frenzied personal attack and someone wanted her dead."

Next to the cat's dinner bowl on the kitchen floor was a vital piece of evidence that David Key had missed in his quick scan of the scene before he fled. It was the first of several bloodied boot prints found at the scene, and it was soon established that they were not left by Kevin Matthews, his sons or emergency personnel.

SC Keane says: "It was a significant piece of evidence. The footprint was quite discernible. You could tell by looking at it that if you found the boot, you would be able to match the boot with that print. It indicated to me that they were in a hurry to get out. If they'd seen that, they would have made some effort to get rid of it."

Sgt Eichner says: "As far as the crime scene was concerned, there was the frying pan and the knives. One of the knives was bent, so from that we could probably assume that the offender was most likely a strong person, and that a struggle took place and that it was a vicious attack, there was no doubt about that. The frying pan and where the knives were found suggested it was not a very organised or controlled situation.

"There was a boot print at the scene. It was large and probably belonged to a male and we knew from the sole that it was most likely a work boot. So those were the sort of things we knew from the scene. We also concentrated on a number of other preliminary things that we do like door knocks, pathology and cause of death. But we had no immediate information about who had done this. One alternative was that this was a home invasion, but they would have to have been very lucky. It had the makings of a long-term murder investigation."

SC Keane: "Has someone come to rob the place or have they come there to kill someone? Whoever it was, they were not armed because they've taken the weapon from the kitchen. So why have they come there? There were no obvious lines of inquiry that night."

At 1am, the Major Crime officers drove to the Royal Adelaide Hospital mortuary, where forensic pathologist Dr Gilbert began his post-mortem examination. Sgt Standing made further notes about six stab wounds to the chest and one to the back, and the defence wounds to Carolyn's hands and arms.

Sgt Eichner: "We would have had a meeting on the night. The main priorities would have been to organise a team from Major Crime, a primary team and a secondary team."

MORE THAN two years later, in a victim impact statement, Carolyn's brother Peter would describe the horror of that night:

"My wife and I were just climbing into bed late on that evening. There was a knock at the front door, it was the police.

(They asked): 'Is your name Peter Tidswell?'

'Yes,' I replied.

'Do you have a sister called Carolyn?'

'Yes.'

'I am sorry to advise you that your sister Carolyn is dead.'

"My heart dropped. The police advised me that they had no more information than that and gave me a number of a detective to call. Still shaking from the news, I promptly called the detective. He advised me that she had been murdered. I broke down in tears and then discovered that I was the only one from our family that had been advised of Carolyn's death. It was then that I realised that I was the one who had to tell the rest of the family. I began to ring my brothers and told them to meet me at my mum's house and that I had some gruesome news. I got dressed and headed off. On the way, I soon realised that the news I had to tell mum especially would break her heart but little did I realise it would change all of our lives from that day forward. On breaking this news to the family, we all cried uncontrollably for what seemed like hours. That personally was the hardest thing I've ever had to do and would never wish it upon anybody."

Yvonne Tidswell remembers: "Allan Dalgleish said to Kevin: 'Has someone notified Yvonne?' I wasn't notified until quarter to 12 that night and she died at quarter to six. (Allan) got on to the police. (He told them): 'Don't come here, I'm on my own. My husband had just died, go to the boys.' So because Allan and my boys competed against each other, he went to Peter. And then Peter rang (Yvonne's eldest son) Geoffrey, who come around here. I was sitting up in bed reading, and he said: 'You'd better get up and get dressed'. I said: 'What for?' and he said: 'Pete'll be here in a minute, and Charlie'. And I thought: 'Pete and Charlie? The only one not here is Carolyn'.

"He said: 'Carolyn's had an accident, I know nothing about it.' And that wasn't until quarter to 12. We went straight down to Kevin's mum's place. Kevin was there, Kevin and the kids were there. Kevin was crying on my shoulder, sobbing and carrying on. The boys were pretty quiet. It was about three o'clock in the morning when we come home and we didn't sleep either. Geoffrey stayed the night with me. We had to get up at six o'clock to go over and tell my mum before she picked up the paper, we didn't know what was in the paper."

Carolyn Matthews's last day was over, leaving her family numb with shock and grief. But Kevin Matthews's tears were the worst kind of charade. How long would his story be believed?

Chapter 8
The hunt begins
July 13, 2001 – July 19, 2001

WALKING OUT of the mortuary at the Royal Adelaide Hospital at 8am the next day, Mick Standing pondered the daunting task ahead. His initial fears remained – this murder had all the hallmarks of a whodunit.

He recalls: "The day after the murder, we had a team meeting and then we sat down and talked about where we were going and what we were going to do. What steps, what investigation techniques we were going to be using. Sifting through whatever information we had and getting a structured approach to the investigation. That old cliché about the first 48 hours being the most important is true. We knew with this one it was going to be a long and difficult investigation until we got some solid information to work on."

Sgt Eichner says: "There were administrative matters to be attended to because it had been declared a major crime – we needed to second officers from the local service area."

The basic facts of the case had been released to the media the night before, and *The Advertiser*'s Rebecca Holmes immediately seized on the crucial element that had also intrigued detectives: "A mother of three was stabbed to death in her West Lakes Shore home last night, in the time it took her family to visit the local video store."

Sgt Standing says: "We knew it wasn't the husband, because he was out with his three boys and they've come home and found it. There was immediate suspicion about the window of time. If you weren't suspicious of immediate family involvement, you'd be lacking in your thought processes. None of us is Sherlock Holmes. The only detectives who solve murders in 200 pages are paperback detectives. For the rest of us, it's a long, hard slog. On the night, it did not look promising at all, but you don't let that deter you."

SC Keane says: "You wonder why a woman such as Carolyn Matthews has been targeted, has been murdered, for no apparent reason."

WEST LAKES Shore is a comfortable, modern middle-class suburb near the beach at Semaphore where the Matthews family spent so much of their time. Football Park, in the adjacent suburb of West Lakes, was home to the local AFL team, the Adelaide Crows. Kevin was a keen supporter and a club member. In 1992, West Lakes had won an international award for being "the best residential development in the world", and signs trumpeted it as the world's best address. McMansions had sprung up like weeds around its man-made lake and the area was a popular choice for young, affluent families. The Matthews family home was a more modest affair, a bungalow without beach or lake views, but it was on a big block in an area that was on the brink of enormous price growth. It was 35km from Davoren Park, in Adelaide's northern suburbs, a region divided geographically from the rest of the city by Grand Junction Rd, or, in local parlance, the "Mullet-Proof Fence". Socially, the two suburbs were a thousand miles apart.

CHRISTINE NIXON recalls how she discovered her closest friend was dead: "It was Friday the 13th and mum rang and she was crying and she said Missy was dead. I said 'no', and collapsed on the floor. My husband made me go back to bed and he took the children out for a couple of hours because I was a mess. And when I woke up I rang my mum back, and I don't know what happened while I was asleep, but I woke up with the feeling that Kevin had done it. I told my mum and she said: 'Why are you saying that? He loved her'. I said: 'It's just a feeling I've got deep down. He did it'. I can't to this day explain why."

DARREN BURGESS awoke to the news on his clock radio. "A mother of three has been murdered in her home at Nambucca Ave in West Lakes Shore …"

He recalls: "But they gave the ages of the boys, and I reckon they were wrong. I said to Kathy: 'It's not Carolyn, the ages are wrong.' Driving to work, mum rang me. She thought it was Carolyn and I said: 'It couldn't be, the boys' ages are wrong.' When I got to work, I thought: 'If it was Carolyn, the police would be there, because I'd threatened Kevin.' But they weren't. Then (my mate) Brad rang me and said: 'Have you heard? Carolyn Matthews has been killed.' As I'm on the phone, (my mate) Andrew's walking across the driveway, pointing at me. I spoke to Kathy throughout the day about calling the police. I was in shock. I straight away thought Michelle had something to do with it. Most definitely."

Darren slept poorly that night. He rang Kathy from work the next day and told her he was going to ring the police. He left his details with Crime Stoppers and was told to expect a call back.

WHILE DAVID KEY had trumpeted his contract killing plans to many people in the lead-up to the murder, he now finally realised he needed to show some discretion. But with the murder weighing heavily on his mind, if not his conscience, he needed someone trustworthy to confide in.

At 8.30am, "most probably" on Saturday, July 14, a pale Key arrived at his mate George's Davoren Park home in Michelle's Seca. (It may have been a day earlier – the day after the murder – but George is hazier than a bong cloud when it comes to specific details and, given Key's prodigious hangover that day, it is unlikely.) The pair went for a drive and Key stopped the car a few streets away.

George told police: "We jumped out and were having a yarn when he turned around and said: 'The job's done.' I just got this horrible feeling through my whole system, like, 'What the hell am I doing standing here talking?'

"Key … sort of come across like, there was a bit of remorse there. But it's like 'It's done. What's done is done'."

George didn't ask any questions. "I told him I knew too much to start off with and I didn't want to know any more about it and it was left at that. I was shaking in an unbelievable way. I had just been with somebody who had took somebody's life away.

"On the Monday after the murder, I was at a neighbour's house having a session with my mate – another couple of bongs, that sort of thing – and I saw a news bulletin on TV and saw the photo of the woman murdered at West Lakes. I immediately recognised her as the woman I saw in the photo David Key showed me. I suddenly had a terrible feeling in my stomach. I had thought Dave just had a big mouth and was full of shit. I felt sick. I knew straight away that Dave must have done the murder."

George confided all of this to his girlfriend and they contacted police, because, George says, he simply couldn't live with himself. He told police:

"What I knew before it happened was actually making me suffer more inside myself because I get anxiety and panic disorder inside my solar plexus area and end up with serious cramps, so I can't tell a lie. I can't put myself in a spot where I have a lot of anxiety around me because I just end up in hospital."

IN THE DAYS after the murder, the police poured resources into the investigation. Port Adelaide detectives and Neighbourhood Watch volunteers visited Nambucca Ave to reassure residents who were understandably frightened by the crime. They also conducted an extensive door-knock of the West Lakes area – which, as Sgt Standing predicted, elicited nothing – and checked out Kevin's story about his visit to the Leg Trap Hotel, retrieving the EFTPOS slip. Within a few days, when they had obtained Matthews's banking and credit card records, they would pick up the paper trail of the Matthews-Burgess affair at hotel and motel reception desks across Adelaide.

At 11am on Saturday, July 14, Major Crime detectives Standing, Eichner, Keane, Senior Sergeant Lyn Strange and Detective Senior Constable Roger Kern returned to Nambucca Ave to conduct a thorough search of the property and an *Advertiser* photographer captured them mid-conference on the front lawn.

Sgt Standing recalls: "On the Saturday, we went back and went through the crime scene again. We looked through the whole house to see what else we could find, any evidence that was overlooked, get a feel for the crime scene, see if the offender had been in the house before and knew the layout, that sort of thing. Kevin Matthews was there with his family members.

"He was briefed on what we were going to do and how we were going to approach it. We let him go and he looked like he was pretty grief-stricken at the time. His eyes were red-rimmed. He wasn't saying a lot. He was sobbing and breaking down. It looked to me like the guy was pretty upset because his wife had been murdered. He was treated as a victim because, at that stage, we had no reason to think that he wasn't."

Also that day, Darren Bland contacted Darren Burgess to say that Michelle had been to Beaurepaires Port Adelaide between 5.10pm and 5.25pm on the previous Thursday, accompanied by a guy with a shaved head, a beard and tattoos.

Sgt Eichner went to Yvonne Tidswell's home, where she gave him a portrait photograph of the family for release to the media. The happy, proud mum's smiling face became the enduring public image of Carolyn Matthews.

The detectives returned to Nambucca Ave at 10am on Sunday, July 15 and conducted more house-to-house inquiries. Sen. Sgt Strange also spoke to Matthews, other family members and Semaphore Surf Life Saving Club members.

Sgt Standing recalls: "I spoke to Carolyn's business partner and people who were involved with her in the surf life saving club. The view I formed of her was that she was a very, very good person. She was a life member of the surf club. For such a young person to be given an honour like that speaks for itself. She was a good lady."

SC Keane and Sgt Eichner, meanwhile, interviewed Michelle's friend Cassandra Hutchison who had contacted police, and the investigation immediately gained focus.

Sgt Eichner recalls: "It was then that she started to paint a picture about Kevin and her friend Michelle, who lived in the same street. Darren and Michelle's relationship, Kevin's behaviour, and the picture started to come together that there was an affair. She knew quite a bit and the information she gave us was very good. It started the ball rolling."

The clean-up of the crime scene was also completed that day. Kevin Matthews apparently had no problem moving his traumatised sons straight back into the scene of their mother's murder.

Later in the day, Darren Burgess drove to the Kmart store at the Ingle Farm shopping centre to pick up his children from Michelle for the school holidays. Darren saw Key and another man in the vicinity.

He later told police: "When they got out of the car, I was a bit shocked to see Michelle because she'd told me she'd sold it and bought another car. I went and had a look at the car. The tyres, mainly the front two, were completely bald."

Darren: "I thought you'd sold this?"

Michelle: "I've borrowed it because the new car has broken down."

Darren: "Well the guy (Key) told me he put new tyres on it."

Michelle: "Well that's got nothing to do with me."

Darren: "You're driving around in a car with a bald tyre."

Michelle: "That's not my problem."

Darren: "So did you hear about Carolyn Matthews?"

Michelle: "Yeah, yeah."

Darren recalls: "I was trying to check her reaction but she didn't elaborate."

The other man was a casual acquaintance of Key who was roped in to stand by while the exchange took place. Key had told him he needed his help in case his girlfriend's ex-husband turned violent; he gave the man $20 for his trouble.

On the same weekend, Michelle visited her mother, Angela Goldup, and was reading *The Advertiser* when she noticed a story on the murder. Her mother later told police she asked her daughter if it was someone she knew. "Michelle said: 'Oh, it sounds like Kevin Matthews's wife – I hope it's not Carolyn', and that was all she said."

Another horrendous crime occurred that weekend, one which would draw much of the media's attention away from Carolyn Matthews's murder, at least for now.

Shane Tidswell recalls: "I think we were lucky because just after my mum's murder, was the Falconio incident. That took us out of the press at the time."

Within days of his disappearance on July 14, 2001, the presumed murder of British tourist Peter Falconio – and his girlfriend Joanne Lees's narrow escape – became a huge story in both Australia and Britain. Drug-running drifter Bradley John Murdoch was arrested in 2003 and later sentenced to life in prison for Falconio's murder.

Kenny, Shane and Daniel Matthews, meanwhile, were trying to come to grips with the devastating loss of their mother, the trauma of finding her slain body and the mystery of why anyone would have wanted to do this to her.

Shane says: "I remember sitting in the lounge room at (Kevin's mother) Irene's place, and there were a lot of people coming over, mostly family, for the first couple of days. After a few days, one of my mates Matthew came in. His uncle, Barry Cole, was actually best mates with my dad. Matt came in and didn't know what to say. He sat down next to us and we were watching TV. His old man and family came in as well, we all grew up together. I didn't say anything."

Sgt Standing recalls: "They were teenage boys who've seen their mother dead on the floor and then tried to revive her. It would have been an absolutely horrendous experience for them. It's a really horrendous experience for anybody to see that. But for young lads like that ... they did a wonderful job trying to save their mum. And they deserve a medal for it. Words can't describe how they would have felt. Little surprise that they weren't even talking to anybody."

SGT STANDING and Detective Senior Constable Scott Duval were tasked with following up the call from Darren Burgess.

Darren recalls: "I was at my niece's birthday party when Mick Standing rang and said: 'I need to speak to you.' So we organised to meet at Kathy's house the next morning. They were there for 2–3 hours."

Sgt Standing says: "I got down there and said: 'Right, what's this information you've got for us?' and he's told me about these phone bills he's discovered and the endless calls and text messages between his wife and Matthews.

"We knew straight away Darren had nothing to do with the murder. We knew where he was on the night of the murder, he was at home. And of course why would he want to kill his boss's wife? If he was going to kill anyone, it would have been Michelle Burgess. He came across as a reserved young man trying to get on with his life after the disappointment of divorce and break-up of his family. The person who really captured my attention was Darren's new partner, Kathryn Morton. She was very supportive of him and encouraged him to be open with me. It was her support that gave him the confidence to tell us everything he knew from the outset. We probably would have got the full story of his relationship with Michelle and Kevin and what he knew, but it may have taken a lot longer. Darren made several references to David Key during the first interview but we didn't know what his involvement was, other than he was some sort of acquaintance of Michelle Burgess."

As well as details of the affair between Michelle and Kevin, Darren handed over the damning phone accounts and a copy of a letter he had written to Kevin. Crucially, he also told them of the call he had received from Darren Bland about seeing Michelle and a man at Beaurepaires who had "a shaved head, a beard and tattoos", talking to Kevin shortly before the murder.

While Sgt Standing was interviewing Darren, Carolyn's brother Geoff was at Royal Adelaide Hospital's mortuary viewing room with Sgt Eichner, identifying the body of his sister. As the eldest son, he shouldered many of the terrible burdens over the next few weeks and he would eventually move to Queensland, forever scarred by the family's darkest hour.

Yvonne says: "Geoffrey, my eldest son, I think he was more hurt in a way than a lot of us because he had to go and identify Carolyn and he managed all the funeral."

Also that morning, Matthews family friend Alison Wenham and her two children went to Nambucca Ave to leave flowers. When they arrived at the Matthews home, there was a young girl standing by the gate.

Mrs Wenham later told police: "I spoke to her and as a result, we went in to see Kevin. He was sitting on a chair in the patio near the pool. There was a blonde-haired female wearing sunglasses with him. He introduced her as a work colleague." She later saw the same woman on TV and identified her as Michelle Burgess.

Before the detectives had ended their interview with Darren Burgess that morning, they made an important final request – help them find Michelle. She had been ultra-secretive about her new Craigmore home, refusing to tell Darren where she was living. So he rang and asked her to meet him at her mother's home, on the pretext of picking up some golf clubs. As Darren left the Goldups' Holden Hill home that afternoon, he spotted an old Ford Fairlane parked at the end of the street with two men inside. When Michelle left, the two officers from the Investigation Support Branch followed at a discreet distance.

David Key, meanwhile, was attending to some administrative duties. He presented sick certificates to his Work for the Dole supervisor and told him he was having trouble breathing and was going to have tests. But, as usual, Key couldn't help but boast about his recent "good fortune" – even though he'd not yet been paid for his brutal crime.

The supervisor described Key's behaviour as chirpy, upbeat, racy and hyperactive, suggesting that a significant amount of the "shitload of speed" he had bought was still circulating in his system.

With a grin, he told the supervisor: "I've had a bit of a windfall."

"Oh yeah, what happened?" the supervisor asked, curious.

"I came into a bit of money, $25,000."

"Oh yeah, how'd you get that?"

"Won it on the pokies."

Key also said he had dropped his old girlfriend from Smithfield and had taken up with an "upmarket lady" from Craigmore. Life, it seemed, was coming up roses for David Key.

The Crime Stoppers phones had been running hot with tips about the case, and one of the most significant calls early in the case was made on July 16.

Sgt Eichner recalls: "A call came through that Scott Rose had information relating to the Matthews murder. (The caller stated) 'Scott and a man named Jamie knew that a man named "Dave" was hired as a hitman by the wife's husband and paid $60,000 to kill her. This "Dave" had since given Jamie about $8000 to buy a car. Dave was allegedly known to police. A lot of people knew about it.' This was the information that pointed us in the direction of David Key. Obviously the next step was to try to locate him. And it wasn't long after that, through the surveillance and telephone intercepts, that we did."

MICK STANDING'S initial fears of a whodunit were proving unfounded. Within four days of the murder, Michelle Burgess and Kevin Matthews were Persons of Interest to the investigation, and David Key was now also firmly on their radar. But the police did not want to alert their potential suspects to the knowledge they had gleaned. On July 17 – the day after the Investigation Support Branch's covert surveillance operation began – detectives also told the media that while Kevin Matthews had told them it appeared nothing had been stolen, robbery had not yet been ruled out as a motive for the murder.

Sgt Standing recalls: "Then we had other information come in about them having sex in a park. That's pretty brazen sort of behaviour. It wasn't as though one person knew about this affair, everybody knew about it but Darren. So by the time we're about five or six days into the investigation, it was pretty well focused on the affair."

CONSTABLE PAUL PALAZZO'S surveillance of Michelle's Craigmore home delivered immediate dividends: David Key, driving away in her red Toyota Seca. Later in the day, Const. Palazzo tailed Key and Michelle, and backyard mechanic Marc English, as they drove to various locations in the northern suburbs. Key had asked English to help him find a new car, because Michelle had decided that the red Seca was too small to be a family car. They visited two car yards on Main North Rd, finding a white VP Commodore at a third yard, David Burton Motors.

Yard owner David Burton later told police they were admiring the Commodore, which was on a ramp at the front of the yard, when he approached and introduced himself.

A jovial Key responded: "Well that'll make it easy, because I'm Dave, too."

English also introduced himself and they spent a few minutes looking over the car's interior and engine bay, before telling Burton they were interested and would be back.

THE NEXT DAY, *The Advertiser* reported that Kevin Matthews had spoken to his friend and Semaphore Surf Life Saving Club president Peter Campaign.

The report noted: "The club – of which Mrs Matthews was a life member – has been caring for the family since the tragedy, cooking meals for Mr Matthews's three sons and walking their dog. Mr Campaign said Mr Matthews was slowly coming to terms with the tragedy. 'Kevin is focused and realises that he has got to be strong for his boys,' Mr Campaign said. 'Personally, he's doing it tough, but that's to be expected.'"

Over the next few days, death notices for Carolyn appeared in the pages of *The Advertiser*, each telling its own story. Kevin's was topped with a small dolphin icon, Carolyn's favourite animal, and read: "Dearly loved and loving wife of Kevin, loved mother of Kenny, Shane and Daniel. Don't know how we're going to make it, it's only your strength keeping us going. Best friend, wife and coaching partner. Miss you always, love Kevin."

Carolyn's beloved sons wrote: "Mum to hear your voice, to see you smile, to sit and talk to you a while, to be together in the same old way, would be my greatest wish today. Love Kenny."

"Dear Mum, peace after suffering. Love Shane."

"Mum, may the winds of love blow softly and whisper for you to hear, that we will love and remember you and forever keep you near. Love Daniel."

And her heartbroken mother, Yvonne, wrote: "Dearly loved and loving only daughter of Yvonne and the late Doug. Missy, thank you for the years we shared, the love you gave, the way you cared. Memorable times will always be treasured. God has you in his keeping, we have you in our hearts. Reunited with Dad. Till we meet again."

ON THE MORNING of July 19, with police tail in tow, Key and Michelle returned to the yard to take the car for a test drive. Key drove, with Michelle in the passenger seat and one of the yard's other salesmen keeping a watchful eye from the back seat. The vehicle, an ex-NSW Police car, was equipped with a V8. After a ten-minute drive, Key was smitten. Burton told them the price of $10,999 was fixed and they naively agreed to it, leaving a $180 deposit. While he arranged registration, they left to get the cash. Bank records show that Michelle withdrew $16,000 of her divorce settlement cash from the bank that day.

They returned to the car yard 40 minutes later, paying for the Commodore with a wad of $100 notes. Michelle began completing the paperwork, giving her old Evanston Park address. A short time later, the details were finalised and new plates were attached to the car.

The police surveillance officer's report notes that at 10.56am, Key left in the Commodore, while Michelle drove off in the Seca. At 2pm that day, SC Kern visited the car yard and seized the contract of sale form. The surveillance officer's report of the afternoon's subsequent events notes:

11.53am–12.25pm: White Commodore followed from 15 Easton Rd, Davoren Park to the Esplanade at Semaphore. Michelle was the sole occupant. She entered the Palais restaurant.

12.26pm: Michelle returns to vehicle briefly with Kevin Matthews.

12.36pm: Matthews and Michelle seen sitting at a table, talking and drinking. Michelle appeared to be crying and laughing and also being serious during the conversation. She took two mobile calls. Matthews kissed her several times and at one point wiped a tear from her eye. After they left the Palais, Matthews and Michelle seen standing on the road. Matthews was hugging Michelle.

12.40pm: White Commodore, with Michelle the sole occupant, followed back to 9 Bluebush Court, Craigmore.

3.20pm: Michelle and Key leave Bluebush Court and park the Commodore on the eastern side of Port Wakefield Rd. There was condensation on the rear window of the vehicle. Michelle was not visible. However, Key was lying across the back seat, with no shirt on, moving up and down in a sexual motion.

That same day, the Matthews and Tidswell families, along with Carolyn Matthews's closest friends, attended a viewing at the Tony Monte Funeral Centre Chapel, in Port Adelaide. Kaylene and Rodney Kenyon were among them. Kaylene approached Kevin and hugged him, and he responded by saying "I did love her" – an oddly defensive statement for a man whose wife had just been murdered.

That evening, Darren Burgess and his new girlfriend Kathy took his son to soccer training at Karbeethon Reserve in Evanston Gardens, a stone's throw from Evanston Primary School, where his estranged wife and Key had first plotted his murder.

He noticed a white VP Commodore among the other parents' cars, but it was 20 minutes before he realised with a jolt that Michelle was sitting inside it. He watched her get out and approach the wife of the soccer coach. At the same time, the man to whom he had sold the battery – and also seen when he'd picked up the kids at Ingle Farm – was stalking across the reserve towards him.

Darren later told police: "He introduced himself as Dave. He wanted me to go somewhere private with him for a talk. I refused. He then proceeded to threaten me. He said he was with Michelle. I took that to mean he was her current boyfriend."

Key got to the point: "If Michelle gets grief, I get grief and then I make a few phone calls, and the person who makes the grief gets dealt with. Do you get my drift?"

"Are you threatening me?" Darren replied.

"No, not threatening you. I am a convicted criminal. I've been to prison. I'm not scared to go back. I'm a very powerful person. I've got a restraint order against me and I can't go within 50m of my kids. I am hoping for court action to see my kids. There's a contract on Michelle's head and mine for $175,000. I am waiting for a phone call tonight to find out who's taken the contract out. Do you know where Michelle lives?"

"No," said Darren.

Key said: "Best you keep it that way. I've got people watching her house. If I go to jail, Michelle would disappear and have her phone on 24 hours a day, seven days a week to answer problems with the children, then disappear again."

Darren says he was not intimidated "in any way" by Key's baffling threats. Key told him he had sold Michelle's red Seca and paid cash for the Commodore. He said he was such a powerful person, he paid $10,000 for a car worth $35,000. He said he was "copping a lot of grief about West Lakes" because Michelle was still in contact with Kevin.

The next day, July 19, Key and Michelle returned to David Burton's car yard, where salesman Terry Vale greeted them, joking: "So you're back to buy another car?"

"Yep, probably," Key replied. Marc English, who was not with them on this trip, later told police: "I believe they bought a car each because Dave is very independent and wanted his own car."

The couple began looking over a blue VN Commodore priced at $6999. Key didn't take long to make up his mind.

"Yep, VN Commodore, that's what I want," he told Michelle.

"Well we'd better get going if we've got to be at the Elizabeth bank before four," she said.

Key turned to Vale: "I've got two words for you – yard change." (Referring to the fact that vehicles would have to be moved around because they intended buying the car.) Vale described them as "carrying on like boyfriend and girlfriend – and the man kept touching the woman's face".

At the same time, Kathy Cowled – who was at the Adelaide train station with her children – sent a text message to Michelle to "say hello". She was surprised when her brother called her minutes later, because she was unaware that he and Michelle were now an item. Key arranged to pick up his sister and her children at the train station. She tagged along while Michelle and Key stopped at the Commonwealth Bank at Elizabeth.

Michelle withdrew $9265 as a cheque made out to Ford Credit, to pay out the finance on the red Seca. She also withdrew $7000 cash, leaving just $425 in the account. At 4.10pm, Key and Michelle returned to the car yard and listened to Terry Vale's spiel about the VN before agreeing to buy it. They continued admiring it while waiting for him to arrange registration, eventually wandering into the office, where a pleased David Burton greeted them: "Well, if it ain't my best customers."

He later told police they both began "talking rubbish" and he can't recall the details, but he did notice that Key was wearing a t-shirt with an obscene picture of a girl on the front with her legs spread.

He recalls: "While waiting for Terry to get back, I followed them out to the road. Michelle mentioned that Dave had been doing burnouts in her car and that the new VN was going to be for him. I checked the back of the VP and noticed rubber near the rear wheels."

They returned to the office to start the paperwork. With a flourish, Michelle produced a white envelope stuffed with hundreds and fifties and announced that it amounted to "seven grand". Burton agreed to drop the price by $200, starting on the paperwork, while Key walked in and out of the office and up and down the car yard. Burton thought he had "ants in his pants".

When he did sit down next to Michelle, he put his head in her lap, and several times moved his head up close to her face, while she said: "Give me a kiss. Come on, give me a kiss." Burton told police they were "very intimate and carrying on like boyfriend/girlfriend". Michelle counted out the money again and signed the contract of sale.

Burton says: "While we were waiting, David was carrying on with Michelle, putting his arm around her and cuddling and kissing her. At times he also grabbed her from behind and made movements as if to have sex."

Terry Vale arrived back at the yard with the registration plates and sticker at 4.40pm. Michelle drove off in the VP, with Kathy and her children in the back seat.

Meanwhile, Key – a parolee with a warrant out for his arrest, a killer with his victim's blood still on his boots, and a driver with no licence – left a cloud of smoke in his wake as he squealed out on to Main North Rd and sped recklessly away.

Police didn't know what to make of these developments. Why had Michelle spent her divorce settlement on two old Commodores? Why was she now openly having a parallel affair with David Key, while continuing to string along Kevin Matthews? There seemed no logic, or ultimate goal, motivating her bizarre behaviour. No one – including her, it seemed – knew where all this was leading.

DEAD BY FRIDAY

Above: Christine Nixon and Carolyn Tidswell, both aged 4, are caught using Yvonne's best gold tea set to "cook" with flour, milk and baby powder on a black goat-skin rug.
Picture: CHRISTINE NIXON

Left: Semaphore Surf Life Saving Club life member Carolyn Matthews, doing what she loved.
Picture: YVONNE TIDSWELL

Right and below: Carolyn and Kevin Matthews on their wedding day, November 17, 1984.

Left and below: Darren and Michelle Burgess on their wedding day, November 20, 1993.

Top to Bottom:

Michelle Burgess's former lover, Darren Bland, outside court after giving evidence on December 2, 2002. Picture: MICHAEL MILNES, *The Advertiser*

Kenny, Shane and Daniel Matthews, about a year before their mother was stabbed to death and their father was accused of her murder.

Top to Bottom:

This picture, from a family portrait, became the enduring public image of Carolyn Matthews after her murder.

Carolyn Matthews's close friend Kaylene Kenyon, with husband Rodney, outside court during the murder trial in August 2003.
Picture: MICHAEL MILNES, *The Advertiser*

DEAD BY FRIDAY

Top to Bottom:

Kathleen Cowled, the "pretty simple woman" who introduced her brother, hitman David Key, to Michelle Burgess.
Picture: MICHAEL MILNES, *The Advertiser*

Jason Colenso planned to write a book about his experiences with Michelle Burgess. He forgot that he was semi-literate.
Picture: DYLAN COKER, *Sunday Mail*

DEAD BY FRIDAY

Telephone Directory

Kind
Exciting
Vigorous
Intelligent
Naughty

The love that I wanted walked into my life.
Although he has a wife.
He's the man of my dreams all in one
No one compares to him

The love that all I wanted all my life
Came to me one day.
He's the man of my dreams all in one
But there is always the threat he will be taken away.
But I want him to stay

Disturbing poetry found in Michelle Burgess's diary.

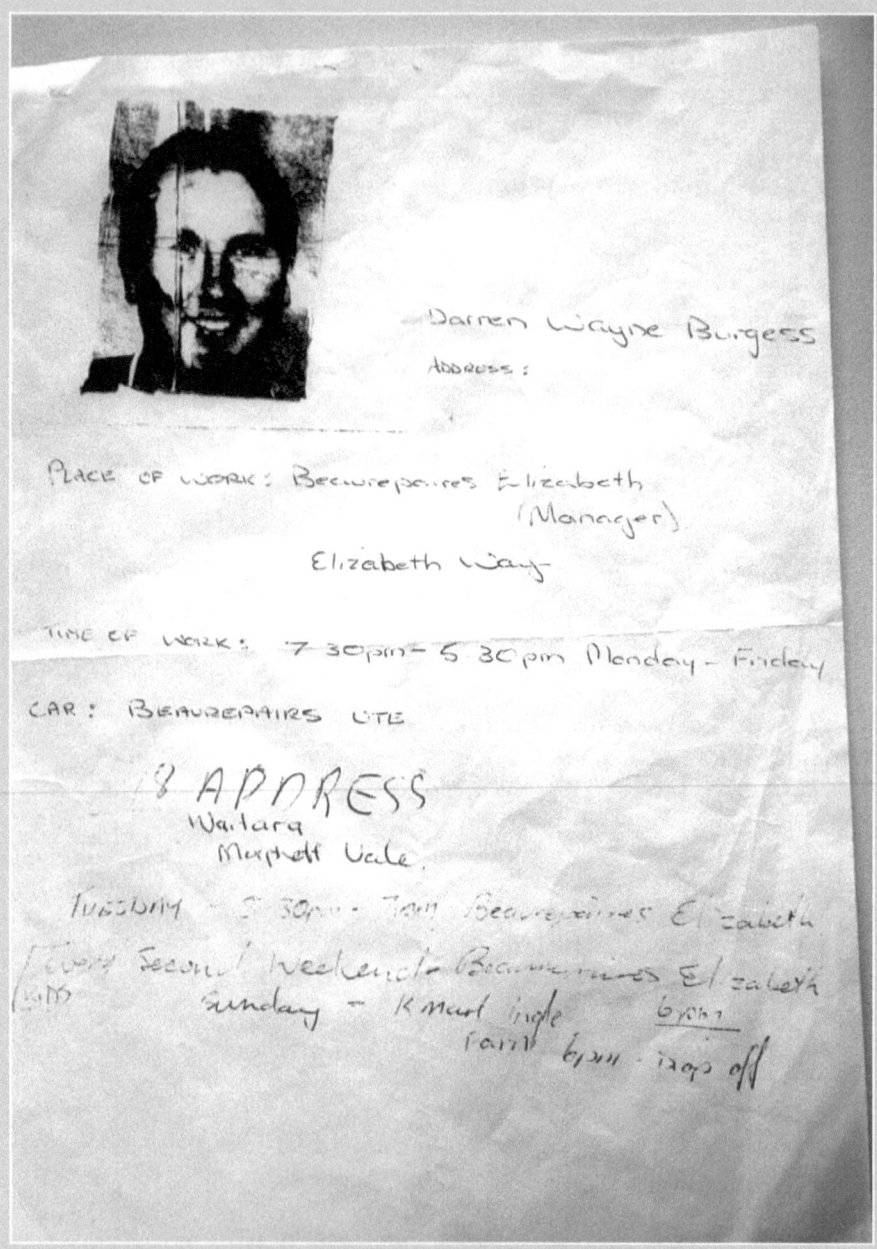

The photocopy taken by police of the contract on Darren Burgess's life, written by Michelle Burgess and found in David Key's wallet. Key ingeniously disposed of the second contract, on Carolyn Matthews's life, by eating it in a sandwich.

Extra details for the murder contracts, scrawled on the back of an envelope by Michelle Burgess, showing that she wanted at least one of the intended targets dead by Friday.

DEAD BY FRIDAY

Top to Bottom:

The street sign that directed children in trouble to the West Lakes Shore home of Kevin and Carolyn Matthews.
Picture: MIKE BURTON, *The Advertiser*

The floorplan of the Matthews's home in Nambucca Ave, West Lakes Shore.

The murder scene inside the Matthews's home. Carolyn Matthews's foot can be seen on the kitchen floor. Picture: SAPOL

DEAD BY FRIDAY

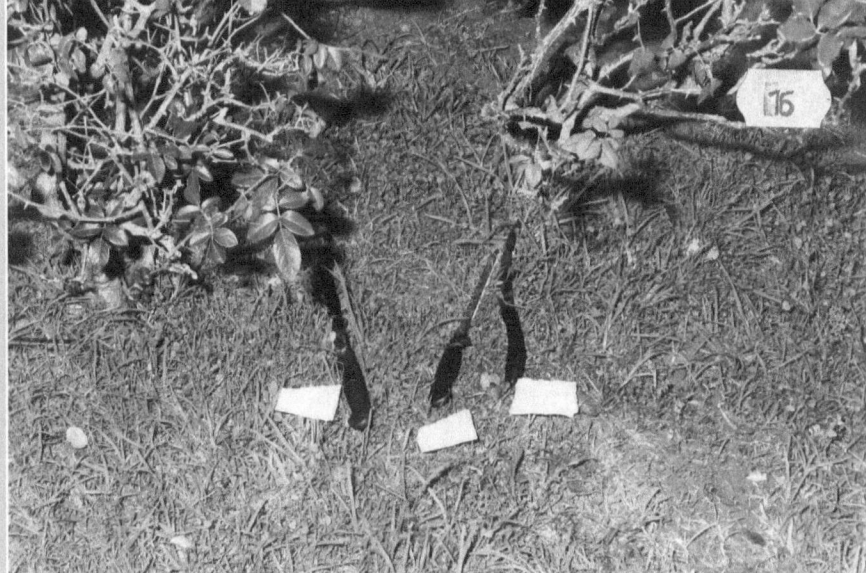

Top to Bottom:

The corner of the kitchen where Carolyn Matthews fought for her life. Picture: SAPOL

The three knives, including the murder weapon, which David Key discarded outside the house. Picture: SAPOL

Top to Bottom:

One of the bloodied boot prints found near Carolyn Matthews's body. Picture: SAPOL

The soles of David Key's boots, which perfectly matched the boot print in Carolyn Matthews' kitchen. Picture: SAPOL

Top to Bottom:

Major Crime detectives Michael Eichner, Roger Kern, Lyn Strange, John Keane and Michael Standing confer outside the crime scene on July 14, 2001. Picture: BRETT HARTWIG, *The Advertiser*

No. 5 Nambucca Ave, West Lakes Shore, surrounded by crime scene tape the day after Carolyn Matthews's murder. Picture: RUSSELL MILLARD, *The Advertiser*

DEAD BY FRIDAY

Top to Bottom:

Detective Chief Superintendent Paul Schramm holds a photograph of Carolyn Matthews the day after she was murdered.
Picture: BRETT HARTWIG, *The Advertiser*

A tableau of Carolyn Matthews's life and achievements at her funeral.
Picture: BRETT HARTWIG, *The Advertiser*

DEAD BY FRIDAY

Top to Bottom:

Kevin Matthews helps carry his wife's casket, flanked by two of his grief-stricken sons.
Picture: BRETT HARTWIG, *The Advertiser*

An artist's impression of David William Edgar Key in court. Police cannot release pictures of the convicted killer because he has a right to privacy.
Picture: *The Advertiser*

Top to Bottom:

Detectives Mick Standing, left, and John Keane, escort Michelle Burgess into their offices for interrogation after her arrest on August 4, 2001.
Picture: MARK BRAKE, *Sunday Mail*

Michelle Burgess's two lovers, Jason Colenso and Kevin Matthews, wait outside court on August 6, 2001, for her first court appearance. Even Colenso seems bemused by Matthews's decision to wear a hat emblazoned with "Forever" on the back.

DEAD BY FRIDAY

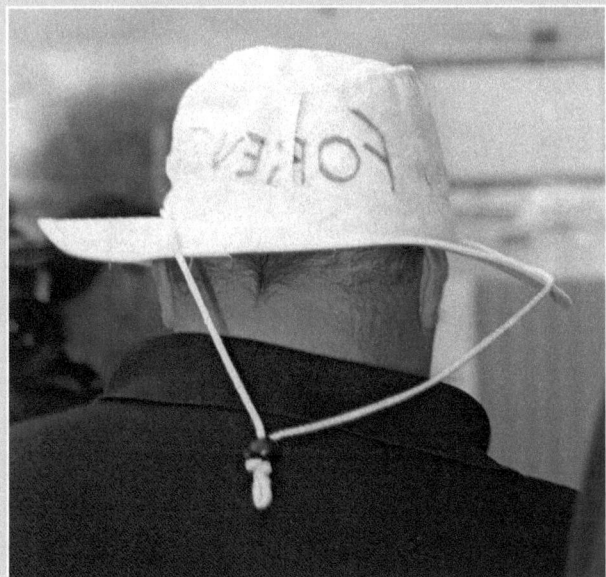

Top to Bottom:

The "Forever" hat.

A media pack surrounded Kevin Matthews as he left court on August 6, 2001, apparently oblivious to the fact that his expression of faith to Michelle Burgess was visible to the world.

Pictures: BRENTON EDWARDS, *The Advertiser*

Top to Bottom:

Kevin Matthews is led into court for the first time after his arrest for murder in August 2001. Picture: MICHAEL MILNES, *The Advertiser*

Kevin Matthews and Michelle Burgess during a court tour of key locations during their 2003 murder trial.

An envelope sent to Michelle Burgess containing a 22-page letter and a love poem from Kevin Matthews.

Kevin Matthews's wedding fantasy poem for Michelle Burgess.

DEAD BY FRIDAY

Top to Bottom:

Michelle Burgess during a court tour of key locations on August 13, 2003.

Kevin Matthews says goodbye to the rest of his life, exiting Adelaide Supreme Court on October 9, 2003 after being found guilty of his wife's murder. Picture: MICHAEL MILNES, *The Advertiser*

Top to Bottom:

Michelle Burgess's parents, Angela and Keith Goldup, outside court on September 26, 2003.
Picture: MICHAEL MILNES,
The Advertiser

Yvonne Tidswell outside court after her daughter's killers were found guilty on September 12, 2003.
Picture: MICHAEL MILNES,
The Advertiser

Top to Bottom:

Carolyn Matthews's memorial plaque at Centennial Park. Her mother Yvonne routinely covers up the reference to "Adored wife of Kevin".

"Carolyn's Walk", at the entry to the Semaphore Surf Life Saving Club, is a memorial to their beloved life member.
Picture: DEREK PEDLEY

Top to Bottom:

Kevin Matthews's stilted attempt at a memorial poem for his wife, a year after her murder.

The picture Kevin Matthews attached to his internet penpal profile in 2009.

Darren Burgess and Kathy Morton, who married in December 2012.

MATTHEWS, Carolyn Wendy.
25/7/63 — 12/7/01
When I look up to the sky I hold myself and wonder why?
Every night I wish for you, but yet my dreams have not come true. I choose to dream of you alive, breathing and living by my side. It hurts to know I can't remember those times that you were so tender. I try to think back as far as you, the memories of love we know were true.
Your beautiful face I can't recall, only from pictures do I know you at all. Your glowing smile and deep brown eyes, always holding in some surprise. I wish I could see you one more time, to tell you these feelings of mine. You will always be in my heart, I love you and wish we weren't apart. Kevin.

CHAPTER 9

The funeral

July 19, 2001 – July 20, 2001

ON THE SAME afternoon that Michelle Burgess and David Key were shopping for the second Commodore, hundreds of people were celebrating Carolyn Matthews's life and grieving her brutal death. They overflowed from the Tony Monte Funeral Centre Chapel in Port Adelaide, many holding single red roses. And with rumours spreading fast, plenty of them already knew that Kevin Matthews was under a dark cloud.

Yvonne Tidswell says: "The minister who did the service (Pastor Peter Marr) had buried my husband. But he knew Kevin was involved because his neighbour had told him: 'The husband's involved with that.'

"Peter said: 'Oh no, no, no.'

"And the neighbour said: 'Oh yeah, I saw him out at the pub (with Michelle). They were carrying on and were asked to leave.'

"And Peter said: 'I wish you hadn't told me that because I'm doing the service tomorrow.'

"So he knew Kevin was involved and he had to stand there and do that service. He hesitated at one part and you can see it on the video of the funeral."

Kaylene and Rodney Kenyon were initially running on time for the funeral, but Kaylene was determined to take some of Carolyn's favourite flowers. Ironically, they were lilies, the death flower, and they were out of season; a frantic search of florists left her empty-handed, upset and late for the funeral. They chapel was full by the time they arrived and they had to wait outside until after the service.

On the funeral video, the mourners milled about outside before the service, holding their roses, signing the guest book, wearing the downcast, grim faces of people coming to grips with a terrible loss. Inside, a tableau of Carolyn's life faced the seated mourners. There were 17 life saving medals and a Semaphore Surf Life Saving Club Certificate of Life Membership dated June 25, 1994. There were also pictures of Carolyn – on her wedding day, with new husband Kevin; with her proud father Doug; a besotted teenager with boyfriend Kevin; in a speedboat on the river. An open wedding album displayed more pictures of their special day.

Mourners lined the driveway as the funeral cars approached, a silver Ford LTD hearse leading the way. Daniel Matthews had the family kelpie-cross, Max, on a lead. The pallbearers, including Kevin, moved forward, and Max scampered through them. Kevin was wearing sunglasses, a black shirt with no tie and a black leather jacket. One hand stayed in his pocket as he reluctantly gripped his wife's coffin with the other and stared at it, only looking away when he was distracted by Max.

As the service began, singer Winston Kay, who sang at Doug Tidswell's funeral only months before, performed a haunting version of the traditional song, *In the Garden*, made famous by Elvis Presley.

"He walks with me and he talks with me and he tells me I am his own ..."

Max sat front row, centre, and behind him the chapel was packed, with standing room only at the back. Kevin sat in the front row with his three boys. His sunglasses stayed on and he did not look around.

During his opening address, Pastor Marr told the mourners:

"We have gathered here this afternoon to share an important and a sad moment in the lives of the family and close friends of Carolyn Wendy Matthews. As we gather here today, we are hurt. We are shocked that Carolyn's life should be taken from us in such horrific circumstances at the age of 37 years. We come today as members of her family or as one of her close friends, to express our sense of sorrow, hurt and loss at her passing."

Max whined quietly.

Pastor Marr said: "We're all here today. Even the dog, because he was special. And as we pay our respects we want to offer our love, our support, our prayers, to Carolyn's family and her loved ones.

"Carolyn was approaching her 38th birthday. Her life has been stolen from her. The events surrounding this death have shocked this nation. To you, Kevin, Kenny, Shane, Daniel ... To Yvonne, Geoffrey, Peter and Charlie, Irene, Sandra, Diane, Vicky, Peter, Julie, Steven and all of your families that are present here today ... Carolyn was a beautiful lady in so many ways and

Carolyn's story, I'd like to invite Mr Peter Campaign from the Semaphore Surf Life Saving Club to come and present some of the events that make up Carolyn's life story."

Peter Campaign stepped forward and, during his eloquent, heartfelt eulogy, said: "Kevin has asked me to speak and reflect on Carolyn's life. She was our daughter, our sister, our friend. How can someone described as a quiet, ordinary, suburban mother of three have such an extraordinary effect upon each and every one she has touched?

"The family, Doug, Yvonne and Carolyn, were responsible for building a bond between Glenelg and Semaphore surf life saving clubs. She pursued and loved Kevin with passion and energy from the moment they met. She captured and captivated the exuberant and high-spirited Bodgie. And a youthful, passionate love affair matured over the years to stand the test of time. The dynamic emotional relationship will always be cherished by Kevin. This pursuit of him led Carolyn to the Semaphore Surf Life Saving Club. We were soon to learn that this angelic wisp of a girl was in actual fact a pocket battleship. Size, gender, status did not phase Carolyn, who could and did stand toe to toe, staking her ground within surf life saving, especially then at a time when the male-dominated association's barriers to females were being broken down.

"After spending some years in the Glenelg Surf Life Saving Club, Carolyn joined Semaphore in 1979, becoming one of the first female bronze holders and also the first woman bronze holder in the club in January 1981, when women were formally accepted into the active service areas of surf life saving. Carolyn went on to gain awards including the advanced resus certificate; radio operator's certificate; and Level 1 and 3 Official accreditation, which she shared with her mother for many, many years, judging and training. In addition to training young surf life savers, Carolyn herself competed and coached at state and Australian championships. She was a member of numerous successful teams and took great satisfaction in coaching the club's gold medal-winning women's open rescue and resus team. A valued member of the Semaphore senior march-past team for many years, Carolyn's contribution to the club is immeasurable. In 1994, in her early 30s, Carolyn was recognised with life membership, which says a lot that such a young person can achieve life membership.

"Carolyn was no angel ... and if she thought people weren't listening to her, she wasn't averse to using colourful language. And as Kevin said to me the other day, when we were talking about the recent circumstances, 'this woman just spat a chewie one day at me and the boys and I certainly know she has a forceful nature and temper'. Carolyn's principal legacy is her sons. The steely, quiet, emotional and physical strength contained within Kenneth; the simmering and demanding passion that ebbs and flows through Shane; the joyful sparkling love of life is painted on Daniel's face. Carolyn loved us all. She never failed to greet us with a smile. Where she found the time and energy to do so much is a mystery.

"We should recognise and acknowledge also that Carolyn was a successful businesswoman. She helped create her own business with her partner Judith, a company which produces bedspreads and curtains in the home for the commercial market. If you need an image to carry in your mind's eye, the family portrait appearing in the media portrays it all. The eyes display a vitality and brilliance that outshines the most perfect diamond and the mouth from which came that chuckle that was her laughter holds a devilish smile masking a wicked sense of humour.

"We cannot allow the passing of Carolyn without recognising the society in which we live ... we must resolve that we will make this world better. We can do that, we must do that. We have to have the courage to try. Remember not the tragedy of July 12, 2001, but the beauty of our sister Carolyn. Go in peace. We will always remember you."

Choking back tears, he somehow retained his composure and returned with quiet dignity to his seat. Pastor Marr later concluded: "Carolyn was a girl who had different tastes to what I had in music. She liked things like the music from *Dirty Dancing* and Whitney Houston. I'd like to give you the opportunity to take yourself to a special place and time that relates to you. We're going to have some music playing."

As Whitney Houston's *I Will Always Love You* filled the chapel, the camera focused on the flowers in the mourners' hands. Kevin and the boys sat like statues, frozen. The camera panned around the room and tears flowed.

Bittersweet memories, that is all I'm taking with me.

Members of the Semaphore Surf Life Saving Club formed a guard of honour outside the chapel, and Carolyn's casket was placed in the hearse.

The mourners shuffled past, each gently placing their flower in the back of the vehicle. Among the last of the mourners was Carolyn's elderly grandmother, Iris Baldock. Behind the funeral director and Pastor Marr, Daniel Matthews led Max and the hearse slowly followed.

After the service, Peter Campaign – who at this stage had no doubts of Kevin's innocence – made a special appeal through the media: "We just keep thinking all this is a nightmare and we will awake from it. Someone, somewhere did this. On behalf of the family, I call upon anyone who can help to contact the police. They are doing a magnificent job."

The mourners adjourned to the Semaphore Surf Life Saving Club's two-storey clubhouse at Point Malcolm Reserve, Semaphore Park.

Yvonne Tidswell says: "There were about 300 people there. My neighbours were there, my closest friends, and they were going home so we went to say goodnight to Kevin, and they said: 'Just wait a bit, we're going to have a little bit of a service'. It didn't even occur to me that it was a quarter to six, exactly a week after (Carolyn's death), on the Thursday. Looking out over the beautiful sunset on the balcony of the life saving club down there. Shows just how two-faced (Kevin) was at the time."

Describing exactly the same moment, Christine Nixon used exactly the same words: "Kevin was two-faced. At her wake they had a minute's silence, exactly a week after she was killed. And he was nowhere to be seen. He was probably texting Michelle on the balcony. No one could find him. I had to leave and the two-faced prick came up and hugged me. He had never, ever touched me. And I hated him. Why would he be coming up and hugging me? I couldn't hug him back. I said to my mum: 'How dare he touch me'. And yes, I still thought he'd done it at that stage. I think he said to me: 'Thank you for coming'. And I thought: 'I didn't come here for you, I came here because someone I was closer to than anyone in my whole life, who knew more about me than anybody, is gone.'"

Kaylene Kenyon says: "At the wake, Kevin's behaviour was pretty strange. On one occasion, he was just standing there, staring at me from across the room. My sister was with me and I said: 'Why is Kevin staring at me like that?' And she said: 'Oh god, I don't know – looks freaky, doesn't he?' I sort of waved. In the end, I turned around to see if someone was behind me, but there wasn't. My sister said: 'He's weird, something's going on.' I ended up moving.

"Out on the balcony, Kevin said to one of his close friends, who had a daughter: 'Come on, are you going let her sit on my lap now? Today of all days. I've just buried my wife.' And so his 16-year-old daughter sat on Kevin's lap for the first time ever. So to me that indicates what kind of a guy he was. And I'm sure (his friend) regrets that. To use 'I've just buried my wife' as a reason for his friend to let his daughter sit on his lap, that's just ...'

Kaylene's voice trailed off, unable to put into words her disgust at Kevin's lecherous behaviour. *Advertiser* court reporter Simonne Reid recalls: "A friend of mine was at Semaphore Surf Life Saving Club after the murder and he was getting some of the young girls to sit on his lap and give him hugs and offer him sympathy that way. When my friend's sister came home, she said: 'There's something weird about him, he's not acting like a man who's lost his wife. He asked me to sit on his lap and give him a cuddle.' There were alarm bells going off all over the place."

Kaylene and her husband Rodney had arranged to leave their children in the care of her parents, after agreeing to stay the night at the Matthews's home. They left the club at 11pm and arrived at Nambucca Ave a few minutes after Kevin, Kenny and Shane had arrived. (Youngest son Daniel was staying at a friend's home.)

Kaylene says: "It was late and we'd had a few drinks and the boys were fairly keen for us to come back, too. So we did go back to their house. And the boys, Rodney, I and Kevin were all sitting outside in a circle just having a couple of drinks, just talking about the whole day. Kevin was in and out, up and down."

"I'm going to bed, I can't handle it," he told them.

Kaylene: "So he went to bed and the boys and Rodney and I continued chatting and then next minute Kevin came flying out of the house."

"I can't hack this, I've got to get out. I'm going to see someone," he told them.

"Are you sure? Because you've been drinking," Kaylene reminded him.

Kevin: "Yeah, yeah, I've got to. I've got to get out of here."

Rodney said: "Well, if you're sure. If you've got to."

Kaylene: "Kevin got in his van and the roller door lifted. Kenny and Shane went to bed. Didn't say goodnight to their father, didn't say a word – just went and closed their doors. Rodney and I just looked at each other. I was thinking: 'What just happened?' Kevin drove out of the carport and Rodney and I went inside and about midnight, Rodney went to bed."

Rodney: "I flaked out on the lounge."

Kaylene: "So we knew something was happening. So I went inside to make myself a coffee, because I couldn't work out what was going on."

SA Police recorded a series of phone conversations that began shortly after midnight on Friday, July 20. The following conversations are excerpts, beginning with a call between Kevin Matthews and Michelle Burgess at 12.02am:

Matthews: "I'm scared … I'm out the front of your house."

Michelle: "Why are you driving around? Put your car in my driveway … I will talk to you when I get there. Do not leave."

Matthews: "The shit was going down. I could not get hold of you."

At 12.09am, Matthews called his home number and Kaylene Kenyon answered.

Kaylene: "Where are you Kevin? Kevin, don't fucking lie to me. I just want to know what's happening."

Matthews: "I needed to have a drink. I needed to get out."

Kaylene: "Kevin, do you want me to come and get you?" The phone cut out. Matthews called Michelle on her mobile phone at 12.12am.

Matthews: "Carolyn's bridesmaid is at home. She reckons I'm lying. She reckons I'm out seeing someone."

Again, his phone cuts out. At 12.36am, he calls Kaylene again.

Matthews: "Hello darling. How are you?"

Kaylene: "Hello Kevin."

Kevin stumbled over his words, having apparently mistaken Kaylene for Carolyn after drunkenly dialling his home number. Then he said: "I'm so sorry to have woken you up and got you out of bed."

Kaylene: "I'm not in bed. I'm wide awake and I'm pacing your lounge room."

The phone dropped out again. Kevin called back a short time later.

Kaylene: "What's happening, where are you?"

Matthews: "I'm supposed to be meeting Marty. They're all supposed to be there. I don't know where they've gone."

(Kaylene recalls: "I think Kevin mentioned the Leg Trap Hotel but I can't be sure of this, he certainly spoke of some hotel. Marty attended the funeral and wake earlier.")

Kaylene: "Don't bullshit to me, tell me what's going on."

Conveniently, the phone cut out yet again. He finally called back 45 minutes later.

Matthews: "I'm shitting myself, I've just driven through a breatho on Victoria Rd. I'm just going to crash somewhere and stay there."

Kaylene: "I'll come and get you. Where are you?"

(Kaylene recalls: "Then the phone cut out again. Almost immediately, Kevin called back again and we had a similar conversation. Then Kevin said he would be coming home.")

Matthews: "I'll be there (home) in about three to four minutes. I'm on Victoria Rd. I'm going to go through the back streets."

At 12.41am, David Key called Michelle.

Michelle: "His wife's bridesmaid, she has turned around and said to him 'I'm not stupid Kevin, do you think I'm stupid? You're off with your girlfriend.'"

Key: "Do you want me to go down and give her a fucking visit, too?"

Michelle: "What a fucking bitch. He buried his fucking wife today, for fuck's sake. I don't know what's going to happen now. The shit's going to hit the fan."

Key: "Baby, do you want me to come down?"

Michelle: "This lady is looking after his kids. She does not need to see me, even though there's nothing going on."

Key: "Why does she think you're seeing Kevin when you're seeing me?"

David Key's stupidity is so absolute it is almost hard to believe. But his casual threat to "give (Kaylene) a fucking visit too" is chilling. He later lamely offers a Homer Simpson-style excuse for his apparent ignorance of Michelle's affair with Kevin: "Sometimes I don't listen. Like, sometimes I'll listen and it goes in one ear and out the other. It doesn't stop in between the ears. I can make myself look like I'm paying attention, but really I'm not. It's fuckin' … I just wasn't payin' attention."

Kevin Matthews finally returned home after 2am, walking into his kitchen to find Kaylene bristling with hostility.

Kaylene: "Don't fucking lie to me Kevin. Are you having an affair?"

Matthews: "No, what makes you think that?"

Kaylene: "I've never thought it before but your behaviour tonight has been really odd."

Matthews: "I need a drink."

Kaylene recalls: "We were at the kitchen bench and Kevin was mixing me a drink as well. We went into the lounge and Kevin put on the wedding video. We talked about the people who were there, what happened on the day. But I think I was still too busy thinking: 'You arsehole.' Then I noticed he wasn't wearing any socks."

Kaylene: "You haven't got any socks on, Kev."

Kaylene recalls: "He just shrugged it off and didn't say anything. He was handling his drink quite well until just before I went to bed about 3.30am. Kevin is a heavy drinker. At a barbecue, he would generally consume about 15 Scotches over 6–7 hours. He had drunk a fair bit that night and seemed to be holding things together quite well until he started slurring his words. When I went to bed, as far as I know, so did Kevin."

There seems little doubt that on the night that he buried his wife – the loyal, loving, hard-working mother of his children, whom he had plotted to kill – a drunken Kevin Matthews drove to Michelle Burgess's Craigmore home to have sex with her yet again.

Kaylene says: "We were gone by 6am. I had been going to stay and Rodney was going to go to work and Kevin and the boys were going to take me home later in the day. I had no inkling that he was involved (in the murder), but I knew that he was having an affair, so when Rodney woke up at six, I said: 'I'm coming with you.' It was purely because of the affair stuff. I didn't really believe then that he was involved.

"Apparently they got up and made breakfast and waited and waited and at 9am, one of the boys came in to get me and I was gone. I actually felt a bit sorry for the boys that I didn't stay, because they'd made me brekkie. But I would have been in Kevin's face about the affair and it wasn't the right time for the boys. So I just got out."

Rodney Kenyon offers his own blunt assessment of Michelle and her apparent powers over men: "She has brainwashed a lot of people. I don't know how, because she's a pretty ugly woman. I think it's the fact that she can suck a golf ball through a garden hose."

Later that day, SC Duval filled out the necessary paperwork to gain access to BankSA's records of Kevin and Carolyn Matthews's accounts, and the Commonwealth Bank's records of Michelle Burgess, uncovering valuable evidence that would later be linked to the crucial events leading up to Carolyn's murder. The damning paper-trail was growing.

Police recorded one final relevant phone call that day, during the evening, between Michelle Burgess and David Key, who was driving on Port Wakefield Rd en route to Dublin to drop off his now-superseded Ford Falcon, which had a blown differential.

Michelle: "Hello, I am just going out for a little while."

Key: "Where are you going?"

Michelle: "Down the other end of town."

Key: "Where?"
Michelle: "You can guess where."
Key: "Kevin?"
Michelle: "Yep."
Key: "Why?"
Michelle: "For a chat. (long pause.) Because I need to chat, all right?"
Key: "You know I'm not impressed."

CHAPTER 10

You're going to go down for it

July 21, 2001 – July 26, 2001

AT HIS SON'S soccer match on Saturday, July 21, Darren Burgess again observed both his estranged wife and David Key at Karbeethon Reserve in Evanston Gardens – Michelle in her VP Commodore and Key in his VN Commodore.

Key later told police that the VN and Michelle's Seca were her payment for killing Carolyn Matthews. And while his powers of deduction were deficient, his arithmetic was not. He says: "I was given $7000 over a period of two months. $500 here, $500 there. Michelle paid me. Which worked out way, way fuckin' under 25 grand."

Earlier that day, at 8.30am, Kevin Matthews and Michelle Burgess had arrived separately at City Discount Tyres at 40 Port Rd, Alberton, where Kevin had arranged for two near-new tyres to be fitted to the front of Michelle's VP Commodore. He later paid $185 each for the tyres.

Also with them was a new player in the game, Jason Norman Colenso, 31, another Davoren Park itinerant with a bad attitude and untidy goatee. He played no part in the murder or its planning but, like Key, he was none too bright and would soon eagerly enter Michelle's world of intrigue and romance. Key and Michelle had briefly seen Colenso on the day of the murder, when they visited a woman named Sandra Hendy at her home, in Charmouth Street, Davoren Park, but that was apparently nothing more than a coincidence. Key knew Colenso from jail, having met him in 1998 at pre-release cottages in Adelaide. Ms Hendy later told police that Colenso started ringing her from Queensland in January 2001, when he was still in jail serving a sentence for driving offences. She agreed he could stay at her home after he was released, until he could find a place of his own. Colenso arrived at her home in June, gave her a hug and left after dumping his suitcases. He came and went over the next few weeks, occasionally dropping by for a meal or to stay the night.

A close friend of Colenso, Rosa Wright, who had known him for seven years, later told police they had first met at a dairy farm in Virginia, where he was working as a milker and calf rearer. His work there was cut short by a prison sentence. She said that prior to his subsequent prison sentence in Queensland, she had become "quite" close to him and they had an on/off relationship. "I am a little older than Jason and I have tried to help him because I think he has a lot of good qualities," she explained.

When he returned to Adelaide in June, she said he was at her house "virtually every day". At night, he would spend a lot of time talking to people in chat rooms on her computer. She confirmed that he was there on the night of July 12 and she had driven him home to Davoren Park at 11pm.

On or about July 21, 2001, David Lane, a friend of Key's associate Marc English, saw Key driving around in the VP Commodore on Peachey Rd in Davoren Park. Key pulled alongside Lane's friend's car and immediately started bragging about his new vehicle's power, explaining: "I got the car for doing a job at West Lakes." Lane's friend had to leave – Key could have talked all day – so Key let rip with a series of burnouts to show them just how great his car was. Key also visited Lane's home a few days later, bringing Michelle's children to play with his children. Again, the entire conversation revolved around his new Commodore and his old XD Falcon.

On July 21, police recorded a cryptic phone call between Samantha Key and her brother at 4.45pm. He told her: "No plan B at the moment because the car's being washed. The car's getting put off the road."

David Key's friend Marc English later told police that he visited Key and Michelle in Craigmore on July 14, although the facts show he was mistaken and the date was almost certainly July 21: "I went to see Dave and Michelle and asked if I could borrow the red Seca. I was only joking but Michelle said I could borrow it. I knew she wanted to sell it for about $10,000 but was yet to advertise it. They asked me to look after the car and not to thrash it. I was unsure how long I would have it for. I kept it parked on the median strip outside my house for about three days. Then it was parked in the driveway and someone broke into it."

For Michelle and Key, English's request was timely. They had fled the murder scene in the Seca and, despite their best efforts, it could still contain traces of Carolyn Matthews's blood. It was better off parked at someone else's house.

On Sunday, July 22, 2001, Darren Burgess returned his son and daughter to his estranged wife, handing them over at that great Australian child exchange point, the McDonald's restaurant.

On Monday, July 23, 2001, David Key finally got around to attending to his Work for the Dole duties again. He used his asthma problem to full effect, bringing with him sick certificates for July 3, 9, 10, 16, 17, 23, and 24. His supervisor recalls that when he arrived, he said: "Come and look at my car." (It was the VN Commodore.)

Supervisor: "Where did you get that from?"

Key: "I won $25,000 at the casino on the pokies."

The supervisor laughed: "Bullshit, you got it growing hydro."

Giving him an odd look, Key opened his boot, where there was a pile of clothing.

Supervisor: "Are you moving?"

Key proudly announced: "I'm moving in with a high-class sheila from Craigmore."

ON JULY 24, 2001, Detective Senior Constable Peter Juers was part of the Investigation Support Branch team conducting covert surveillance on Persons of Interest in the Carolyn Matthews murder investigation. At 11.11am, he was keeping tabs on Kevin Matthews, who had parked his Nissan Nomad van in the northern car park of the Old Spot Hotel on Main North Rd, Salisbury Heights. Michelle parked her VP Commodore two spaces from the van at 11.13am.

SC Juers entered the Highway Bar via a different door to Michelle at 11.37am. He observed Michelle and Matthews sitting at a table together. They were the only two people in the bar. She was wearing blue jeans and the black Adelaide Crows club jacket which rarely left her shoulders. Matthews was wearing a light blue t-shirt and blue jeans. SC Juers's report noted: "Matthews and Burgess were drinking and talking, but I couldn't hear what they were saying because I was at the bar about 6m away from the table. It was an animated conversation and Matthews conducted most of it. Burgess had her head bowed a lot of the time as Matthews talked".

At 11.45am, Constable John Baldwin came into the bar and SC Juers quietly briefed him. They casually shifted to a table directly adjacent to

Matthews and Michelle. She remained hunched over the table with her head bowed while Matthews spoke in a low tone close to her. At 11.50am, Matthews became more animated and leant back in his chair, declaring: "You know you're going to go down for it, too many people know about it." There was no response heard from Michelle. She was sniffing and possibly crying. Const. Baldwin discreetly made notes of the conversation on a Keno ticket.

The officers exited the bar to the northern car park at 11.52am and, at midday, Michelle left, closely followed by Matthews. Constable Greg Hillier, whose target was Michelle, observed her standing next to the driver's door of the Commodore with Matthews.

His report noted: "They hugged for about 40 seconds. Matthews moved his face close to Burgess, as if to kiss her. They continued to hug. Matthews walked around the car and appeared to be looking at the tyres. Burgess opened the boot and they looked inside and then closed it. They both walked around to the driver's door and had a conversation. They kissed and Matthews stepped back from Burgess and pointed his right index finger at her. He poked her in the chest twice.

"Burgess lowered her head. Matthews tried to kiss her but she kept her head lowered. Matthews walked off to his blue Nissan Nomad van and reversed it up behind the Commodore and stopped next to the driver's door. They had a conversation. At 11.59am, they both drove out on to Main North Rd, Burgess driving north and Matthews driving south."

That evening, trouble magnet David Key struck again. He was involved in an incident with another driver, a woman, on Main North Rd, Bolivar. His sister, Samantha Key, later told police that when she arrived at her mother's home the next day, Michelle's VP Commodore was in the driveway. David was there, but he said Michelle was at her place, ill. He related the road-rage incident to his sister, saying that a woman had cut him off as he was pulling into a service station. She stopped and abused him and tried to grab Michelle's daughter from the car. Key said he called police and the woman was arrested because she'd smashed the grille on the car. He had a blackened left eye and a bandage on his left hand, and explained to his sister he'd punched a tree after the incident because he "would never hit a woman".

Key later told police: "It could have been me she was trying to run off the road. I had a fear because I had the kids in the car, so I forced her off at the

BP petrol station on Port Wakefield Rd at Bolivar so I could have a go at her over her driving and she attacked me and kicked my car."

He said he later gave evidence against the woman in court. She also allegedly assaulted the police and resisted arrest. If Michelle hadn't arrived on the scene shortly after, Key would probably have ended up marrying his attacker, given how much they had in common. The fact that Key took the high moral ground in this incident showed his extraordinary hypocrisy, not least because of his claim that he would never hit a woman – only days after he had stabbed one to death. He was driving under suspension at the time and was one of the most reckless and unsafe drivers to ever sit behind a steering wheel. During one of his many passionate condemnations of Michelle Burgess, Sgt Standing revealed that on one occasion, Key drove down the same road at 200km/h, with Michelle and her two children in the car: "(She is) a woman that would allow her kids to be in the back seat of a car being driven (by Key) at 200km/h down Port Wakefield Rd. They're screaming their heads off in terror and she's laughing. You've got to wonder about a woman who would allow that to happen to her children."

THAT EVENING, Kevin Matthews hosted a barbecue to mark Carolyn's birthday the next day. It is more likely that he was aiming to deflect the growing suspicions of family and friends, rather than out of any genuine desire to acknowledge the 38th birthday of the wife he had just had murdered. He invited his closest mate, Barry Cole, and his wife Nat, along with Rodney and Kaylene Kenyon, who brought 15 fresh T-bone steaks from their farm.

Kaylene Kenyon says: "He still seemed like Kevin, I can't say that I saw anything different. We all watched the wedding video and then he wanted to play the funeral video and Nat said: 'This is just sick, I can't handle it.' In the end, it was just me and Kevin watching it, and I said: 'This is just too sick, Kevin' and I ended up going outside, too. There was a lot of talk about the boys that night and how they were going."

Rodney says: "I asked Kevin if he had heard anything from the police and he said: 'No, not yet, bits and pieces'."

After his guests had left, Matthews made a whispered phone call to Michelle at 10.54pm, careful not to let his boys hear. Michelle discussed with him how he was coping. He finished the call by saying: "Good night, I love you."

A few hours later, Michelle and David Key were given a small taste of what it was like to come under attack in your own home. At 2.40am on July 26, 2001, Constable Philip Kataras and Constable Leanne Attard, from Elizabeth police, attended at 9 Bluebush Court, Craigmore, to investigate a complaint of property damage. Key told them he had seen several youths in the street running away from the house, when he was on his way home from a friend's house. When he saw the smashed window, he tried to pursue the youths but they had already fled. The window was on the bedroom of Michelle's young son, who must have been terrified by the attack. The officers noted that Key, who mentioned that he was a parolee, "was very irate and said he would do anything to protect Burgess".

Later that day, around lunchtime, Sgt Eichner and SC Keane went to Kevin Matthews's home. On the surface, it was two detectives visiting a murder victim's husband to ask a few more questions. In reality, it was a carefully orchestrated interrogation designed to elicit as much incriminating evidence as possible. Crucially, Matthews was being treated as a witness rather than as a suspect – officially at least – because the detectives still did not have sufficient evidence to back their suspicions. Once he became a suspect, they would be required by law to formally caution him, almost certainly leading to Matthews calling his lawyer and refusing to answer further questions.

SC Keane recalls: "By that stage, we knew he was lying about the affair, so we thought: 'Well, what else is he lying about?' We wanted to go through his story again and see if he would change his attitude in relation to his relationship with Michelle. We wanted to hear from him the story from start to finish and to question him on some things we were aware of."

Matthews sat down with the two dour, stony-faced detectives and watched nervously as they set up their tape recorder and opened their notebooks. He had no idea just how much incriminating evidence that the intensive investigation had already gathered – nor was he likely to find out today. So far, he had lied at every opportunity and the detectives expected nothing different now. But every lie that Kevin Matthews told could later return to haunt him in court, should this case make it that far. The entire Major Crime team knew that they were building a strong case against Michelle and Key. As Matthews had told Michelle, "you're going to go down for it, too many people know". But Kevin Matthews's exact role in the murder was yet to be established. Was he a killer or was he an accessory? His lies so far indicated that he had much to hide.

Sgt Eichner recalls: "When he was interviewed about the affair, it was well known they were having an affair and we had evidence of it, but he still wouldn't say he was having an affair. Now, it may not have done him very much harm if he said so. So you can't understand his reasoning and why he was doing such things."

SC Keane says: "Just because he was involved in an affair didn't mean that he was involved in the murder. Why he continued to deny it was just beyond me."

Early in the interview, Matthews addressed the "threatening phone calls" made to his home in the months before Christmas, saying that on one occasion, the caller stated: "I know you're up the river at Morgan, you've got a boat with Bodgie written on it and a dog named Max. You're with a heap of people and you'll die before New Year's Eve."

On the affair claims, he said simply that Darren Burgess ended up "not being a friend", but Michelle was. He said he didn't have much to do with her up until September, 2000. He went to their house for Darren's birthday party and they had a bet on the AFL grand final. But since then, "our relationship has grown a lot stronger".

Keane interrupted, asking: "All right, how did that come about, do you think?"

Matthews: "Oh, I don't know, I mean, it started off that she rang me up one day at work ... 'cause I was Darren's boss at that stage ... she wanted to meet with me and she said he'd kicked her out, or she'd kicked him out, I can't remember to be honest. She wanted to have coffee. She said she didn't want me to tell Darren about it. She wanted me to look out for him. Apparently he used to work in Mildura and he went psycho up there or something. She just said, watch out, you know, he might sort of get a bit spastic or something. And ever since then, we just sort of, you know, have, um, had a lot of contact. Um, she came with, with Carolyn and me and the two boys to, um, well she met us down at Glenelg for a surf carnival. Been around here probably, um, two or three times. Carolyn's spoken to her on the phone. I speak to her on the phone daily."

Keane: "Were you seeing her regularly prior to Carolyn's death?"

Matthews: "Regularly? Yes we used to go to the pub just about every day at lunch time and have a drink. That was when I was in me old job. Prior to that, I didn't have the opportunities and freedom as much to do it. We probably had lunch 3–4 times a week."

Keane: "She came to your work on July 12?"
Matthews: "Yes."
Keane: "What time was that?"
Matthews: "About 5.20pm."
Keane: "And what, she wanted some tyres on her car?"
Matthews: "Yep, she's got one bald tyre on her car."
They asked if he'd been to Michelle's new home at Craigmore.
Matthews: "Yep, yep been there."
Keane: "Was that before or after Carolyn's death?"
Matthews: "Oh, before. Before her death. Yeah."
Keane: "Oh. So you haven't been up there since?"
Matthews: "Nup. Oh yes, I have. No I haven't. I don't think so because … yeah, I think I have. We weren't having an affair. We had a really good relationship. You know, a kiss and cuddle relationship. And like, you know, I do with a lot of me friends but I … I … I … have not been having an affair with Michelle."
Keane: "So you've not had a sexual relationship with Michelle Burgess?"
Matthews: "I have not had a sexual relationship with Michelle Burgess."
Keane: "Well, Detective Sergeant Eichner, do you have any more questions?"
Eichner: "Not really. I just want to ask you Kevin, have you been completely truthful with us today?"
Matthews: "I have been completely truthful with you today."
Eichner: "Are you sure about that?"
Matthews: "I'm positive about that."
Keane: "I know I've asked you before Kevin, but you're quite sure and quite adamant that you've never been involved in a sexual relationship with Michelle Burgess?"
Matthews: "Yeah, I haven't, I haven't, we're just good friends."
Keane: "And if I was to tell you that we've got it from very good sources that you were, what would be your comment?"
Matthews: "I would say that they're just shit stirring."
Keane: "All right."
Matthews: "And I would say that they're possibly, possibly responsible for some of the hang ups and stuff. I mean, people, this has just been going around and around and around and it's been so fucking frustrating and she's actually come down here and spent time with, you know, Carolyn and

that. And look, I mean, I really, you know, I love the lady, I love the lady like a sister, but I'm not having a sexual affair with her."

Eichner: "All right. And you've got to understand that by misleading us, it's not helping the investigation at all."

Matthews: "I want this ... I mean this is just bullshit. I mean yesterday was Carolyn's birthday. And we want this to ... we were quite encouraged by the newspaper thing that said you get 91 per cent. I don't know if you read that ... unsolved murders in South Australia. We've got a high ... so the whole family is encouraged by that."

Eichner: "All right, perhaps we'll leave it there, the tape's going to run out soon."

The detectives left at 1.46pm (after an earlier, brief interruption when Kevin's mother arrived and was told politely but firmly to return later). Eight minutes after the detectives left, Matthews called Michelle to relate what had just happened but, now clearly aware that it was likely their calls were being monitored, their conversation had the stilted flow of a daytime TV soap.

SC Keane recalls: "They probably were aware that we were listening to what they were saying. There were a lot of statements made that were self-serving. But they still said things that helped us down the track."

Matthews informed Michelle that he had told the police they were "just good friends".

Matthews: "I just told them the truth. I said 'shit, my relationship with Michelle is a huggy-kissy relationship'. They even asked me whether you were capable of bloody doing this. I said 'no fucking way, she loves me too much to want to do that'."

Michelle: "Oh, so I'm a suspect."

Matthews: "Oh, it doesn't matter ... everybody is at the moment."

Michelle: "Some people have just got nothing better to do. But I mean, they've got to look at everything ... if you and I were having an affair, then why were Carolyn and I friends?"

Immediately following this call, at 2.06pm, Michelle called her other lover, Key, unaware that he was now the centre of his own daytime drama.

Michelle: "Where are you?"

Key: "Waikerie."

Michelle: "Fuck."

Key: "Why?"

Michelle: "What's the time?"

Key: "Two-ten."

Michelle: "Do you know where the Evanston Primary School is in Gawler? You go there, where I met you at the school that morning. Meet me there."

Key: "What time?"

Michelle: "As soon as you can get there."

Key: "Oh."

Michelle: "I'm leaving to go now. Why is that?"

Key: "You don't want to know."

(A short while later)

Key: "I love you too, baby. This is fucking hurting me. I don't know what you're going to do. Fifty, fucking … You didn't want me to get knocked off …"

Michelle: "Hey …"

Key: "I know what you're going through because you didn't want me getting locked up."

Michelle: "Well, I might be now after what Darren said to the cops."

Key: "What did he say to the cops?"

Michelle: "Oh, he's given them my phone bill and all that and put everything on me."

Key: "Has he?"

Michelle: "Yep, so the cops want to talk to me now. They're going along the lines that Kevin and I had an affair and I was psychotic enough to do it."

Key: "Bullshit."

Finally, Key drops into the conversation the fact that he has some problems of his own at the moment. He was, quite literally, surrounded by police.

Key: "I got Ds sitting here as well."

Michelle: "Hey?"

Key: "I got Ds here."

Michelle: "Because they were interested in me being … ah … You? What, so they're going to talk to me as well now?"

Key: "Yeah. Well, they got me. I ain't sayin' nothin'."

ASKED LATER by police to explain the day's events, Key said he had left Michelle's home and visited his mother. As he was driving back, he received a call from Colenso, who wanted him to go to the Riverland town of Morgan to help "do something about his ex-missus". Stupidly, Key agreed, picking up Colenso and a third man, Trevor Jenkins, and embarking on an unspecified but ominous-sounding mission.

He told police that when they arrived: "(Jason) said: 'That's the bitch's fucking house. (We'll) go round the corner, fuckin' bally up (cover their faces), fuckin', we'll give him (presumably a man with Jason's ex-girlfriend) a frickin' hiding.'

"(I thought) yeah, whatever. I was that out of it. I was just going with the flow. So we went round the corner, ballied up, had the baseball bat, pulled up in front of his house, locked up and went over and fucking banged on the door. I'm sitting here, I've got the baseball bat, and the curtains in the window moved.

"Jason started yelling: 'Come out here and face the music, you cunt. You think I'm fucking full of shit? Told you I'd get up here, you weak cunt.'

"He just kept going on with it. I said: 'Come on Jason, this is a waste of time, let's go.' So we went.

"I thought: 'Fuck it, we'll go and see dad at work,' so we went to Waikerie. I said: 'Dad, look, I could end up back in jail soon and I might have hurt someone and I might end up getting charged over it.'

"Dad said: 'Yep, all right, not a problem, just let us know.'

"We left there and we came back over the ferry and shot up through Waikerie. Sort of brought a bit of attention to ourselves. Came around corners screeching and flooring it. We flew out of there just before Blanchetown. There was a police officer on the side of the road setting up for radar. Actually it was quite a smart way the way police did it. They held the traffic up and got me in amongst a whole heap of traffic."

Key later told a psychologist that he was driving at speeds of up to 300km/h that day, but had no recollection of the trip to Morgan. He insisted that the VN Commodore's speedometer went up to 300km/h and he broke it when he hit this speed. Years later in court, Crown Prosecutor Steven Millsteed put a series of questions to Key which dispelled any doubts about his intellectual capacity.

Millsteed: "Police were chasing you?"

Key: "They were trying to keep up with me."

Millsteed: "Of course, at 300km/h I don't suppose they were making any progress."

Key: "No, if you were sitting on such a high speed, would you expect anyone to catch you?"

Millsteed: "How affected by drugs were you when you were travelling at 300km/h back to Elizabeth?"

Key: "I was well and truly out of it."

Millsteed: "Were you?"

Key: "Yes I was. That's why I was sitting at a high speed. I was taking a major risk. We turned it all into a game when the police started chasing us, cat-and-mouse style."

At 4.40pm that day, Sgt Alan Dennett, of Gawler police, was sent to Barossa Valley Way, Concordia, to intercept a vehicle travelling west at high speed. He had permission to use road spikes, but the VN Commodore was caught in heavy traffic, so he didn't need to deploy them. As the vehicle approached, Dennett motioned for it to pull over. He approached the driver, who got out.

Dennett: "Can you bring your licence with you, driver."

Key: "I haven't got one."

Dennett: "None at all?"

Key: "No."

Dennett: "Are you unlicensed or disqualified?"

Key: "Probably disqualified. It runs out sometime this month."

Dennett: "I'll make some checks."

Key: "I've probably got a parole warrant, too."

Dennett: "What is your full name please?"

Key: "David William Edgar Key."

Dennett: "Date of birth?"

Key: "17 August, 1974."

Dennett made checks via the police computer and ascertained that the disqualification had ended on July 23, but a parole warrant had been issued on July 9, presumably because Key had not maintained contact with his parole officer.

Dennett: "David, because of the parole warrant, I have to now place you under arrest."

By this time, several other police officers had arrived. Among them was Detective Senior Constable Jeff Carruthers, of Nuriootpa police, who questioned Key about his movements that day. But when SC Carruthers indicated he was going to search the vehicle, Colenso became aggressive and intervened. He was also arrested on an outstanding warrant. Michelle rang Key just as the police were about to handcuff him, and they allowed him to take the call and break the good news. News of Key's arrest was quickly relayed to Major Crime, whose immediate concern was the preservation of potential evidence. Sen. Sgt Strange spoke to SC Carruthers shortly after Key's arrest, advising him he was in possession of a murder suspect and to immediately seize Key's boots.

Key, Colenso and Jenkins were taken to the Elizabeth police station, along with Key's precious Commodore. At the charge counter, Sgt Dennett told Key to remove his boots. SC Carruthers examined the soles and the boots in general. The boots had a distinctive pattern on the soles similar to the one described to him by Sen. Sgt Strange.

Shortly after 5pm, Michelle called Key and he told her he was under arrest and in the process of being locked up.

Key: "They're taking all my possessions, like my clothes."
Michelle: "You're kidding."
Key: "Nup. They've ripped my boots off me."
Michelle: "Oh, Dave."
Key: "I'm going down, baby … What did they say? What did Kevin say?"
Michelle: "Kevin?"
Key: "Mmmmm."
(Silence).

Sgt Standing and SC Duval soon arrived at Elizabeth police station, with a photograph of a bootprint taken at the murder scene in Carolyn Matthews's kitchen. Sgt Dennett showed them Key's boots, which were now in a plastic evidence bag – the sole pattern clearly matched the print in the photograph. Sgt Standing and SC Duval went to the visitors' room in the charge area and spoke to Key. SC Duval was holding the boots. Sgt Standing recalls that Key was sitting on the floor when they walked in and he somehow rose to a standing position without using his arms. He was clearly still operating at 300km/h.

Standing: "I understand your name is David Key. K-E-Y. My name is Detective Sergeant Standing from Major Crime Investigation Branch. I believe these are your boots."
Key: "One of my pairs."
Standing: "I will be seizing these boots."
Key: "On what grounds?"
Standing: "The tread pattern from these boots is similar to that found at a homicide recently. Your clothing will also be seized."

The colour drained from Key's face. There was nothing more to be said. At 8pm, the detectives went to the rear of the police station and searched the VN Commodore. There was little inside it, aside from Key's clothes, which were photographed. In the meantime, Michelle arrived with two unknown men, who are not named in police records. But, courtesy of Key's stupidity, the investigation was about to take an extraordinary twist.

Sgt Standing says: "We went back into the station and Detective Duval copied the contents of a wallet taken from Key. I saw that one of the pieces of paper had a photograph of Darren Burgess on it and details written on it, including his place of work and start and finish times. I saw that there were two different styles of handwriting on the paper."

It was a disturbing discovery; while the detectives couldn't yet be certain, it had all the hallmarks of a murder contract. And with Key already a prime suspect in Carolyn Matthews's murder, it was reasonable to assume that there would be a matching document relating to her death. Sgt Standing approached Michelle.

Standing: "Michelle, I believe you are the owner of a red Toyota Corolla Seca."

Michelle: "Yes."

Standing: "Where is that vehicle now?"

Michelle: "It's at Marc's (Marc English) place."

Standing: "Where's that?"

Michelle: "42 Hogarth Rd. Why?"

Standing: "I have reason to believe that a person I believe to have been involved in a recent homicide may have driven your vehicle. I wish to seize it and have it forensically tested."

Michelle: "When do you want it?"

Standing: "We'll collect it tonight. Can you and your friends go and get it and bring it to the Elizabeth police station?"

Michelle: "Yes, we'll go now."

She returned with the car at 9.40pm and police took it into the city, where it would later be forensically examined.

Key's unrivalled stupidity in delivering himself – and evidence directly linking him to the crime scene – straight into the hands of Major Crime detectives, had made their job significantly easier.

Sgt Standing said: "The boots had cracks in them and that's where we got the blood, and also one of the eyelets. They had Carolyn Matthews's DNA. And the contract in the wallet. So Key was a cooked goose."

Questioned later by detectives on the location of the Carolyn Matthews murder contract, Key explained: "Carolyn's contract made a sandwich, as in, I mean, I had made a sandwich. I was in the kitchen of Michelle's house making myself a sandwich and it's like, pull the document out, don't need this no more, tore it all up, spread it over my sandwich and I ate it. That would have been on July 13 or 14 at Bluebush Court. I et (sic) the contract."

"Why did you do that?" An incredulous Sgt Eichner asked him.

Key: "I thought, if the police can't prove there was a document, then it never existed. But I was wrong."

Eichner: "Did you do any sort of research ... on Darren Burgess's particulars?"

Key: "I didn't get a chance to. So fuck it. Because after that incident, after Carolyn Matthews died, Michelle pulled out. Michelle said, fucking: 'Don't worry about doing Darren – I'll do him'."

That night, Key gave permission for Michelle to collect the VN Commodore and all his possessions, including his wallet with the contract inside. He said she later told him she had burnt the Darren Burgess contract. At 9pm, Michelle arrived home in her Commodore to find a phalanx of police, armed with a search warrant, waiting on her doorstep. She got out of the car and one of the officers approached her.

"My name is Carruthers. I am a detective from Nuriootpa CIB. These other officers are Detective Day from Kadina and the officer-in-charge of Williamstown police station. What is your name please?"

"Michelle Burgess."

Carruthers: "Michelle, we've been asked by Major Crime taskforce to attend your address here this evening. Your partner, I understand, Mr David Key, is that correct?" – "Yep" – "He is in custody at the Elizabeth police station. Major Crime taskforce have seized some shoes and clothing from him and they have asked us to come here and see if there is clothing of a similar description at the house."

Michelle: "Mmmmmm."

Carruthers: "All right, that is our purpose for being here. We intend to search the property with a general search warrant."

They found a large pile of clothing and children's toys and other items.

Carruthers: "You've only just moved in, have you?"

Michelle: "Yeah, I've only been in here for about three or four weeks. I've been trying to find room for everything. Like, I recently went through separation and sold the house out at Williams Street and had to find a house here and my ex-husband doesn't know where I am and, uh, that's a mess if you want to know, a mess."

Carruthers: "I see."

Michelle: "If you want to get personal, I mean, I've had threats from him and I've had threats from my ... like, he's given my sister threats and now, now my front window gets smashed last night. It's just one headcase after another."

The detectives asked which bedroom Key was using and Michelle replied: "My bedroom."

As SC Carruthers continued to explain what they were looking for and blood was mentioned, she said: "That's my blood, if you want to know. I've been sick (coughs theatrically). I've been coughing up a bit of blood. I've been to the doctors and all that, if you wanted to check that out."

A newspaper was found lying on the floor of the main bedroom, between the bed and the window, folded and open to an article about the murder of Carolyn Matthews. The window broken early that morning was also examined.

Sgt Standing, who visited the house several times in the course of the investigation, said: "I think Michelle Burgess lived in a fantasy world her whole life. She was the worst housekeeper you've ever seen. She was living in a pigsty, it was dreadful. To live in that squalor with children. The way she looked after her children was absolutely abysmal. The stink in the house was unbelievable. And look what she did when they sold the house and she got her share of the money. She paid a car off and bought two others. And it's all gone. It's just ridiculous."

The day after the raid on her house, Michelle seemed to have recovered from the shock of David Key's arrest – completely. At 3.30pm, SC Carruthers happened to be visiting the Elizabeth City shopping centre, adjacent to the Elizabeth police station, when he saw Michelle's VP Commodore in the car park. He watched as Michelle and Jason Colenso emerged and "placed their arms around each other, holding each other close and affectionately" as they walked towards the shops.

CHAPTER 11

Interrogations
July 27, 2001 – August 2, 2001

IN A CONTRIVED phone call at 7.32am on Friday, July 27, Kevin Matthews and Michelle Burgess took another shot at a daytime Emmy. SC Keane, the unfortunate officer tasked with listening to the 2874 calls recorded by SAPOL's Telephone Interception Section to and from Kevin's and Michelle's phones, would later cull this list to 150 calls relevant to the investigation. He must have rolled his eyes each time the pair put on such performances for his benefit. This call began with Michelle informing Matthews that Key had been arrested.

Matthews: "For what?"

Michelle: "Well it started off as fuckin' speeding."

Matthews: "Yeah? Who's Dave? Is that your boyfriend?"

Michelle said: "That's my boyfriend, right."

Matthews: "Oh yeah."

Michelle: "Yeah, yeah, so they've decided they're going after him now they've decided he's prime numero uno."

Matthews: "Oh, you'll protect your boyfriend at all costs, won't you?"

Michelle: "Fuckin' oath. I tell you what, there's a lot of people who are going to stand up for him."

Matthews's "coded" plea to Michelle is crystal clear – Don't let me down. Later that day, SC Duval handed the photocopy of the Darren Burgess murder contract to Sgt Standing. At 4pm, they visited Beaurepaires in Elizabeth, where Darren Burgess identified the photo of him as being cut from a family portrait. He also identified the handwriting as that of his estranged wife, Michelle, pulling out an old letter from her to double check.

His assessment was later confirmed by police forensic comparisons. After Sgt Standing left, Darren rang Kathy, who asked what the document was. Darren called Sgt Standing to pose the same question.

"I'd better come back and talk to you," Sgt Standing replied, deciding that Darren needed to know that his life could be in danger.

"We believe it's a contract on your life," he told him when he arrived.

Darren was stunned.

"So, would it be a good idea if Kathy and I moved out of our house?" he asked.

"Yes, that'd probably be a good idea."

Darren rang Kathy and told her to pack her bags; they would be staying at his parents' home for the foreseeable future.

THAT EVENING, a listening device planted at Michelle's home delivered crucial evidence. Sgt Standing was monitoring the feed when he overheard a conversation that began at 8.31pm. He lost sound at 9.05pm because of technical problems, but the 34 minutes he did hear were deeply disturbing. The audio feed revealed Michelle to be utterly ruthless and possessed of a vocabulary that would make a shearer blush. Michelle and Colenso were interrogating Scott Rose, the man who wisely refused when Key had offered $900 to burn Carolyn Matthews's van.

Sgt Standing explains: "The terms of the conversation relate to the murder of Carolyn Matthews, who the people were who had told the police of David Key's involvement and what to do about them. It was obvious from what I heard that Michelle Burgess and Jason Colenso were not only going to try to identify witnesses but cause them harm. Michelle Burgess stated that she would kill those responsible."

The initial sounds on the recording were of a TV in the background and children crying and arguing.

Michelle: "You get in your room. Move. In your fucking room."
Unidentified male: "Go on, in your room."
A child continued to cry.
"Mummy?"
Michelle: "What?"
Child: "Um ..."
Michelle: "Quick ... anyone for coffee?"
"Nup."

Michelle: "In your room, be quiet."

Colenso: "All right, simple. No fucking yelling around ... fucking."

Michelle: "All I want to know is if it's you saying it. Is it you?"

Scott Rose: "It's not me. I'd never dob, mate, never. He's my mate. I'm not a dog, mate. You look over the years, mate and I've looked after him."

Michelle: "This is what we heard from them, right? Apparently you're supposed to have got dropped off like, in a cop car last week, right? Around the corner, right? Wait till I finish. After the murder, you were supposed to go around, like, telling the young bloke that fucking um ..."

Colenso: "I hope not."

Michelle: "... that Dave had done something you were supposed to do and get paid $900 after the murder. That's all I heard."

Rose denied it.

Michelle: "As soon as I find out who it is, they can go six foot under and I'll do it myself. And that's no fuckin' lie."

Rose: "Well fuck, I can tell you now it wasn't me, mate."

Michelle: "It's someone from that area. I haven't said shit you know and there's only three possibilities I can think of."

Rose: "Name them."

Michelle: "You were one and Nicole and Mark were the other two; Jamie, I'm not sure about, I don't know him well enough. I'm only just saying, like, judging by the things I've been told by Dave and the way I've looked at the situation and getting information from both sides of the fence, I've come to those three conclusions. And whoever they are, they're an idiot. They'll be dead, because I'll kill them. I'm not fucking kidding because this is bullshit. And the police have known for a lot longer, so someone's been leaking it slowly.

"They don't know a lot but they're going to pin it on Dave. Like, and they know, hey, for them to be at Elizabeth police station within five minutes of him being there ... within five minutes ... if they didn't know, they knew they had to be there at a certain time. Cos the CIB were getting down there. They've wanted Dave for a very fuckin' long time. So some cunt has been doing it and I'm mad as ... And Dave, fuckin' Dave's as mad as ... And because he's not here, fuckin' I'll do it, I don't give a shit.

"But I need to know who it is and I want to know now. Cos I want to know who would have a grudge bad enough to fuckin' do that and still be his mate on the fuckin' phone. Because they are a back stabber and they will find out what a real stab in the back is. Cos Dave's not goin' down for this. I won't let it happen.

"They've had us under surveillance since it happened. So someone's dobbed Dave in because it's all about Dave, it's not about anyone else. Well it's about me as well because I'm with Dave. But they want Dave and they're going to nail him. And they're going to keep him in jail until they can nail him. That's the way I look at it – the longer Dave's in jail now for that other thing, the worse off he is."

(The children ask if they can come out.)

Michelle: "Shut up, I'm talking. Shut your mouth."

Crown Prosecutor Steven Millsteed later quotes in court a damning statement also recorded that night. As Michelle mused over whether Debbie Richards could have been the police informer (for the record, there was no police informer, only the call to Crime Stoppers), she said: "The thing that happened that night didn't happen as it went to plan, all right? Fuckin' looked good and I pushed Dave, that's why Dave done it himself, with some help. But I'm telling you, she didn't know."

The phrase "with some help" was crucial. Sgt Standing believed that as well as setting up the murder, goading Key into a frenzy and handing him the murder weapon, Michelle was actually the first one to physically attack Carolyn Matthews with the knife.

He says: "I was at the post mortem and I saw what I saw. I think she's probably put the first one (stab wound) in to spur him on to do something. That's my personal belief. There's no way I can prove it. One of the wounds was a little lower than the others. If she did it, that was the one. She is shorter than Key.

"To me, of all the crooks and people I've ever dealt with, she was the most vicious. To do what she did. To hire someone to commit a murder. Then to stick the knife in. Then this bloke with her has got to put up or shut up. And he's not the sort that's going to shut up, so he's gone and finished the job. (Carolyn) had quite a few stab wounds.

"He wouldn't have admitted this because it would have been a loss of face for him: 'I'm in for murder.' He did admit she egged him on. He can say that, but he can't say that she started it. He's said himself he's not the sharpest tool in the box. He's dead right there."

Another statement, by Jason Colenso, also points to Michelle's direct involvement in the act of murder. (It is worth noting that of the dozens of people who were approached to co-operate with this book, Colenso was the only one who demanded payment.) He wrote to the author:

"I will tell you everything but I want to be paid. I will tell you everything including (Carolyn's) last words on this Earth. You want the truth, you'll get it and I will even tell you who did the first stabbing on her."

His offer was declined.

The surveillance of Matthews and Michelle continued on the following day, Saturday, July 28. Const. Palazzo's surveillance log showed that Matthews left his home in the Nissan Nomad van at 12.38pm, arriving at the beachfront Palais hotel at Semaphore at 1pm. At 2.10pm, he observed Matthews and Michelle together outside the hotel. They hugged and walked west towards the beach. A minute later, they stopped and talked near the water's edge. Matthews handed Michelle an unknown object. They walked east, back towards the Palais, talking and occasionally pausing. At 2.34pm, Michelle leant over and whispered in Matthews's ear. Colenso, meanwhile, was walking in an easterly direction along the beach at the same time, about 50m away, with Michelle's children. Detective Sergeant Shane McMahon took photos of both groups.

At 3.39pm, Michelle and Colenso exited the Palais. Const. Palazzo followed Matthews back to Nambucca Ave, while Sgt McMahon followed Michelle, Colenso and the children, who were in the VP Commodore, to Davoren Park.

ON JULY 30, Major Crime received the crucial lab results they'd been sweating on – the DNA found on David Key's boots belonged to Carolyn Matthews.

Early that morning, Matthews met up with Michelle and Colenso at City Discount Tyres on Port Rd, Alberton. Kevin had kindly arranged for Michelle's Commodore to get new rear tyres to match the new front set. He seemed to have no issue with the fact that Colenso – a complete stranger to him – was now constantly shadowing his lover.

The tyre store manager recalls: "Kevin was engaged in intense conversation with the woman on the driveway. I didn't speak to any of them. The tyres were changed by a staff member. At lunch time that day at the Alberton Hotel, I saw Kevin. He was apparently drinking quite heavily."

And all the while, the police watched and their cameras clicked away. It was the same the next day, Tuesday, July 31, when the trio again rendezvoused, this time at the Edinburgh Castle Hotel in Currie St, Adelaide, at lunch time.

On Thursday, August 2, Kevin Matthews was followed to the rear car park of the Walkers Arms Hotel, on North East Rd, in the affluent inner north-eastern suburb of Walkerville. He was talking on his mobile phone when he emerged from his van and walked in to the hotel at 10.18am. A few minutes later, Michelle arrived in her Commodore, chauffeured by Colenso. The trio emerged at 12.48pm, deep in conversation. Apparently oblivious to the hordes of surveillance police, Colenso and Michelle later drove to Nambucca Ave, arriving at the Matthews's residence at 2.52pm. They were seen standing in the front yard, and left at 2.57pm. At 3.28pm, Michelle rang Matthews and told him she needed to speak to him urgently.

Matthews: "Have you got dramas?"

Michelle: "Oh, real big ones."

They arranged to meet at Semaphore jetty at 5pm. It's likely that Michelle had just been listening to the news on the car radio, learning that police were holding a press conference at 3.30pm to announce details of an arrest and murder charge in the Carolyn Matthews case. A short time later, Matthews called her back to tell her he couldn't meet her because the police were at his house – they had caught someone and needed to talk to him. He said that he'd left the detectives at the house and told them he was going to pick up Shane, who was walking home from somewhere.

Michelle: "The police have got Dave."

Matthews: "What for?"

Michelle: "They've arrested him for murder."

Matthews: "Have they? You're joking."

Michelle: "No, and more arrests are to be made."

Matthews: "Hmmmm."

Matthews arrived home and led Sgt Eichner and SC Keane out to the back yard, where they again told him that an arrest had just been made, closely watching his reaction.

Sgt Eichner recalls: "The purpose of going to interview Kevin on August 2 was principally to advise him of the arrest of David Key. And to speak about the alleged affair again with Michelle – and about who Michelle was with at Beaurepaires. We believed then that Kevin may have been involved in the murder or covering up for Michelle in some way."

SC Keane says: "We wanted to put to him if he knew the bloke who was with Michelle that day, and the fact that that was Key and he had now been charged with Carolyn's murder. We wanted to put to him that this bloke was with you Kevin, and within 45 minutes your wife's been killed. It was also to get things going on the phones between Kevin and Michelle."

When they told Matthews a man had been charged with his wife's murder, he replied: "I got a phone call from my sister saying the same thing."

Keane: "I am going to ask you some more questions in relation to this matter."

Matthews: "Right."

Keane: "You're not obliged to answer these questions unless you wish to."

Matthews: "No, it's cool."

Keane: "Anything you say can be recorded and given in evidence."

Matthews: "Yeah."

Keane: "Do you understand that?"

Matthews: "No, I understand."

But Kevin Matthews clearly did not comprehend the significance of the rights he had just been advised of. He was now officially a suspect. However, since he did not request a lawyer, the detectives were free to question him.

Keane: "And you realise that we're here now to speak about the death of your wife?"

Matthews: "Yeah, I understand."

Keane: "All right, you understand that someone has been arrested and charged in relation to the death?"

Matthews: "You've told me and my sister's told me."

Keane: "All right, what time did your sister tell you that?"

Matthews: "I think the phone rang as youse were at the door. That's who I was on the phone to."

Keane: "Right, did she give you any details at all?"

Matthews: "She said that Jeff rang her and said that somebody's been arrested."

Keane: "Right. Do you know a male by the name of David Key?"

Matthews: "No, but I believe after speaking to Michelle that he is Michelle Burgess's boyfriend."

Keane: "When did you speak to Michelle?"

Matthews: "Oh, I seen her today when we went to Walkerville … went with Jason to the Walkerville club on North East Rd."

Keane: "That's today, is it?"

Matthews: "Yeah, we went there for lunch."

Keane: "Right. Was there some discussion about David Key?"

Matthews: "No, she just said that ... she's been telling me that her boyfriend's been arrested for breaking parole or something."

Keane: "Right."

Matthews: "And he was questioned about a homicide."

Keane: "Right. This is Michelle Burgess who told you this?"

Matthews: "That's correct."

Keane: "Well, what homicide did she say he was being questioned about?"

Matthews: "She didn't say. She said she didn't know. I said, 'Is it related to ours, to Carolyn?', and she said she didn't know."

Keane: "You still maintain you're not having a sexual relationship with Michelle?"

Matthews: "I maintain that I'm not having a sexual relationship with Michelle."

Keane: "I guess what I'm trying to say is, are you surprised at the connection of David Key and Michelle Burgess?"

Matthews: "I am surprised at this connection because I don't understand why Michelle, who's a friend of mine and a friend of Carolyn's, why her boyfriend would do this."

Keane: "Well, the investigation is continuing in relation to Michelle."

Matthews: "Yep."

Keane: "She could well be involved in the murder of your wife as well. Do you understand that?"

Matthews: "I don't believe that."

Keane: "Sorry?"

Matthews: "I don't believe that."

Keane: "Well that's what I'm putting to you, anyway."

Matthews: "Yep."

Keane: "Why is it that you don't believe that?"

Matthews: "Because she's such a good friend. What motive would she have to do that?"

Keane: "I don't know. What about if she's such a good friend, why is she associating with a bloke that we allege killed your wife?"

Matthews: "I don't know. I've never met this David."

Keane: "Well, we're alleging he was, in fact, with Michelle at your place of work late afternoon on the day your wife died. And the allegation is that after they've spoken to you and left, they've attended here, they've attended here within perhaps half an hour and your wife was murdered."

Matthews: "I can't believe that. I do not. Why would Michelle do that to me?"

Keane: "Well, we were hoping that perhaps you could tell us that."

Matthews: "Why would Michelle do that to me, why would she do it to Carolyn?"

Keane: "We don't know. Is there more to this that you haven't told us?"

Matthews: "No, there isn't."

Later in the interview, SC Keane said: "Is it a case that since you found out who might be responsible, that you're sort of trying to cover up for her because she's a friend?"

Matthews: "No, I wouldn't. Me and my family and my children need this to be resolved. I have been going downhill badly in the last three days. It's just starting to get to me. I thought once the funeral's over ... there's no contact with any police officers, nobody's telling us anything, we don't know what's going on."

(Throughout the entire police investigation, Matthews never contacted police seeking an update; all contact was initiated by the detectives.)

Keane: "I guess that's part of the investigation. It has been since this started. We've become aware of certain things which we've been inquiring into and following up, which has culminated in this man being charged today with murder."

Matthews: "Well, do you think he really done it?"

Keane: "There are substantial ... plenty of evidence to indicate that he has done it. And as I said to you, the indications are that Michelle is involved."

Shortly after the interview ended at 4.12pm and the detectives left, a tearful Matthews turned on his best phone performance yet for the police.

Between sobs, he told Michelle: "They (police) said you were involved ... you weren't, were you? You wouldn't do that to us, would you? They believe that you were involved and if I have had an affair with you then I'm an accessory or something. I will never be able to trust anyone again. I've just had a detective around here. Is your boyfriend's name David Key? They said that he done it. They've got evidence that he done it and they said that you're involved ... but Carolyn was your friend."

Michelle told him Key was nowhere near Carolyn Matthews on the night of the murder. He recounted his conversation with SC Keane and Sgt Eichner, in which he was also told that Key's bootprint was found in his wife's blood.

Matthews: "They just said he's definitely the one and they said that you're implicated and they said youse come down and youse had an argument and it got nasty or something."

In another conversation with Michelle around the time of Key's arrest, Matthews said he was "not happy" about the suspicious reactions of police, friends and strangers: "It's on TV that I'm fucking doing it and I'm getting it from the school that the kids are doing it. I can't even go to West Lakes (shopping centre) and do the fucking banking without people looking at me." That conversation concluded with both Matthews and Michelle pledging to each other: "Forever".

Earlier that afternoon, at 2.30pm, Detectives Standing, Eichner, Keane and five other officers had gone to Michelle's Craigmore home. The villa was deserted, but an hour later, Colenso arrived in Michelle's Commodore, driven by another man, James Hill, a bystander who found himself in the wrong place at the wrong time – in the middle of a murder investigation.

Hill had been at his Davoren Park home when Michelle and Colenso arrived and a long discussion about car parts ensued. Michelle asked Colenso to buy her some cigarettes and Hill went with him for the ride. But instead of returning home, they drove to Michelle's home to pick up the VN Commodore – where they were greeted by the police welcoming committee.

The officers searched the VP Commodore, seizing a mobile phone, wallet and other papers and ID belonging to David Key. Colenso had a Nokia mobile phone containing Key's SIM card, and these were also seized. Colenso refused to speak to them, explaining that he intended to be a witness for Key's defence.

At 5.40pm, Detectives Standing, Eichner and Keane arrived at 15 Easton St, Davoren Park and found Michelle.

Sgt Standing recalls: "(Aside from when she picked up Key's belongings from the Elizabeth police station) the first time I spoke to Michelle was the day we searched her house. We didn't go anywhere near her (earlier); that was part of the plan. When you investigate a murder and you've got people you think are responsible for it, you try to get sufficient evidence to give you reasonable cause so you can go and speak to them. You only get one crack at these things and you don't want to blow it. By the time we searched the house, my opinion of Michelle Burgess was about as low as one person can have for another."

Standing: "Your full name is Michelle Burgess?"

Michelle: "Michelle Elizabeth Burgess."

Standing: "Michelle, we would like you to come back to your house with us at 9 Bluebush Court. We need to search your home and we need you to be present."

Michelle: "OK."

Standing: "You are not under arrest. I make that perfectly clear. You are not under arrest, OK?"

Michelle: "Can I grab my mobile phone?"

Standing: "Yes, you can grab your gear, yes. I must warn you, I am going to tell you, you are not obliged to answer any questions or anything like that. Anything you do say will be recorded, OK?"

Michelle: "OK, no problems."

A short time later, Sgt Standing spoke into the tape recorder he was carrying: "We drove to 9 Bluebush Court. Burgess did not speak, other than to give directions and to speak to her mother on her mobile. We arrived at 6.50pm. Michelle, before you get out of the car, the procedure is going to be we're going to search your home. We need you to be present. I do have a search warrant and what we would like to have happen first is the inside of your house will be photographed before we start the search and as we are searching, if we locate anything it, will be photographed and seized. Do you understand that?"

Michelle: "I understand that. Am I allowed to be inside?"

Standing: "You will be, yes, yes, no problems. That's why we came and got you. The situation with these friends of yours ... You want them here?"

Michelle: "Yes, I want them here."

Standing: "Well, they won't be allowed to be inside while this is going on. They'll have to wait outside, OK?"

At 6.15pm, Sgt Eichner found pages from *The Advertiser* dated July 13 on the floor of the western side of the double bed. Michelle confirmed it was hers and it was seized, along with a black 2001 diary found in a cardboard box in the wardrobe. Michelle insisted it only contained "stuff relating to the Family Court".

In fact, it also contained more damning evidence. In the back of the diary, Michelle had committed to paper the kind of wordplay normally used by lovesick schoolgirls. In an acrostic poem, she had used the letters from Kevin's name to spell out the qualities that she – and she alone – believed he possessed: Kind, Exciting, Vigorous, Intelligent and Naughty. Also in the diary, she wrote a poem that gave a subtle but disturbing hint of the terrible events she had later orchestrated:

> The love that I wanted walked into my life,
> Although he has a wife,
> He's the man of my dreams, all in one
> No one compares to him
> The love that I wanted all my life came to me one day,
> He's the man of my dreams all in one
> But there is always a threat he will be taken away
> But I want him to stay.

After finding a letter on the side table in the main bedroom, SC Keane read the first line and asked Michelle: "This is written to 'My darling sweetheart and kids.' I take it that's yourself, is it?"

Michelle: "Yes. I received it on Wednesday."

It was a long, rambling letter from Key, written for him by another remand centre inmate. Key, too, had been inspired to great literary heights by his love for Michelle, having dictated a spontaneous and original love poem:

> Roses are red,
> Violets are blue,
> And fuck I love you.

Keane: "All right, we'll be seizing that for the time being."

During the search of the bedroom, various items of clothing were seized, and when Sgt Standing asked what she was wearing on the day of the murder, Michelle replied: "Virtually what I've got on."

Standing: "OK. Have you washed those clothes since then?"

"Yes," Michelle replied, apparently oblivious to the insult.

Standing: "What shoes have you been wearing?"

Michelle: "I only wear these shoes."

Standing: "They're the only ones you wear. OK. I ask you to remove those shoes and the jacket you were wearing that night; we'd like to take that with us, please."

Michelle: "It would only be the Crows jacket."
Standing: "OK, where's that?"
Michelle: "It's in the other room. It's the only jacket I own."

At 7.35pm, Sgt Standing did a walkthrough of the house with Michelle to check that none of her property had been damaged. She was issued with a receipt for the seized property. SC Keane says she seemed unperturbed by Major Crime detectives going through her house with a fine-tooth comb.

Sgt Standing recalls: "It didn't seem to worry her. She was her normal calm self, with a cocky attitude. For some reason, Michelle formed a very bad opinion of me. One would have reason to do that. I think she thought I was a bit full-on. I think she complained about the way I spoke to her in relation to her children (and her treatment of them)."

Asked what was going through his mind as the search proceeded, he had no hesitation in revealing his feelings: "That she's a cold-blooded murderer. She showed no emotion about anything at all except herself. Every comment she made to me and other officers was in the form of sarcasm or abuse. I thought she most definitely was involved in the murder of Carolyn Matthews and I was going to be lucky enough to get sufficient evidence to lock her up and charge her with it.

"Her parents turned up the day we searched it. And to listen to her speak to her parents and one of her sisters, you would have thought she was in charge of the whole world. It was all about her. Not about her children, not about her ex-husband or about anything else. It was all about her and the inconvenience in her life and what these horrible detectives were doing to her house."

The interview with Matthews at his home and the raid on Michelle's home were both carefully timed, besieging them both when they felt vulnerable and fearful after news of Key's arrest for Carolyn's murder.

EARLIER THAT DAY, just a few minutes after Matthews, Michelle and Colenso entered the Walkers Arms, Detectives Standing and Duval had gone to the Adelaide Remand Centre in Currie St to take the first step on the long road to justice for Carolyn Matthews. They stood waiting in a cramped holding cell, as David Key was led in by two Corrections officers. SC Duval, a talented young officer who would rise to the rank of superintendent in charge of the Drug Investigation Branch in just a few years, was tasked with informing Key of his arrest: "David William Edgar Key, I am arresting you on suspicion of having committed a serious offence, namely, the murder of Carolyn Matthews at West Lakes on Thursday, July 12, 2001. Do you understand that?"

He did. His rights were explained, including his right to a phone call.

"Is there anything you wish to avail yourself of in respect of that right?" Key, oblivious as usual to what was actually being said, replied: "No comment." But when his right to legal representation was also fully explained, he knew exactly what to say: "I want to see my lawyer."

He was told that his clothing at the remand centre would be seized. At 10.43am, Key was taken to a Major Crime interview room on the fourth floor of the police building in Angas Street. At 10.53am, Duval again advised Key of his rights. A call was made to a solicitor but, by the time the tape restarted, Key had already forgotten her first name. Then he forgot her last name. She wisely advised him to not answer any questions. His only other comment was that he wanted to let his "fiancée" know where he was. (He was about to be taken to the city watch-house.) SC Duval refused on the basis that the call could impact on the investigation.

Standing: "What is your fiancée's name, please?"

Key: "Michelle Burgess."

Since he had been taken into custody, Michelle had been cooing sweet nothings in his ear in phone calls to the remand centre. "I love you," she told Key. "The kids are missing you. Don't tell the cops anything."

Key persisted with his "no comment" mantra throughout the 40-minute video interview, but it mattered little to the detectives that he wasn't prepared to co-operate or confess; irrefutable physical evidence and many long months in a cell would give him plenty of reasons and opportunity to change his mind. Key was taken to the city watch-house and officially charged with murder. At 4.33pm, the police medical officer took body samples from Key and noted injuries to his right hand and healing deep abrasions to his left anterior tibial (lower leg) area.

His subsequent appearance in Adelaide Magistrates Court late that afternoon, flanked by three guards, lasted just 15 seconds. Major Crime officer-in-charge Superintendent Paul Schramm would not say whether there was a connection between Key and his victim, but tantalised the media by revealing that "there might be further arrests".

That evening, Kaylene Kenyon spoke to Kevin Matthews on the phone.

She recalls: "He told me the police had charged someone who was a friend of someone that they knew. Kevin said that he didn't know this man. I said: 'Who's the friend of the family?'

"He said: 'Me and Carolyn know her, but we don't know her boyfriend.'

"I said: 'Who is it? Do I know her?'

"Kevin began to cry and said he had to go."

The next day, on the front page of *The Advertiser*, Carolyn Matthews's radiant smile shone again.

Chapter 12

Forever

August 3, 2001 – August 6, 2001

JASON COLENSO dropped off the Burgess children to their father on Friday, August 3, just as he had done the previous week. His presence in their lives appalled Darren, who was still coming to grips with the fact that his estranged wife had hired a hitman to kill him. "Knowing full well what she had done, it was pretty hard," he told the *Police Association of SA Journal* in 2010, in the only previous public interview he has given.

There was no guarantee that Key's arrest meant the contract was null and void. For their own safety, Darren Burgess and Kathy Morton would ultimately spend 2½ months staying at his parents' home. In the *PASA Journal* article, written by editor Brett Williams, Darren said the presence and input of Sgt Standing and other Major Crime detectives was a great comfort to them.

"Mick was pretty good and always has been," Burgess said. "He was straightforward and didn't bullshit around. He looked after us very well. And Michael Eichner, John Keane, they were all good."

Kathy found that, when she felt angry and/or frustrated, she could vent to Sgt Standing. "When you were feeling like you needed a shoulder to cry on, he was there," she told Williams in the interview. "It was never too much for him. He was just a phone call away. And when you called him, he'd come around and see you and he'd let you know that everything would be OK." Sgt Standing found the couple to be "wonderful people" for whom he still has "a lot of time".

"You saw the adversity they had in their lives and realised that a lot of people would have fallen apart ages ago," he said. "They hadn't. Kathy was brilliant. She's a very strong person. She stood by Darren all the way through it. And he certainly didn't back off or bow to threats or show any signs of weakness. He knew what was required and he stood up."

CONST. PALAZZO watched closely as Kevin Matthews, Michelle Burgess and Jason Colenso met up again at the Semaphore Palais for two hours, from 11.30am on August 3.

His surveillance log notes:

11.54am: Trio observed on path towards Semaphore Jetty.

12.02pm: Trio stops and talks. Various conversations ensued until 12.57pm, when Colenso gets into Commodore and exits immediately. Michelle and Matthews continue talking; Matthews kisses her on the forehead and hugs her, patting her on the back and touching her hair. Matthews shakes hands with Colenso.

12.58pm: Michelle and Colenso get into car. Matthews shakes both his hands, spread fingered, in front of his body, as he speaks to Colenso. Commodore leaves car park, as does Matthews. Followed to Military Rd where observations cease.

The pressure on both Matthews and Michelle was now intense. They still had no idea exactly what evidence the police had gathered, and they feared that Key, despite his assurances, could be selling them out to save himself. They were well aware that police were monitoring their every move and every phone call and they'd finally learned to keep their mouths shut. But the Major Crime team was already satisfied; they had enough evidence to make their next move.

Sgt Eichner recalls: "We believed we had sufficient grounds to arrest Michelle Burgess. She'd met with Kevin Matthews at Beaurepaires; her handwriting was on the contract; the denial of the affair; the conversation at the Old Spot Hotel; and no alibi on the day of the murder."

At 5pm on August 4, 2001, Michelle got the knock on her door she'd feared. Colenso answered it, and the door swung open to reveal six grim-faced detectives. Fortunately, Michelle's children were with Darren.

Sgt Standing recalls: "Colenso answered the door wearing only tracksuit pants. We told him what it was about and he didn't want to let us in. Burgess was in the bedroom getting dressed – you can leave it up to your imagination what they were doing before we got there. She was told she was under arrest. It came as quite a shock to her. She couldn't believe it."

Peering coldly over his spectacles at Michelle, Sgt Standing spelt out the situation in a statement for the record: "Michelle Burgess, my name is Detective Sergeant Michael Standing from the Major Crime Investigation Section. The time is ten past five. We are at 9 Bluebush Court, Craigmore. Michelle, I am arresting you on suspicion of having murdered Carolyn Matthews on Thursday 12th of July this year at 5 Nambucca Ave, West Lakes. You are not obliged to answer any questions or say anything about this matter. I warn you that anything you do say will be recorded and may be given in evidence. Do you understand that?"

Michelle: "Yes."

He completed reading her rights and she requested a phone call to her parents, Keith and Angela Goldup, and that Colenso accompany her to the interrogation she was about to face. But there was no way police were allowing Colenso into the interview room. Detective Senior Constable Les Jolly remained at the house, conducting a brief interview with him. He refused to answer questions about the murder. Like David Key before him, he had no idea how he had landed himself a "high-class sheila from Craigmore", but he was thrilled at being caught up in the middle of a murder investigation. On the journey to the Major Crime offices in the city, SC Keane and Detective Senior Constable Rosalie Delurant travelled with Michelle in the same car.

Keane: "Detective Keane is my name. I wasn't sure, did you arrange for your parents to come in too, or what?"

Michelle: "Ah, they didn't say whether they were coming in or not, all right? I think they might go to my brother's first."

Keane: "What will we do if you want someone there? At this stage, we will be objecting to Jason being there because we're not sure at this stage whether he's involved with this incident and he may well be spoken to by police as well. We have no problems with your parents or someone else being there."

Michelle: "I want Jason there because ..."

Keane: "Well as I said, we're not happy with that because of the situation; we don't know how much Jason is involved with this. When we get back there, ring your parents and see if they're happy to come in, all right?"

At 5.55pm, the car pulled up outside the Angas St police building. The *Sunday Mail* had already been tipped off. Three hours before their weekly deadline, the police had gift-wrapped a fantastic Page 1 story – now they just needed the picture. The presence of media only added to the enormous pressure on their suspect. Sgt Standing noticed photographer Mark Brake readying for their arrival and said: "Michelle, is it all right if you don't have a cigarette at this stage? It looks as though there is a chap there with a camera so we would rather go straight inside. Is that all right with you?"

Michelle: "Yes."

Brake captured the moment perfectly. SC Keane led the way, striding purposefully up the steps towards the building, clipboard under his arm. Behind him, Sgt Standing and SC Delurant escorted Michelle, who was the only one looking at the camera. One hand was clutched protectively to her chest, with shock and trepidation written on her face. On the *Sunday Mail*'s front page the following day, Michelle's face was pixellated for legal reasons. Inside the police building, SC Delurant took her to a balcony for a cigarette and then the toilet, before depositing her in a fourth-floor interview room to face her interrogators.

Sgt Standing, emotionless, started by clearing up some details. "When we were at your house, I advised you of certain rights. You have requested Jason Colenso present. That person is not acceptable to police for being a person present during the interview for a number of reasons. One is I don't believe he can give you appropriate advice. Second, we don't know what extent he has involvement in this matter. We are still making enquiries. We will give you a phone and you can make another call, perhaps arrange for your parents to come. There will be no further interview with you until such time that they arrive. Do you understand that?"

Michelle: "Yes."

She was handed her mobile phone and she called her father; her parents arrived at 6.20pm. Stunned at their daughter's predicament, they sat quietly as Sgt Standing and SC Keane went about their work. Michelle agreed to answer "what she can" which in itself was a victory for the detectives, who had feared she would immediately call a lawyer and clam up. It quickly became apparent that Michelle had ensured her story matched Matthews's; the detectives would have to work hard to knock holes in it. She was a cunning and manipulative woman, but her belief that these talents could allow her to safely negotiate an interview with two experienced homicide detectives – without a lawyer – was a major error of judgment. Perhaps Michelle believed she could bat her eyelids and the detectives would immediately turn their guns on their colleagues, set her free, and join her at the nearest hotel for Scotch and cuddles. The questions, from both officers, were rapid-fire and, initially, Michelle was confident with her answers.

"Where were you on July 12, 2001?"

"During the day, I was with Dave, driving around."

"Dave who?"

"David Key."

"Who is he to you?"

"Boyfriend."

"How long have you known him?"

"A month and a half."

"What car were you in?"

"Red Toyota Corolla."

"Do you know Kevin Matthews?"

"Yes."

"What is your relationship with him?"

"He's my friend."

"How long has he been your friend?"

"For a while, since a lot of the stuff with my ex-husband and myself has been going on."

Michelle admitted visiting Beaurepaires at 5.30pm on July 12, but insisted Jason Colenso was with her. The detectives exchanged glances. Was she serious? There was little to no physical resemblance between Colenso and Key, who was seen by several independent witnesses.

Michelle: "It was 'cos we went down to go and get some tyres, 'cos I needed some tyres for my car. And Kevin, I rang up Kevin and he said he'd get me some second-handies (known in the tyre trade as take-offs – near-new tyres that have been removed from cars being fitted with different tyres, for example, with mag wheels) for nothing. And we went down there, and by the time I was down there, he was already closed up and he was going home. So he said for me to go back another time."

"Where did you go ..."

"Uh, we ..."

"... after you left Beaurepaires on that night?"

"We started heading back up towards Grand Junction Rd, heading towards Elizabeth."

"And who was driving your car at that time?"

"Jason was driving my car."

"During the course of the day of July 12, did you have any communication with Kevin Matthews at all?"

"Um, yes I did."

"And what were those communications?"

"The tyres, going down there, making sure I was going to be on time. That was it."

But Michelle "can't recall" how many calls she made to Matthews that day.

"On July 12, in fact you had 19 telephone calls with Kevin Matthews, would that be correct?"

"If you say so; I assume so, I don't know."

"The first call you had with him was at 6.30am in the morning and lasted for 21 minutes and 35 seconds. What was that conversation about?"

"I honestly can't remember. I know I asked him about the tyres."

"For 21 minutes and 35 seconds?"

"And making sure … and also to do with a telephone bill that my ex-husband had been ringing me up about. That he reckons he gave Carolyn and Kevin. And a fax that Kevin received from Darren."

"Was there any other conversation?"

"No, it was mainly during the day. Because my ex-husband kept ringing me."

"You had another phone conversation with Kevin from 8.46am in the morning that lasted for 8 minutes and 52 seconds. What was that conversation about?"

"I honestly couldn't … I … I can't tell you every single conversation … I don't remember."

Michelle continued nervously babbling about the tyres and the phone calls, then addressed the affair allegations head-on.

"Because we have had enough about the stuff that my ex-husband was ringing up talking to Carolyn about, talking to Kevin about, talking to me about, and it was … we've … we've had enough. Carolyn and I and Kevin, we had sat down and come to an agreement and … about what was going on way before this happened."

"And what was going on?"

"There was accusations that were going on from just the day after Christmas last year. It was a phone call saying that … to my house, my old house at Williams St, Evanston Park, that I was having an affair with Kevin."

Standing: "Yes?"

"Kevin Matthews and everything went out from the water from there. It was affairs. We were meant to be having an affair. And Kevin and I were always in contact, which we were, and so was Darren and so was Carolyn. We were all texting each other, they were always ringing each other. And that's how all this has gone … we had, Kevin and I, never had an affair, we were friends. Carolyn and I and myself and Kevin, we all sat down and Darren refused to sit down with us to talk about it. And we sorted the situation out without Darren."

"And when did this happen?"

"Oh, around February, March sometime. Darren didn't have a problem with ringing up Carolyn and ringing up Kevin and ringing up myself and threatening us and saying he was going to get us and everything else because we were having an affair and it wasn't true."

"When did you first meet Kevin Matthews?"

"Kevin Matthews? I met him years ago at a Beaurepaires Christmas dinner at the Bridgeway Hotel."

"I understand your ex-husband is Darren Burgess?"

"Darren Wayne Burgess, yeah."

"Yeah and he was employed by Beaurepaires."

"Yeah and he still is."

"What was the work relationship between Kevin Matthews and Darren Burgess?"

"Well Kevin was his boss. For a while, yes, until he recently got demoted."

"And what caused the break-up of your marriage with Darren Burgess?"

"The phone call, the affair phone call. We'd been having problems for over three years."

"And you're saying there was no affair between yourself and Kevin Matthews."

"There was no affair whatsoever."

"Did you ever have a telephone account for $1200 for one month's worth of calls?"

"To Kevin yes, and Darren knew about that and he was also using my mobile phone at that stage. We were all texting each other. Carolyn was texting. We were all texting each other."

"Who paid for those calls?"

"I borrowed the money off Kevin and I paid him back because Darren went off his tree. And Darren turned around and said: 'You've got to find a way to pay it.' And Kevin and Carolyn lent me the money and I paid them back."

"And how did you do that?"

"I paid them back after I got the money from the house settlement."

"Right. Did you then have any other substantial telephone accounts?"

"I think there was probably about one more."

"You had one that was at least $900."

"I think so, yeah."

"And who paid that?"

"As far as my knowledge, I think that's still unpaid."

"And did you have one for about $1600 at one time?"

"I honestly can't remember. Probably. There's a few phone bills floating around. I know there's one from Telstra that I still haven't paid."

"Did you ever go away and spend time away from home with Kevin Matthews?"

"No."

"Did you go to Melbourne with him at any time?"

"No, I did not. And I know those three days that Darren is talking about and I went up to McLaren Vale."

"What sort of places did you meet Kevin Matthews in?"

"Coffee shops, pubs."

"Which ones?"

"OG, Hampstead and there's one in town up at North Adelaide."

"On July 11, the day before Carolyn was murdered, you had a substantial number of phone calls with Kevin Matthews. What were they about?"

"I think they were also about the phone, the fax, the phone bill that was going on."

"On the 9th of July, you had a number of different phone calls with Kevin. What were they about?"

"I honestly can't remember."

"When did you first meet David Key?"

"I met him at my son's school. His sister."

Michelle said she has a "boyfriend-girlfriend" relationship with Key and he had been staying at her house for three or four weeks.

"Getting back to the 12th of July, what was David doing that day?"

"We were with each other during the day."

"You were together all day, were you?"

"Most of the day, we were down at Davoren Park because we had the kids. We were driving around."

"Did you go to a bank with him?"

"I can't remember."

"There is a photograph taken in a Commonwealth Bank."

"Oh yeah, that's when I deposited the cheque from the house."

Standing showed her the picture. "Which person in the photograph is you?"

He indicated the blonde woman in the picture wearing a black top, Crows jacket and brown boots. She identified herself and David Key in pictures marked 12.34pm and 1.01pm.

"Where did you go after that?"

"We went back home."

"Then where?"

"Down Davoren Park."

"When did Jason Colenso meet up with you that day?"

"Probably in the late afternoon, around three or four o'clock."

"And you stated he was in the car with you when you went to Beaurepaires Port Adelaide?"

"Yes."

"How was it you went to get tyres at Beaurepaires?"

"Because I knew Kevin and I needed some tyres and because Kevin and I were talking and Carolyn, we were all friends, we were all talking and I needed some tyres and I rang him up and he said he could get me some ... some second-handy tyres."

"That was one of those 19 telephone calls you had with him that day?"

"Yeah."

"Where was David Key?"

"He ended up ... I don't know who he was ... he went off in some other car."

"What car was that?"

"Um, what do you call it? I forget what model, what do you call them? Like, um, you know the old-style Commodores?"

"And whose car was that?"

"I honestly don't know; I'd never met him before."

Sgt Standing also made particular reference to Key's footwear in the bank security picture and Michelle agreed that he was wearing boots.

"Do you know where David was while you were at Port Adelaide visiting Kevin?"

"I don't know where he was."

"When did you see him again after that?"

"On the way back to Elizabeth. Just driving along Main North Rd."

"Where was Jason Colenso living at that time?"

"I don't know. I know how to get there but I don't know the name."

"How did he arrive at your place that day?"

"Dave went and picked him up."

"Why?"

"I don't know. They just said they wanted to go cruising, wanted to go out."

"So they came back to your place?"

"And picked me up."

"Picked you up?"

"And the kids. And Dave went his way. Oh, I said to him, I said to Dave: 'I want to go and get my tyres'."

"And where were your children while you were at Port Adelaide?"

"They were at my mother's house."

"On July 2 this year, you had a phone call with Carolyn Matthews that lasted for five minutes. Can you remember what that call was about?"

"I honestly can't remember. I can't remember the phone calls, actually."

"When was the previous time you contacted her to that?"

"Oh we'd been talking fairly regularly. We'd ..."

"What, weekly? Daily?"

"Oh weekly, sometimes daily. She was helping me through the situation I was going through with Darren and we were discussing a lot of things, you know, questions that Darren kept raising."

Sgt Standing questioned her on what happened to the house settlement cheque.

"How much is still in the bank?"

"None."

"What happened?"

"Bought a VP Commodore and also a blue Commodore and also paid off some other bills."

"What other bills did you pay off?"

"Ah, um, ah ... I had the loan for, for the credit."

"How much was that?"

"I think nine thousand. And just other little bills here and there. And paying for stuff because my ex-husband hadn't been paying ... hasn't been caught up in maintenance, so a lot of money was used to get the kids stuff."

She was asked for an explanation as to why she had bought two additional cars when she already owned one.

"Because I was selling the Toyota and Dave didn't have any cars that were working. He had two Fords that were broken down. He needed a car to drive around and I wanted a bigger car, so we went and bought some cars and I paid off the red one so I could sell it and put the rest of the money that was going to be sold into the bank account for the kids."

"You're saying you bought David a car. This is a chap you've only known for a month and you bought him a new car."

"Yes, well it was in my name and I said, like, the agreement was that he drove it around. If we busted up, you know, or anything like that, the car stayed with me. I would sell it and keep the money."

"Now, going back to Jason being with you to go down to Beaurepaires. Just refresh my memory again, how did that come about?"

"Dave and, I don't know, Dave received a phone call, he wanted ... Dave wanted to go out for a ... cruising around town and all that. So Dave went out and picked up Jason, they came back and picked myself up in the car and I ... Dave was in another car. Two cars rocked up to the house. I, um, said to Dave: 'Well I've got to drop the kids off because I want to go and get some tyres, I'm taking this car.' I drove down to Beaurepaires Port Adelaide and Jason came with me."

"OK, and did he go in the shop with you when you were in there?"

"He ... I walked in first and then Darren Bland came over and had a word with me and then walked out."

"What was that about?"

"Ah, because a few years ago, I think about three or four years ago, Darren Bland and I had an affair and I had told Darren. Darren had confronted him and he wasn't happy about it. As soon as he saw me at Beaurepaires, Darren Bland came walking over and said: 'Michelle, when you're finished here, I'd like to talk to you.'"

"Right."

"I turned around and went: 'Yeah right whatever' and he said: 'Right, I'll see ya' and walked back. Jason came into the front of the store and was standing there for about two minutes and then went back and sat in the car."

"So, OK, you've taken the red Toyota down to Beaurepaires to have a new tyre fitted."

"Well, second-handies, yeah."

"Which tyre on the vehicle needed replacing?"

"Back, and, um, the fronts. Well they all needed replacing, probably mainly the front ones."

"Did Kevin Matthews inspect the tyres on the car when you got there?"

"He had a look at them and said: 'They do need replacing' and I said: 'Well, fine' and he said: 'I can't do it now, 'cos all the roller doors are shut,' and he said he was going home and he asked if I could come back."

Standing: "We've spoken to two people who saw you at Beaurepaires on Thursday. They saw you there and they saw the other person you were with. Can you describe Jason to me, please."

Michelle began a lengthy description of Colenso. Sgt Standing pulled out a picture of Key and said: "The description of the person that was seen with you at Beaurepaires in fact is the same or similar to that of David Key, not Jason. Do you have anything you'd like to say about that?"

"David Key was not there. Well he wasn't with me. David Key was not there with me. Jason was there with me."

"OK," Sgt Standing replied, clearly less than convinced, provoking a fit of righteous indignation from Michelle.

"No, well, in all honesty ..." she spluttered.

Michelle's parents interrupted, urging her to "just calm down".

SC Keane remembers: "From the reactions on their faces, they must have had some sort of doubts when they heard some of the things that were put to her and some of the things that she said."

Michelle: "David wasn't there. It was Jason and myself were there and I know it's Darren Bland. Because I dobbed him in to Darren and he's nasty with me and turns around and threatens me that if he ever sees me he wants to beat the crap out of me. He hates my guts and wants to get ... like Darren."

"Just calm down," her parents urged again.

"There was another person who saw you at Ultra Tune ... sorry, at Beaurepaires that day other than Darren Bland. The description of the person he gave also fits David Key. You may like to comment on that."

"As I said before, in all honesty, David Key was not with me down at Beaurepaires Port Adelaide. He was not there."

"You're a hundred per cent sure on that?"

"I'm a hundred per cent sure of that. David Key was not with me."

"So where was David Key when you saw him after you left Beaurepaires?"

"He's been driving, heading towards Elizabeth on Main North Rd."

Sgt Standing grilled her on how it was that she just happened to come up behind him on Main North Rd. Sgt Standing changed the topic to Key's boots.

"What sort of boots did David Key normally wear in the time that you knew him?"

"Black boots."

"And where are those black boots now?"

"Apparently you guys have got them."

"What happened to the laces out of those boots?"

"They were handed in a package I received from Dave when he was arrested, along with his wallet and mobile. They could be anywhere. Whether they're in the house or car, I don't know."

"Have you had much conversation with Kevin Matthews as a result of his wife being murdered?"

"I've been talking to him. Yes, quite frequent."

"When was the last time you spoke to him?"

"Today."

"Today? OK. For your information DNA has been located in the form of a blood sample. Blood has been found on one of the boots belonging to David Key and that blood is Carolyn Matthews's blood. Do you have any idea how that may have got there?"

"I would not have a clue."

"You understand what the implication of that is?"

"Well, yeah."

"And what's that?"

"Well then if Dave did kill her then, only, it'd be me as well with him or something like that."

"Well, the implication is that the person who was wearing those boots at that time is responsible for stabbing and murdering Carolyn Matthews. I ask you again, were you with Dave on that day?"

"I was with him during the day and like I said, between the time I was down at Beaurepaires Port Adelaide and the time we met up, I'm not sure of the time when we saw him down at … I don't know where he was."

"Why was Dave arrested on July 27?"

"He was arrested for a high-speed chase and bail. I think the reason was bail."

"Was Jason Colenso arrested at the same time?"

"Yes."

"What for?"

"I don't know."

Sgt Standing questioned her on how she came to meet Jason Colenso. She insisted it was before the murder because he was with her on the night of the murder. She said the first time she met Jason was when they went to the wreckers at Dublin several weeks before the murder. Sgt Standing pressed her for the exact time she met Jason. Michelle became flustered and ended up saying two to three weeks before the murder, which was around the end of June.

"Was there ever a confrontation between you and Carolyn?"

"There was only ever one confrontation and it wasn't even a confrontation, it was like sitting down and arguing and that was about January or February. We'd had enough and wanted to sit down with Kevin and Carolyn and Darren and discuss the whole situation. Clear it all up because I had had enough of it, Kevin had had enough of it and Carolyn had had enough of it. My marriage broke up and we didn't need another marriage to break up."

"Well, did Carolyn think you were having an affair with Kevin?"

"At the beginning, yes, she did. But after Kevin, myself and Carolyn sat down and discussed it all, we all came to the conclusion that it was, you know, Darren being an arsehole."

"All right, so you say the Friday before her death was the last time you spoke to Carolyn Matthews?"

"Yes."

"We have some information that Kevin had asked you to be his mistress."

"No."

"Did that ever happen?"

"No."

Standing: "Just one other thing. Since the death of Carolyn Matthews, have you given Kevin Matthews any money?"

"Yes, I have."

"How much was that?"

"I think it was about four grand. I owed him money for them paying off my bill. And Carolyn and himself had given me money every now and again when I needed it. So he was strapped, didn't have any money and I was being a friend and he's paying that back."

"When did you give him that money?"

"Oh, probably the week after."

The detectives paused and came to a silent agreement – they had heard enough lies for one day. Sgt Standing casually announced: "Well, at this point in time, you'll be arrested and charged with the murder of Carolyn Matthews."

At 8pm, when asked to undergo a forensic procedure, Michelle finally asked for a lawyer. The Goldups left the interview room while their daughter was led out and allowed to smoke another cigarette. When the lawyer arrived, the forensic procedure request was refused. He may also have mentioned to Michelle that she should have called him before opening her mouth to the detectives – accused murderers have nothing to gain from speaking to police.

The interview officially concluded at 8.42pm. Michelle was taken to the city watch-house and charged with murder at 9.14pm, just in time for the *Sunday Mail*'s first edition. Bail was refused and after being searched, she was placed in a cell.

SC Keane says: "During her interview, she made no admissions, just lied about everything. Her lies basically dug her in deeper. She said Colenso was with her and we could prove that he wasn't."

Kevin Matthews was aware of Michelle's arrest, and had already had lengthy conversations with Colenso, who told him he'd also let Kev know about the charge, and Kev was "going off his brain". Crucially, Matthews replied: "Yeah, well he's gonna make sure he wasn't in the car with her."

SC Keane called Matthews at 9.24pm and officially advised him of the good news – a second person had been arrested and charged with his wife's murder.

Darren Burgess recalls that he had picked up his children for their regular fortnightly visit the day before Michelle's arrest. The day after her arrest, they walked around to the deli to pick up the *Sunday Mail* and there was their mother on the front page.

Darren says: "I had to tell the kids the truth. Their mum had been arrested for murder. Some people have said to me that was a bit hard. It was during the next week that it hit my son because we had to put him in a new school. I had no choice because of where I lived. The school counsellor rang up after he'd been at school for an hour and said: 'This is too hard for me, you need to get him professional help'. I asked Michelle's parents to back off a bit and give the kids a chance to settle into their new environment and give me some space. They went straight to lawyers and started filing applications. I would have been accommodating but they didn't want to wait."

Michelle's arrest was the talk of the town. It even overshadowed that afternoon's Showdown X between Port Adelaide and the Adelaide Crows. Although stricken by her arrest, by that afternoon Crows fan Kevin Matthews had his head right; a Showdown, after all, was a Showdown. He rang the Semaphore Surf Life Saving Club to see if anyone was there watching the game. Carolyn Garland, who was running the bar, told him the place was empty. He arrived with his three boys soon after.

Carolyn recalls: "He made a call and said: 'Is it OK if some mates come down?' When they arrived, I thought, 'Who the hell are you?'"

One of the men was Colenso and she put his name to his face when he appeared on the TV news after the football game. The other man was equally mean-looking and had a teardrop tattoo on his face. When the trio went out to the balcony to smoke, talk and drink, Carolyn pulled the boys aside and asked them to help her move some tables.

"I just wanted to get the boys away from them," she says. "Kevin used his credit card and I rang Peter (Campaign – to check whether she should accept it) and he said 'just let it go'. It came to over $80. He had Scotches and beers and (after they watched the game) gave Colenso and the other man beers to take home."

After they left, Kevin watched the TV news coverage of Michelle's arrest the previous night.

Carolyn recalls: "(Kevin said) 'She's the one that gave Carolyn a cat, she's a good family friend.' I thought that was odd. A good family friend? Colenso came on TV and he was being interviewed. He said he was a good family friend of Burgess. I was scared."

Kevin left with his boys soon after the news item, his mood not helped by the Crows' eight-point loss to Port Adelaide.

Earlier that afternoon, Sgt Standing and Sen. Sgt Strange were walking through the foyer of the police building when they came across Michelle's parents.

Sgt Standing later made notes of their conversation: "Angela was visibly upset and had been crying. DSS Strange and I spoke to them concerning the activities of Jason Colenso and his association with Michelle. Keith had first seen Colenso when he went to his daughter's house on the evening of August 2 when police were there searching the premises. Angela says the same. She might have seen him on another occasion, not sure when. She says on the night of July 12, 2001, Michelle picked her children up from her home and she thought Colenso may have been the other person in the vehicle. But she didn't actually see him. Keith Goldup says he remembers the night of the 12th. He didn't get home until 6.30pm and his grandchildren were still there when he arrived. He recalls Michelle coming to collect her children but he didn't see who was in the car either. Keith was forthright and direct, Angela was nervous and sobbing."

KEVIN MATTHEWS had become the Adelaide media's most wanted man. And it was Channel 7 crime reporter Jessica Sullivan (now Seven newsreader Jessica Adamson), who had been laying the groundwork for the big scoop. Michelle Burgess was scheduled to appear in Adelaide Magistrates Court on Monday, August 6 and there was a massive media turnout. Matthews had been advised by detectives not to turn up at court, but he feared that if he did not demonstrate his solidarity to Michelle, she could turn on him. He arrived with Colenso and waited outside Court No. 2 for almost three hours, until Michelle's case was finally called at 12.30pm. She was brought into court surrounded by five sheriff's officers.

Adamson says: "I'd been in contact with Jason Colenso for two weeks leading up to the court appearance. He was adamant in the several phone calls I had with him that Michelle had nothing to do with it, that Kevin had nothing to do with it and he was very keen for Channel 7 to do a story pointing that out."

In court, Adamson found herself sitting in the front row, between Matthews and Colenso, for what she describes as "the most bizarre court appearance of my career".

The moment Michelle Burgess was led into the dock, handcuffed, both men began behaving like love-struck teenagers.

Adamson: "Despite the fact that Michelle was under arrest, in handcuffs and charged with murder, she still held this extraordinary power over these two men. They were both competing for her attention. Everyone saw it – the media, the family and the detectives working on the case. Still to this day, I wonder what it was about her that drew men in so deeply.

"Both of them were making hand gestures, mouthing words to her, trying to get her attention and she, in turn, was responding to them both. She mouthed the words 'get me out of here' and she was pretty distressed. Kevin, on one side of me, had a hat in his lap, like one of those Greg Chappell (cricket) hats and I could see that it had something written on it, but he was trying to hold it up to her without letting anyone else see what was written on it. It wasn't until we got outside court that I realised what he'd written on the hat."

Michelle's lawyer, Stephen Ey, asked Magistrate Sue O'Connor to order a report on her suitability for home detention. But the prosecution had all bases covered. They cited "ongoing investigations as to further offences; lack of alibis; and the threat at this stage there could be hampering of the investigations if bail was granted".

Ms O'Connor told him: "In my view, your client doesn't qualify for bail at this stage."

Ey replied: "What concerns me is this young woman has two young children and she has been separated from her two young children."

But it was to no avail. Michelle would be spending her 28th birthday, the following day, behind bars. She became distressed when she realised bail would be refused. When Michelle cried, so did her parents. And across the room, "Kev" and "Jase" both comforted "Mish" with their mime acts.

Kevin Matthews slipped on his sunglasses as he walked out of the court building, firmly planting the hat on his head. It was written on the inside in texta, but the media pack could clearly see the word "Forever" through the back of the hat. When reporters quizzed him about it, he denied it had anything to do with the court appearance. He later claimed that it was the first hat he'd picked up off the rack as he left the house. The media crews buzzed around him like flies. This guy was gold. He stalked briskly down the street. One reporter asked: "Mr Matthews, can I just ask why you were in court today?"

"Nup," he replied.

"There's been speculation, Mr Matthews, that you may be implicated. Do you want to reassure people that you're not?"

Matthews remained silent, hiding behind his sunglasses and sucking furiously on a cigarette. Adamson was relieved by his silence because he had already agreed to an exclusive interview. She recalls: "Kevin Matthews was pretty stressed that day. He wasn't expecting the huge media turnout – God knows why. I think it took him by surprise and he really didn't know how to react."

That night, every TV news broadcast ran the footage of Matthews's court exit, jamming the "Forever" hat on his head and maintaining a sullen silence as the media pack engulfed him, with a bemused Colenso trailing behind. When she saw the footage, Kaylene Kenyon was furious: "That 'Forever' hat, that was just terrible, I wanted to punch him. What a fool."

Adamson and her cameraman Rob Brown met Matthews at his home shortly after the court appearance. Colenso was also there. When Matthews opened the door, the first thing Adamson noticed was the Scotch on his breath.

She recalls: "He was extremely agitated, he was shaking, he was sweating, he was smoking and he was in quite a state about the media turnout at court. So we were standing in the doorway that leads to the kitchen, where Carolyn had been murdered and Rob, the car alarm in his vehicle went off and he had to go out and turn it off, leaving me in the house with these two men which ... wasn't that much fun. Thankfully he didn't take long. He came back and we decided to do the interview outside."

Before they went into the backyard, Matthews told Adamson: "I told you I didn't want to be on camera, but it's obvious I've been on camera that much today, I think I don't give a rat's. The only thing is you've got to understand I'm getting fuckin' haunted. Starting to get to the angry stage."

"That's cool," said Adamson agreeably, as Matthews poured himself a Scotch. He offered her one, but after agreeing it was a "good idea", she demurred. They moved to the backyard, where Brown set up his camera. Matthews sat down, but continued to smoke, waving for them to wait.

"I'm not going to go on camera with a cigarette in my mouth, so just bear with me. I'm also paranoid of the fact I want to get this done before the kids get home. And I don't want to come out of this looking fucking stupid, either. So I need to know sort of what you're going to ask."

"Yeah well, you know ..." Adamson began, but Kevin interrupted.

"We've got a cat running around here that she gave Carolyn, for freak sake, you know, and her and Carolyn had a good relationship."

"Oh, really?" Adamson said, quickly reassuring him: "I'm not going to shaft you."

"Frustrating thing is that some of the stuff in the paper about me phoning ... it's all totally wrong, you know. What happened that night, I've never seen anything so scary in my friggin' life, I tell you. It was brutal."

Brown peered around from the camera.

"You might want to take off the sunnies because all I can see is Jess (reflected)," he told Kevin. But Kevin had no intention of exposing his guilty eyes to the public: "They're optical prescription."

Brown: "Oh, OK. Yeah, that's fine."

Adamson recalls: "And it was like the flick of a switch. As soon as we started the interview, Kevin put on this calm, loving husband façade and talked about how horrified he was by Carolyn's death, how terrifying it was for him and the children to come home and find her."

She opened her questioning: "Kevin, why did you go to court today?"

Matthews: "The police contacted me and said there was a family friend involved. I'm just totally not convinced that the person they're naming is involved. I mean, if you knew the relationship between her and Carolyn and I, I mean, I just can't believe it. So I figured they were going to get ... I thought today was about giving evidence so they could, you know, convince them, but it wasn't about that at all."

Adamson: "It must have been pretty awful for you and the boys to come home to that, that night. Does it still haunt you?"

Matthews: "Yeah it haunts me, it haunts me terribly. The boys seem to be holding up reasonably good. The issue with the boys is they try not to deal with it, they try and avoid it, they don't want to talk about it. They don't want to read the papers about it, they don't want to do counselling. They've gone to counselling and they don't want to continue with that. Personally I don't want to go to counselling. I think I might have to eventually. It's just a nightmare. I'm trying to be as strong a supporter for the kids as possible. Unfortunately, I don't know if I'm doing a good job of it. But I will say the support we've had from family and friends and 700 mourners at the funeral has been nothing short of miraculous."

Adamson: "What was she like? She was your wife and the mother of your children."

Matthews: "I suppose the majority of her focus was around the children and the family. Her involvement in the life saving club. You've got to read the hundreds of thousands of cards in there. I mean, the support and help she gave Michelle when Michelle was going through a divorce because her husband was being a dickhead about it. So she supported her. And then Michelle came down and supported us. Carolyn, she'd just help anybody."

Adamson: "How much do you miss her?"

Matthews: "Heaps. Absolutely heaps. You just don't know what you've got until you miss it."

(Adamson recalls: "The thing that struck me the most about the interview was that when I asked him about what Carolyn was like as a person and whether he missed her, he tried to look like he cared, but he didn't have any tears. He was trying to pretend to cry, but no tears came out. It really hit home that this was a man who knew a lot more than he was letting on … that he was calculating.")

Adamson: "What happened that night?"

Matthews: "We basically walked inside. The oldest son Kenny found Carolyn on the kitchen floor."

He went on to explain in detail their vain attempts to revive Carolyn.

Adamson gently broached the interview's most important question: "Having gone through what you've gone through, you're obviously deeply upset. How do you cope with, obviously, the finger-pointing going on in your direction? Everybody says: 'Oh. it's someone you know.' How do you cope with that?"

Matthews: "We've heard rumours from other schools saying the kids done it and covering them up doesn't help. Then we heard reports of Carolyn having an affair, we've heard reports of me having an affair, we've had reports of us getting into pornography. It's just so much bullshit, you can't even go shopping without people looking. You can't even go out the front and check your letterbox without people driving past and looking. It's just a nightmare."

Adamson: "What would you say to those people?"

Matthews: "Well it's fucking obvious we didn't do it, but I know how people gossip and stuff like that, but I don't need to hear it and the kids don't need to hear it."

Adamson: "What do you say to those people pointing the finger at you?"

Matthews: "Get a life. Get a life, go to page 36 and read the funny pages. We don't need this shit at the moment. I didn't kill Carolyn and my boys didn't kill Carolyn and I believe that nobody I know killed Carolyn."

All the other TV stations had captured Matthews's damning post-court performance earlier that day, but only Adamson and Brown captured the mind-boggling encore – Matthews's red, Scotch-bloated face, hidden behind sunglasses, trying vainly to shed crocodile tears for his murdered wife, then proclaiming the innocence of the woman accused of killing her. The city of Adelaide was agog. What was this man thinking? And, more to the point, what was he hiding?

Adamson wrapped up the interview; she had everything she needed. In fact, she had far more than she could ever hope to squeeze into a TV news story. But Brown kept the camera running.

(Adamson explains: "Major Crime knew we were going down there to do the interview and they actually asked us to keep the camera rolling. Just in case we could pick up anything more. As soon as the camera was turned off, he went back to his agitated state of pacing the backyard and begging me not to make him look like an idiot on television. He seemed completely obsessed with wanting to talk about what a great person Michelle Burgess was, and what a great friend she had been to Carolyn.")

Matthews: "I wasn't unhappy with anything I said there."

"No, you've come across very well," Adamson reassured him.

"I mean, Jesus Christ, I tell you what, I don't know, you'd have to be pretty sick and twisted to have killed somebody and walk back into the same house."

Adamson didn't miss a beat: "Oh, with your kids as well."

(A decade later, she says: "As soon as he said that, it was chilling, because we knew exactly what he had done. It was just a matter of time before he was charged.")

Matthews: "Exactly. Carolyn's mum, it's just a shocker. Carolyn's brother died when he was 20, Carolyn's dad died the day before last Christmas and now she's had a daughter that's murdered. It's just getting too much. That night was the fucking scariest thing I've seen in my life. I mean, as I had to physically hold Carolyn's hair back in maximum head tilt because it was flowing forward in the blood ... I couldn't put a hand on the forehead. It was just ... Nobody told us how many times she was stabbed ..."

Adamson noticed more media gathering outside the house. She was determined to hang on to her exclusive.

"You can probably tell them to move on; that would be great," she told Kevin. But she needn't have worried. Kevin was enjoying the undivided attention of an attractive young journalist – even if she was grilling him for incriminating information.

"I'm not talking to them," he reassured her. "And to be honest, if somebody comes down and says that Jessica sent me, I'm not talking to them until you contact me first."

Brown chipped in: "You're better off just saying nothing. Don't open your mouth."

Adamson decided to wrap it up: "All right guys, thank you. Thanks Kevin, I really appreciate it." He tried to offer a handshake and she pointed out: "That's your Scotch hand."

Matthews: "Yeah, I know. I've been drinking shitloads of it."

Adamson: "I've been too and I don't have an excuse."

Within hours, Sgt Standing and other officers were at Channel 7's studios with a warrant. They viewed the tape at the studio before taking a copy.

Adamson says: "It was fascinating being there when they watched it because they're experts in being able to watch people's body language and behaviour. They, too, were struck by the fact that while he tried to look like he was crying, when he was talking to me about Carolyn, no tears were coming out."

Sgt Standing formed an immediate opinion of what he had seen: "I was in Major Crime for 22 years before I retired. I've been a detective since 1974. Kevin's the only person in my experience that has stepped up and told the media that the police had arrested the wrong person who had committed a crime against him and his family. Now, you gotta scratch your head and wonder about a guy that would go public and say that the police have arrested the wrong person for the murder of his wife. This suggests that (A) he knows who did do it and (B) perhaps there was something between him and the arrested person. It was absolutely bizarre. I think the general feeling in the public was that this bloke's got something to answer for."

CHAPTER 13

Kev and Jase

August 7, 2001 – August 29, 2001

THE SNOWBALLING media obsession with the murder case had an immediate and unexpected benefit for the Major Crime detectives. The day after Michelle Burgess's court appearance – and Kevin Matthews's appalling TV interview – Kathy Cowled's conscience and fear of arrest finally tipped her over the edge.

As the person who lit the fuse by putting her brother, David Key, in contact with Michelle – with full knowledge of what Michelle was seeking – there was every chance she could end up facing charges as well. The arrest of her brother had shaken her badly; Cowled, like so many others, had thought he was full of shit and that Michelle was just a drama queen. She never dreamt that they would actually go through with Michelle's wild threats. But the fact remained that her actions were the catalyst that brought together Carolyn Matthews's killers.

Cowled confided in friends, who urged her to go to the police before they came to her. It was an enormous struggle for the young mother, who would later be described in court by a lawyer as "intellectually limited", while a more charitable judge called her "a pretty simple woman". At 11.15am on Tuesday, August 7, 2001 – Michelle's 28th birthday – Cowled entered the Gawler police station and timidly approached Constable Craig Curtis at the front counter.

Cowled explained that she was the sister of the man charged over the West Lakes murder and she had some information about the murder. Pressed for further details, she said her brother's girlfriend had told her they had been approached by the murder victim's husband, saying the only way he could get out of their marriage was to kill her and that he was prepared to pay for it. Const. Curtis knew a break in a murder case when he heard one. He immediately contacted Major Crime and spoke to Sen. Sgt Strange. By 2pm that day, Cowled was in a police car talking to detectives Eichner and Strange at Elizabeth.

The next day, they took her statement for the record. Sgt Eichner recalls: "That's when it all became quite clear as far as the events leading up to Carolyn Matthews's murder, why they occurred and how it was done.

"We had seen the contract, when Mick Standing and Scott Duval had arrested Key, and they took a copy of it. But the real significance of it wasn't known until Kathleen Cowled spelt it out to us. We then spoke to Kathleen a number of times, (and she later gave us) writing on the back of a letter that helped us identify Michelle's handwriting."

Cowled's statement was the missing link that tied Key, Michelle and Matthews together; an independent witness whose every word would significantly boost their case. The detectives listened, spellbound, occasionally interjecting with questions as Cowled related how and why she had introduced Michelle to her brother; details of the murder contracts; and, crucially, her knowledge of Kevin Matthews's role.

AS THE POLICE dossier of evidence on Kevin Matthews grew further, so did the suspicions of the Tidswell family. On the same day Cowled made her statement, a sceptical Yvonne Tidswell was grilling Kevin Matthews at her Netley home. Two of her sons, Geoffrey and Charlie, were also there. Yvonne, who had seen the footage of Kevin at court with Colenso, asked him who he was. He told her: "He's a friend of Michelle's. The TV cameras were hassling us. I just gave him a lift to his car around the corner."

Charlie Tidswell says: "Geoffrey said to Kevin: 'Someone said you were having an affair', and he said: 'No, I heard that Carolyn's having an affair'. And mum's gone: 'What? When's Carolyn going to have time for an affair? It was all about the kids and the club.' I thought Kevin's story was pretty hard to believe.

"And as soon as I saw that hat, I thought, well, that's just proven that you're guilty. Geoffrey blasted him. (He said:) 'What the fuck were you doing? The cops told you to stay away from court.' (Kevin said:) 'No, someone said go to court.' Obviously he wanted to go anyway because if he didn't show up, she would have gone: 'Well he's not supporting me, I'll dob him in anyway'. So when I saw that, I thought: 'What are you hiding?'

So then you start thinking: 'Is he capable of doing something?' He could have been involved with anything with that callous bitch. I said to the boys: 'Have you ever seen that hat before?' (They said:) 'Oh yeah.' But they hadn't seen the 'Forever' on it. Was it R&R (rescue and resus) forever? The boys couldn't work it out."

But sufficient doubt about Kevin's exact relationship with Michelle remained in the minds of Carolyn's brothers for him to leave his mother-in-law's home in one piece. If they had even an inkling that he had caused Carolyn's death, Major Crime would have had a new homicide case on their hands. Matthews knew that too and couldn't get out of the house quickly enough; he was only there a few minutes and that same afternoon he was back on the phone to Kaylene Kenyon, asking if he and the boys could come and stay at their property – but they never arrived.

THE NEXT DAY, August 8, Jason Colenso rang Darren Burgess, who later told police: "He first spoke to my partner, Kathy. He wanted to drop some stuff off at work and meet me at work. Kathy told him to just drop the stuff and go. Then he asked to speak to me. He carried on about dropping some gear off. Some (children's) clothes. I told him if he wanted to drop anything off, to drop it off at the Goldups'."

"Who are they?" Colenso asked.

"Michelle's parents. Do you know where they live?"

"Yes … Can I ask you a personal question?"

"No, you can't ask me anything."

"Are you a Crown witness?"

"No, it's none of your business."

Darren hung up, but it would not be the last time he heard from Colenso, who was now viewing himself as Michelle's protector and "white knight".

ON AUGUST 11, mechanic Darren Bland was interviewed at Port Adelaide police station by Major Crime, and more of Michelle's life of infidelity began to emerge. It was becoming clear that she changed Beaurepaires lovers like they were bald tyres.

Bland told the detectives about his lengthy affair with Michelle and his decision to move interstate. When he had returned to Adelaide from Melbourne in 1998, he worked at the Beaurepaires store in Ridgehaven for a couple of months, transferring to Port Adelaide where he worked as assistant manager, then manager. Kevin Matthews, by now the regional manager, was his direct superior. He confirmed that he had contact with Michelle after his return to Adelaide.

Bland: "Initially, it was probably just to reaffirm that there was no more relationship to be had. I think I saw her on a couple of occasions socially when I was out – once with a mutual friend and one night we went out for drinks and I think she was there with Darren."

SC Duval asked him: "Anything of a sexual or physical nature after your return from Melbourne?"

Bland: "No."

In mid-June, 2001, Bland quit his job as manager of Port Adelaide Beaurepaires. He explained that the move was prompted by the fact that he didn't like the way the company was being run and he "didn't need the stress that was going with it at that stage". In a move that undoubtedly cost him money and career options, he moved across the driveway to take up a position as a mechanic at the Ultra Tune store.

Duval: "Did you make any observations of Kevin Matthews?"

Bland: "We were in close proximity. Kevin would be out the back or in the driveway or out the front making a lot of mobile phone calls. Up to a couple of hours a day, spread across the day."

Duval: "Was there a rumour at Ultra Tune and Beaurepaires about Kevin and Michelle having an affair?"

Bland: "I had heard talk of it, yes."

Duval: "Around this time, did you approach Kevin in relation to this affair on more than one occasion?"

Bland: "Yes. Because me and Kevin had developed a friendship over time, I didn't want (an affair with Michelle) to affect him the way I was. I told him to cease it if he was."

Duval: "Did you ever ask Kevin if he was having an affair?"

Bland: "I believe I did, yes. I believe he said he wasn't."

He went on to describe in detail the events on the day of the murder, including his confrontation with Michelle after she arrived at Beaurepaires with "a bit of a weedy-looking fellow with a bushy, messy-looking beard". Crucially, he was able to identify Key from an array of photos the police showed him, which would later help refute Michelle's claim that she was with Colenso that afternoon.

IF KEVIN MATTHEWS'S relationship with David Key had seemed odd, it had nothing on his camaraderie with new acquaintance Jason Colenso. Matthews had stayed at arm's length from Key for obvious reasons, except for their unscheduled meeting at Beaurepaires on the day of the murder. But Colenso was a different matter. "Kev" and "Jase" were now allies, even mates, united in their efforts in trying to free poor, innocent "Mish". But Matthews seemed as oblivious to Colenso's relationship with Michelle as he was to Key's; it simply didn't fit the fantasy of his "future bride". There were dozens of phone calls and text messages between Matthews and Colenso intercepted by police in the ensuing weeks. Most involved more of Matthews's self-serving rubbish, but others helped add pieces to the jigsaw the police were assembling.

AROUND EARLY to mid-August, Amanda Tidswell agreed to meet her brother-in-law for lunch at the Ramsgate Hotel at Henley Beach. She recalls: "We had been getting some really bizarre phone calls from him. He would be drunk and then not remember the conversations. He asked me to go to lunch. He wanted to talk to me about his side of things. He didn't want to eat. While we were there, he was on the phone continuously. I don't know who he was talking to, but he would get up and go out and then come back. I'd made the effort to go down there. I was very conscious that people around us were watching him. I know that, at that stage, I knew he was a suspect. But he was trying to convince me that he hadn't done anything wrong."

ON AUGUST 12, 2001, Kevin Matthews took up the Kenyons' offer of a visit to their farm to give himself and the boys time out from the growing media circus. Despite Rodney and Kaylene's belief that Kevin was having an affair, they still didn't suspect that he was connected with Carolyn's murder; it was unthinkable.

Kaylene says: "We actually believed him and told him if they needed to get away from it all, they were welcome to our house, because we lived out the back of Strathalbyn on 80 acres. I think now that he was probably wondering what we knew. So we had them up for the day for a barbecue. It was to give the boys a bit of breathing space. Our kids took them for a couple of motorbike rides. What struck me about that whole day was the alcohol he was giving the boys. The oldest was only 16. I said: 'What are you doing, Kevin? Why are you giving the boys alcohol?' And he said: 'They're all right, it's only a little bit.' I said: 'Well, Carolyn wouldn't have liked it, it wouldn't have happened if she was here.' He was drinking Scotch and he was giving them (vodka) Cruisers ... He wanted to know what we believed."

Rodney: "It was as though he wanted to know who was on his side."

Kaylene: "We felt like we were being watched and started locking up our house. We were really nervous. It turned out the police were keeping us under surveillance."

After arriving home that evening, Matthews sent Colenso the first of several text messages: "Jase have M phone me Monday I'm going spastic here."

8.45pm: "Be warned: I have been told that my phones are tapped and cops looking to set up a panzy (sic) to push a motive and possibly fabricate evidence."

8.50pm: "Got to the stage where I'm getting pissed off with the bullshit. Both you and I know that Michelle is innocent. DB set her up."

The following day, Major Crime had arranged for an expert podiatrist to examine David Key at the Adelaide Remand Centre. Sara Jones, a Senior Lecturer in Podiatry and Deputy Head of the School of Physiotherapy at the University of SA, examined Key's feet, making notes of his foot structure in relation to his stance and gait. Later that month, at SAPOL's Central Crime Scene Section at Netley, she examined a pair of Great Divide brand, Size 9, six-eyelet lace-up boots with synthetic uppers and steel supporting shanks in the insoles. She re-examined them on September 7, 2001, and compared the shoe-wear characteristics with Key's feet. In terms of toe position, heel position, foot size and foot shape, the wear on the boots was consistent with foot impressions obtained from David Key. If any doubts remained about linking Key to the murder scene, these examinations dispelled them.

Also on August 13, Matthews called Colenso and told him to be sure to pass on his messages to Michelle, asking if she was interested in "going fishing at Semaphore jetty" and to let him know if she said yes or no. Colenso also told him he had spoken to a couple of people and the consensus was that Key was "fucked".

The reference to Semaphore jetty, which would become a fixation with Matthews in the following weeks, appears to relate to some sort of agreement struck during their final meeting at that location, shortly before Michelle's arrest.

At 2.20pm, Matthews texted Colenso: "I am loosing it and almost suisidal. Can't help it. In the dark. At the monmoent. Lost a wiff and cops blaming best friend. (sic)"

2.31pm: "Very drunk at moment. Starting to loop the plot. Sorry. Shit happens, then some."

Matthews received a text from his son, Kenny: "Pick up Kenny from school."

Matthews replied: "When?"

Shane Matthews texted: "Are you going to pick us up?"

Eventually, he replied that he was on his way. Mercifully, he was already too late.

Shane: "Vickie (Kevin's sister) has got us."

Matthews: "Life is like a box of chocolates."

At 4.43pm that day, Colenso called Michelle and passed on Kevin's message.

Michelle: "Well, do you want to know what I know? They knew straight away that Dave's done it."

Colenso said he'd "checked out a couple of things" but couldn't tell her over the phone. He'd been to see Key, who wanted to know whether Michelle had talked. Michelle, clearly already comfortable with jail vernacular, said three or four people were "going Crown" on her. She told him that all she had said in prison was that Colenso was with her when she left Beaurepaires Port Adelaide and they drove back to Elizabeth to pick up the kids. She said Key was in another car with some guys she didn't know. Colenso talked about bashing Crown witnesses. Michelle wanted to know why Colenso had been hanging around with Matthews. But Colenso changed the subject, saying: "think of AC/DC's favourite hit, Bon Scott sang it." (A detective has noted: "Dirty deeds done dirt cheap?" in the transcript of this conversation.) Colenso told Michelle he'd been to see some friends and "that's been arranged". The implication is chilling.

5.05pm: Michelle called Colenso, who said he'd been out in the Commodore looking for people. He told her that everyone knew that Michelle was his girlfriend except Key (and, apparently, Kevin Matthews).

5.31pm: Matthews called Colenso. Colenso said he'd spoken to Michelle. Matthews said Key was guilty and Colenso agreed. Matthews said he didn't see how Michelle was involved. Colenso said he told Michelle about going fishing and she said no.

Matthews: "So no Semaphore jetty?"

Colenso: "Yeah."

Matthews: "She knows what it means if she says yes to Semaphore jetty. It's up to her. To be honest, I'm not fussy either way."

5.38pm: Matthews called Colenso and again asked whether Michelle was definite about not being interested in fishing at Semaphore. Colenso said she didn't want to do anything. "She said to say ditto."

Kevin said that meant he knew she was innocent. "Michelle has done so much for Carolyn and the boys." He again asked about fishing at Semaphore jetty and said Michelle had promised to go fishing. But Colenso told him she "didn't want to do anything stupid".

Matthews texted a family friend at 6.35pm: "Please tell your wife how much I appreciate you both and the support. I weaken at times and need it. Thanks and we love you all."

6.37pm: Matthews texted Michelle's phone, even though he knew it was in Colenso's possession: "The bad wolf told red riding hood lift your top so I can suck your tits. No she said, lifting her skirt, eat me like a fucking BG."

Ten minutes later, after his erection had apparently subsided, Matthews again texted Colenso: "Have her call me tomorrow bud."

On August 14, Michelle appeared in Adelaide Magistrates Court again. Crown Prosecutor Kos Lesses told the court she was "directly involved in the offence and assisting the primary offender".

"It was calculated and premeditated. There are ongoing investigations which may involve the possible arrest of a third offender, who may be known to this lady," he told the court. Burgess again sought bail, which was again refused because of the risk that her release could jeopardise Major Crime's investigation.

On August 15, at 11.30am, Matthews texted Colenso: "Tell her to be strong. She has nothing to hide. Don't let Dave or any lies he may say about her get the better of her."

2.19pm: Matthews called Colenso, who told him that Key had told him to "take out the witnesses". Matthews returned to his favourite rant, about how helpful Michelle was to Carolyn.

The police were concerned by Colenso's casual threats. Darren Burgess recalls: "They offered me witness protection on August 17 – the Friday night before my friend Andrew's wedding, which I was going to be in with Darren Bland. I'd just got to mum's and Mick rang me and asked where I was. He said: 'Stay there, don't go anywhere, I need to talk to you.' He came over by himself. He said they'd intercepted a phone call from Michelle to Colenso about what they planned to do. He said: 'We're going to offer you witness protection. We'll put you into protective custody and come and get you when we need you.'

"I said: 'I've got a job and I'm not going to run and hide. That's not me. I've got a wedding tomorrow and I'm the best man. I'm not going to let these people run my life.'

"I'd planned to stay at Andrew's for the night but Mick said: 'No, you can't do that. I'll pick you up and take you to the wedding tomorrow. There might only be a one per cent chance but I'm not willing to take that chance. I'll drive Kathy home to pick up what she needs and bring her back to your mum's place.'

"I've got a feeling the police were there at the wedding as well. Colenso rang Kathy that night and left a message on her voicemail, laughing."

Sgt Standing recalls: "I was very concerned about Darren's safety, it was a big issue. On the weekend he was best man at his mate's wedding, we had pretty strong evidence that there was going to be an attempt on his life that weekend. I recall taking him and his partner to various places to make sure they were safe. We took it very seriously, we couldn't afford not to. Just because David Key was in custody didn't mean the contract had expired."

At 3.21pm on August 17, Matthews called Colenso to confirm with Michelle that "a month's salary is still OK".

4.47pm: Michelle asked Colenso to do an "urgent job" for her. She spoke cryptically, acutely aware that they were not the only parties to the conversation: "Remember I was telling you about ... he's going to the other place as well ... I want you to be careful because the thing here is they're going to arrest a third person."

She told him that "the thing that we have been discussing needs to happen on the day I go to court as a back-up".

"I've spoken to a few people about that," Colenso assured her.

Michelle emphasised that if it was not done that day, "she'll never get out". She said there were a couple of things she needed to discuss on "a proper line" and she also said yes to Kevin's question about a month's salary.

5.01pm: Matthews called Colenso, who told him he had Michelle on the other line. "Ask her: Semaphore jetty, mobile, yes or no? She'll know what I mean. I want to know if she wants to go fishing or not."

The call was immediately terminated by prison staff – inmates are banned from speaking to third parties via authorised phone calls.

5.26pm: Matthews called Colenso and told him "about his burdens", police notes say.

Crown Prosecutor Steven Millsteed later made reference in court to a phone conversation that evening between Michelle and Colenso: "There was a reference to Key and Colenso says: 'It's Jason here, not Dave. I bet you regret meeting him.' Burgess says: 'Fuckin' oath.' Colenso laughed. Burgess said: 'I'd like to thank your (Key's) sister.' Colenso says: 'Yeah, isn't she a fuckin' idiot? Bright spark. And my prints are on that too.' Burgess: 'On what?' Colenso: 'That contract.' Burgess: 'Hey?' Colenso: 'On the contract, my prints are on that.' Burgess: 'So are mine.' Colenso: 'Mmmm. What are we going to do? What are we going to do?' And the conversation petered out."

6.21pm: Michelle and Colenso discussed Wednesday's court appearance.

Colenso later told Matthews that Michelle had received a letter from Key, and she "feels sick" whenever she hears from him.

6.34pm: Michelle called Colenso and asked him to "go and find Dave and find out what he's been saying".

Michelle had good reason to be worried about Key – he had been saying plenty. In 2003, a man who was an inmate of Adelaide Remand Centre in August 2001 approached police to give a statement about Key. By that time, he was a free man and was not looking to cut himself any deals. He just "wanted to help". The tale Key told him was a mixture of fact and fantasy – his stories would change as his allegiances shifted over the next couple of years.

The inmate told police he had met Key in August 2001 and they shared a cell in the reception area for about 2½ months. Key would boast about the murder but, like most people who knew Key, the inmate dismissed the stories as bullshit – at least until Key was actually charged with murder. Later they shared another cell and when Key received three letters he couldn't read, he asked his cellmate to read them to him. The first was from Kevin Matthews, advising Key to keep his mouth shut – the job had been well organised and well planned and he would see him when he got out. The letter also said if he wanted money or cigarettes, to ring him. The second letter was from Michelle. With typically flawed logic, it said that with Carolyn out of the way, they could now take care of Kevin and get on with their lives. She told Key she loved him, missed him and would be in to see him. On the same day, he received a letter from Colenso, which explained that he was taking care of Michelle and he would take care of any problems; they would both be in to see him soon.

Key's former cellmate wasn't the only one who talked to the police. Another man, a convicted rapist, was interviewed at Holden Hill police station by SC Kern on August 23, 2001 about recent conversations he'd had with Key.

They had met in the kitchen in B Division at Yatala Prison in January 2001, before Key was transferred to Port Augusta Prison. He knew him as a burglar, car thief and amphetamine user who would constantly filch cigarettes. Their paths crossed again in August 2001, in G Division at Yatala.

The inmate noticed Key's name on a cell door and, when he squinted through the peep hole, Key immediately asked for a cigarette. The man told Key to be cautious about what he said because the prisoner in the next cell was disgraced magistrate and convicted paedophile Peter Liddy. They talked for an hour and again on Saturday, August 18, 2001, through the bottom grille on Key's cell door. Key volunteered full details of the murder, including his role in it. The inmate immediately returned to his cell and took notes.

The following day, Key gave further details, including his cunning plans to stymie the evidence police had gathered. He'd organised a fake receipt to show that he had bought his boots at a garage sale the week after the murder – garage sales, of course, being the type of businesses which always issue receipts for transactions – and when police had checked his feet and gait, crafty Key said he had walked differently to throw them off track.

He had also organised an alibi for the night of the murder, involving a party near Michelle's home and half a dozen people had promised to tell police he was there. Key was clearly proud of his efforts; he would be a regular Perry Mason by the time the case went to trial. It was also more than enough for Key's latest confidante – the next day he was in a police interview room recounting every word.

AT 7.32PM ON AUGUST 19, Matthews sent a text to Michelle's phone (which he knew was in Colenso's possession): "Tried to phone. See you 9am. Fuck I miss you."

8.11pm: "Tell her I'm thinking of her and love her."

8.13pm: "Massive heartache. Waiting from 9am to 11am Let M know."

8.20pm: "Will phone back in 30 minutes."

9pm: "Why Michelle phone you twice and not me? Whatever."

9.33pm: Colenso told Matthews that Michelle couldn't talk to him because of MJ (presumably an unidentified person's initials). They decided to get Michelle to call Kevin the next day.

9.38pm: Matthews sent a text to Colenso: "Jase don't be offended but want to know, are you interested in M? Please don't take offence and be honest mate. Text reply buddy."

Colenso's reply – which is not divulged in police records – seemed to satisfy the easily placated Matthews, who replied:

9.56pm: "Cool. Speak to you after court Wednesday. Forget tomorrow bud."

The police believed that there was every possibility that, despite their stern warnings of dire consequences, Jason Colenso was planning to do something very stupid on Monday, August 20, 2001.

Sgt Standing rang Darren Burgess the day before and told him: "It's supposed to happen on Monday while you're at work and we're going to put a few things in place. A couple of cars will follow you to work and the Elizabeth police will be doing regular patrols past the business."

Darren recalls: "My cousin Kym came to see me and told me he would not let anyone harm me. He brought a bloke into work who was so big that he had turn sideways and duck to walk through the door. Kym said, 'This bloke here lives in the area. Anyone gives you a hard time, he will be around here quick-smart. He won't let anyone hurt a Burgess'."

Beaurepaires also hired a security guard. Police cars cruised slowly past the business all day. The tension was high, but the day was an incident-free anti-climax. The next morning, the same arrangements were in place. But the security guard assigned on this day was unaware of the circumstances. Darren brought her up to speed and told her: 'If he (Colenso) turns up, I'll talk to him and you get on the phone to the police.'

Finally, Colenso arrived. The white VP Commodore cruised past Beaurepaires. The local police, unaware of this, kept up their patrols. Colenso came past again and again. He suddenly pulled into the Beaurepaires car park, got out of the car and strode aggressively towards the showroom.

"That's him, get on the phone, I'll do what I can to keep him here until the police get here," Darren calmly told the guard as he watched Colenso approach. Colenso walked up to Darren and began gesticulating and ranting about family photos being cut up and sent to Michelle's parents. But this was just small talk; Colenso had a point to make.

"If this makes it to court, you won't," he told Darren.

"What are you talking about?" Darren asked.

Colenso repeated the threat.

"Oh. OK," Darren said, while thinking: "Who does this idiot think he is?"

Satisfied that he had delivered his message, Colenso turned and walked out of the showroom. There was still no sign of the police. "What can I do to keep him here?" Darren asked himself. He wanted this clown locked up, right now.

"How about you go and earn yourself some money instead of driving someone else's car around," he called after him. Colenso halted and took the bait.

"What are you talking about?"

"That's my car you're driving."

"No, it's not – Michelle gave it to me."

"Well, it's my money that bought that car."

"I'm going to come over there and smack you one," said Colenso, enraged.

"Well Jason, I'm the one that's standing here, you're the one that's getting ready to go. Go get yourself a job and get your own car."

Colenso – who had two women in the car with him – was speechless. He jumped in the car, tossed a parting "fuck you" out the window, spun his tyres and sped off. When the local police finally arrived minutes later, the senior officer said to Darren: "Well, you'll go into witness protection now, won't you?"

But Darren, who was fuming at their slow response, retorted: "No, I was trying to keep him here. If you'd done your job and got here fast, you'd have him by now. How about you go out and get him?"

Sgt Standing rang him a short time later and congratulated him on his efforts. Still pumped with adrenalin, Darren said: "How about you come and pick me up and we'll go and get him together? I'm fucking sick of it. I want to be there when you get him."

Sgt Standing sighed. "Darren, just go home."

WHILE COLENSO had been building up the courage to confront Darren Burgess, his phone was bleating with pathetic text messages from the lovesick Kevin Matthews.

12.25pm: "Jason, tell M my sister is supporting her as well please."

2.25pm: "Message for M from Chook. Says he loves her heaps and will see her on Thursday. Let me know answer and I will pass on for her."

2.28pm: "Please ask Michelle to write to me please. Tell Michelle a beginning, a middle and if she wants it, an end. Just be strong. She will be happy one day, I know it."

4.25pm: "Taken four Valium to get some sleep. Will phone you AM. Goodnight. Tell Michelle sweet dreams."

At 4.31pm, Colenso and Michelle had a phone conversation in which he told her about his earlier confrontation with her ex-husband.

5.15pm: Matthews called Colenso, who boasted about the "fright" he'd given Darren Burgess. But Matthews was more concerned about Colenso passing on the message from Chook that he loves Michelle with all his heart.

5.54pm: Matthews texted Colenso: "Will try to stay awake until you phone me. Need to know what Michelle said or any messages. Tell her I'm sorry I got her involved in this nightmare."

5.58pm: Matthews texted Colenso: "Also am following up the issue of the screw. Am going to fix it. He will never do it again. Fact: Future looks better now."

6.31pm: Michelle called Colenso, who told her the message from Kevin about Chook. They discuss talking to Key. Michelle said if she talked to Key, she wouldn't get out.

At the Gepps Cross Hotel at 7.45pm that evening, Colenso – sitting slack-jawed in front of a poker machine – was oblivious to the two police officers who strode up and stood either side of him. As they frogmarched Colenso from the hotel, Senior Constable Robert White and Constable Paul Ward told him he was being arrested for intimidating a Crown witness. He was handcuffed and put in the rear of their police vehicle. The officers conducted a preliminary interview in the car, advising him of his rights and that he would be taken to Elizabeth police station. He was belligerent and full of complaints.

White: "I warn you that anything you may say may be taken down and may be used in evidence. Do you understand that? What are you doing there, Jason?"

Colenso: "This is breaking my fucking hands. Right, OK, there's no need for this, OK?"

White: "Mate, when I put the cuffs on you, they were fine."

Colenso: "They are not fine, all right? You got … fucking holding the fucking chair down, all right?"

White: "I put it that way so you are secure."

Colenso: "Mate, I am secure in a fucking cop car, all right? You know that and I know that, OK? I gave you no hassle, no nothing and I get my circulation …"

White: "So what are you saying? That the cuffs are too tight, are they?"

Colenso: "Yes, they are way too tight."

White: "Fine, all right, I'll loosen them up for you shortly."

A few minutes later, after the cuffs had been loosened and Colenso had finally stopped whining, he asked: "Who's got my car?"

White: "Jason, that's going to be looked after by police. As prisoner's property, it's going to be conveyed to Elizabeth police station."

Colenso: "So are youse going to do your usual trick?"

White: "What's that, mate?"

Colenso: "Get me in the cells, give me a kicking while I'm handcuffed?"

White: "Why would we do that, mate?"

Colenso: "Come on, you're talking to a bloke from the old school, not fucking today's …"

White shook his head and cut him off: "You've been watching too much TV, mate."

They arrived at Elizabeth police station at 8.15pm, and Colenso was formally interviewed. (The transcript does not identify which officer is speaking.)

"This is in relation to an incident on Monday, August 20 at Beaurepaires, Elizabeth. What can you tell me about that matter?"

Colenso: "Well, first I was at Midas because I had to get a mag wheel. I got a card and a quote there. I had a phone call from my girlfriend. She was pretty upset about all the lies that had been said. I seen Darren there and I spoke to Darren because he claimed in court that …"

"Darren who, mate?"

"Burgess. Claims that his two kids were in the car when I got arrested with David Key in that high-speed chase, right? And I confronted him about the lie and he reckons that Michelle was with us as well and he has written it in court to gain custody of the kids from his ex-wife Michelle. I've got documents from the police that it was just me, Dave and Trevor that got arrested that day. So he's perjured himself. And I spoke to him about that today … When I left Midas I was about to turn right and I seen Darren standing there, you know, like, arms folded, thinking, you know, in the middle of the showroom floor. So I went around there and stood at the door and spoke to him. There was a security guard there and I put the allegations towards him about the lies he'd said. I said to him: 'This won't even make it to court'. I said to him, you know, we'll get the kids back through the court. Because he perjured himself, he lied."

"You say 'we'll get the kids back'. Who do you mean, 'we'?"

"Me and Michelle."

"Who is Michelle to you?"

"A very good friend."

"Can you remember the exact conversation at Beaurepaires?"

"Just that Darren was trying to egg me on and trying to get me fired up but it wouldn't work because I just … I just told him … because he, like … Michelle's mum and dad, he sent a parcel to Michelle with all the kids' photos … with Michelle and the kids all cut up, you know? And I said to him: 'Fucking what's the go there?' (It is believed that the pictures were sent by another family member, not Darren Burgess.) I said, I said, I said: 'Where do you get off taking two kids to a psychiatrist trying to fuck 'em up in life and stopping them from seeing their mother?

"There was no conversation about that Carolyn Matthews or nothing, it was just about the kids … I can't understand where you guys are coming from. I didn't know he was a Crown witness and if I had known that, I wouldn't have went near him … I'd never touch him. I know better. Because when Michelle and I used to drop the kids off, so he could have weekend access, he would actually intimidate us. Wouldn't let us try and leave the car or nothing."

"When you refer to Michelle and the kids you say 'we'. Do you have a relationship with Michelle?"

"Nup."

"You've just been there as a friend, is that right?"

"Yep, helped her out. Darren interrogates the children to try and find out who I am because when (his son) comes back he's shaken up because his old man's telling him his mother's a murderer and things like that.

In my eyes, that's not on, right? You're innocent until you're proven guilty."

"You seem to have taken this photo business with the kids to heart. Can you explain what's in that?"

"I love them kids. I been with them kids as well. Taking (the boy) … kicking a football with (the children)."

"How long have you known the kids for?"

"Six weeks, maybe more. They're good kids, you know. I've got no kids of my own. When I was looking after Michelle when Dave got locked up. And I sort of, like, bonded."

"How does it make you feel that Michelle is where she is?"

"She's innocent and it does irate (sic) me. And when it comes to trial and they finally realise that, we can sue the arses off of youse. You've got Blandy from Port Adelaide and the other woman – I don't know who she is – but they're all saying Michelle had an affair with Kevin, right? If you were to really do your homework … Look and think: these four people all know each other and they have all got a grudge against Michelle. You know what I mean? It's just … fuck, you don't need to be an Einstein to work that out."

"When did you become involved in this?"

"As soon as Dave got arrested, he rang me and asked me to look after Michelle, which I did … kept an eye on her. She was going through a hard time and every time the police came around and tore the place up whenever they fucking felt like it, Michelle looked towards me. And they've denied her rights so many times it's not funny."

"Did Dave ask you to do anything in particular (for Michelle)?"

"He said to have fun – but I said no."

"What do you mean, have fun?"

"Exactly that and then he hung up, so I don't know. He wanted to know where the VN was. I said: 'Michelle's parents have got it.' And he said: 'What about the house?' And I said: 'It's already been vacated, all Michelle's gear has been taken over to Michelle's parents' house.' So he said: 'Oh, OK, no worries, have fun' and the phone cut off. I haven't heard from him for weeks."

"You're alleged to have said to Darren Burgess today: 'Well if it makes it to court, you won't make it to court'."

"No, no, no. I said, I said: 'All this bullshit won't even make it to court. It'll all be thrown out."

"You deny that?"

"I fucking deny big-time on that."

The "big-time" denials continued, but to no avail; Colenso was charged with attempting to prevent a person from attending court as a witness. He was deposited in the cells at Elizabeth police station, to appear in Elizabeth Magistrates Court the next day. Police also believed that Colenso had a baseball bat in the boot of his car at the time he made the threat.

AN ACCUSED armed robber who we'll call Emily was extradited from Perth to Adelaide, arriving at the city watch-house on August 4, 2001. The following afternoon, she was let out for four hours to mix with other prisoners in the foyer area of the cells. One of the three other women was Michelle Burgess. Emily later told police that on the first night, over tea and coffee, they had the obligatory discussion about the crime each of them was accused of.

The next day, Monday, Emily went to court and was remanded in custody, along with Michelle. Emily was transferred to Adelaide Women's Prison at Northfield and, after two days, was moved to A-wing and given a cell of her own. Another two days later, she saw Michelle again. Michelle said she'd been in the infirmary before moving to C-wing for a couple of days. She said she had moved out of C-wing because she was having problems with another prisoner and was instead allocated a cell in A-wing.

Michelle and Emily became friends and began spending time together each day; they saw TV stories about Michelle's arrest. Michelle explained that she had moved on from her last boyfriend and was now with a man named Jason Colenso. But they were having some issues and she was often in tears over her frustration at being locked up. Michelle was paranoid about her cell being bugged but, after about a week, she began to relax in Emily's presence. They were both lying on the beds in Emily's cell after lunch one afternoon when Michelle volunteered that David Key had "done it" and it was quite brutal. She claimed Key had come to her house after the murder and she had "freaked out" and washed his clothes. She began telling Emily about her affair with Kevin and included lurid details. Emily had no interest in this sort of thing and politely told Michelle she needed to have a sleep. Michelle was so friendly she even arranged for a man named Don to offer to be Emily's bail guarantor – and he duly turned up in court with Colenso when she appeared on Monday, August 20, 2001. When she returned to the prison, Michelle told her she was stressed because Jason had been harassing her ex-husband for being a Crown witness and for stopping Michelle from seeing their kids. When Emily returned from court the following day, Michelle was deeply distressed because Jason had now been arrested for harassing a Crown witness. She feared that one of the conditions of her home-detention bail would be that she not see Jason. She had also lost all patience with her ex-husband and really hated him.

Emily later told police that Michelle joined her at 6pm to watch the evening news. When she saw the report on Jason, she said she thought that she was now "sunk" and was expecting Major Crime to "pull something big" on her in court on Thursday. Michelle moved the conversation on to the murder and admitted she knew more than she had been letting on. Michelle went on to describe the conspiracy and the murder itself in chilling detail, fully implicating herself in the crime. Conveniently, though, she placed herself in the car outside the Matthews house while Kev committed the murder. And yet, she was able to recount Carolyn's terrible death, literally blow by blow, and seemed to take great satisfaction from it. She told Emily that if she didn't get home detention bail, she would consider an escape bid because she no longer had Jason to help her. There was also the possibility that she would flee interstate using Kevin Matthews's speedboat.

Emily couldn't listen to another word. She felt physically sick from listening to Michelle's chilling description of the murder. Another prisoner asked her if she was OK and she explained what had happened. Within minutes, Emily was transferred to a different wing of the prison.

A Correctional Services Officer later told police that at 10.50pm on August 21, 2001, she was working in the Movements Area when (an inmate) called out to her. She said: "Miss, Emily's freaking out. She needs to get out of here. Michelle's told us everything about the murder ... how she did it, what the lady's face looked like and when she did it."

Emily had locked herself in her room, but was persuaded to go to a room with a Prison Manager to discuss the incident. When they sat down, the young woman began shaking and burst into tears. Through her sobs, she explained what she'd been told and said: "I don't want to see her and I can't go back into A-wing. I feel sick."

Emily was released on home detention the following day, to live with Colenso's associate Don in Davoren Park. By the time she arrived at his home, Michelle had already left messages for her on his answering machine. But Michelle was too late – and Major Crime duly took Emily's statement.

JASON COLENSO had appeared in Elizabeth Magistrates Court that morning. Crown Prosecutor Robyn Cork asked that the case be moved to the Adelaide Magistrates Court so it could be heard in the same court as the "closely related" case involving Michelle Burgess. He was remanded in custody. Now only Kevin Matthews remained free.

But amid Michelle's confession and Colenso's court appearance that day, Matthews was dealing with more important personal issues. Police records list another string of text messages and, while the replies are not listed, his motivations are clear and predictable – money and sex.

10.46am: Matthews sent a text to solicitor Chris Patterson: "Chris how are you going with Carolyn's last pay cheque and the three MLC claims and two super claims? Can't understand the hold up. Kevin Matthews."

7.54pm: Matthews sent a text to an unknown mobile phone number: "I love my wife but am so lonely. Female friendship, is that wrong?"

8.01pm: Matthews to same unknown number: "Hello I'm trying not to get arrested as it is. At least 25–30 will do. I'm serious."

8.23pm: "Hello I'm the gingerbread man. I have to deal with wife's murder, rumours and a friend being charged. All I need now is them to charge them or Nat to top it off."

8.28pm: "Hey, the way things are going and the corrupt investigation, will you visit me behind the glass wall? Don't believe what you hear. I miss and love you all. Fact."

8.46pm: "PS my phone and mobile as well as home bugged so beware when talking about the large shipment. You know what I mean, the one with school crayons."

9.27pm: Text to Chris Patterson: "Chris need last pay cheque and insurance to pay bills. What's hold up?"

And as the month wore on, Matthews's desperation escalated.

August 26, 10.06pm: Matthews sent a text to an unknown number: "Got me sitting next to an eligible 25–35 at the wedding? No bushpigs! Bodgie."

August 27, 6.50pm: Another text to Chris Patterson: "You did not phone as promised regarding my claims for Carolyn's three life and two super claims. I don't understand why they are not straight forward. No one is talking to me."

7.07pm: Text to Chris Patterson: "Chris, Judith, Carolyn's partner just told me you have not requested Carolyn's last pay cheque. I need this $1980 plus the cash in the draw. What's going on?"

August 28, 2.21pm: Matthews called Michelle's mother, Angela Goldup. She told him Michelle "didn't get out". She asked Kevin not to call any more. Kevin asked Angela to tell Michelle he had been in contact with her (Angela). Angela told Kevin to trust her and that if she needed to call him, she would.

11pm: Matthews's text to Chris Patterson: "Please help me ASAP. I need funds even in dribs and drabs."

August 29: Matthews sent a text to a young woman, from the Semaphore Surf Life Saving Club, who we'll call Joanne. The first message he sent her, according to police, is cryptic, and ends with "a kiss from one sexy person to another".

She replied: "Who is this?"

He replied: "A friend who cares for you as a friend. Have you dropped that deadbeat boyfriend yet? Hey just trying to put a smile on your face, don't get too excited. It's Bodgie."

Joanne: "How you going Flash, long time no see."

A few minutes later, Matthews texted another friend: "Dale, have you got Hayley's mobile number? I met her at Troy's grand final barbecue last year. She was the nutter."

Dale: "No."

That afternoon, Joanne sent a text to Matthews: "I sent you a message last week to your old number. I'm still with my boyfriend. How are you going? I've been thinking of you."

Matthews: "I'm struggling. Did not mean to pry in your personal life. In our last heart to heart you were not happy. I care and you deserve the best."

Joanne: "Thank you. I've been thinking of you too and how this tragic mess must be upsetting you."

Matthews: "I've done nothing wrong. Please believe I would not hurt a fly."

Joanne: "You are not prying. I've said this to you before, if you need to talk or need help with anything just give me a call. I was never ever in doubt Bodgie."

Matthews: "Sounds good. I will talk to you soon. Let you go now darling love you heaps as a treasured friend. We will get together soon for a drink. Let me know when you're free. My shout. Sweet dreams."

Joanne: "Love you too Bodgie. I will see you very soon."

Matthews texted her again late that evening: "Each time your name appears on my screen I smile like this. How happy you make me. Guess where I'm going next week? Pitjantjatjara Lands, northwest of Marla, sat to thurs, have to take sleeping bag and pillow."

For the Major Crime detectives, this development was a concern. Their unstable final suspect was leaving town, apparently bound for a remote location where they would be unable to monitor him. What was he up to now?

CHAPTER 14

The third offender

September 1, 2001 – September 26, 2001

PETER CAMPAIGN, the president of Semaphore Surf Life Saving Club who had spoken so eloquently at Carolyn's funeral, planned Kevin Matthews's trip to the APY Lands and was to accompany him. As a public servant with many decades of experience working with Aboriginal issues, he had extensive knowledge of, and an abiding love for, the culture and heritage of the Aboriginal people; he had strong links with the people of the APY Lands and believed it was the perfect place for Kevin to find some peace and quiet.

Peter was one of Kevin's staunchest supporters. Not for one minute did he entertain the notion that "Bodgie" could have had anything to do with his beloved wife's death. He'd known them both too well for too long – Kevin since he was a Nipper and Carolyn since she'd joined the club as a teenager. Peter did everything he could to help the family, assisting with their finances, helping arrange the clean-up of the crime scene so the family could move back in and defending Kevin to anyone who would listen. He hoped the trip would give Kevin some respite and distraction from his grief, and also escape the pressures of the ongoing murder investigation. Kevin agreed to the trip – he was more than happy to put some distance between himself and the Major Crime detectives.

But before they could leave as planned on Saturday, September 1, SC Duval called Matthews at 10.30am and asked him to view a photo ID of the three knives found outside the house on the night of the murder. Matthews told him he wanted his solicitor, Bill Morris, present. It was ironic that he was finally insisting on legal representation for a procedure which was routine and unlikely to incriminate him. He would have been much better served calling in the lawyers for his two earlier police interviews, when he would have been advised to say absolutely nothing. The three men met at Port Adelaide police station at 12.04pm.

Morris: "What is the purpose of today?"

Duval: "To show Kevin a photo ID pack and to identify some knives found at the scene."

Matthews: "Do they have blood on them?"

Duval: "Some of them could. I can't guarantee that they haven't as they are straight from the forensic science centre."

Morris: "Are you all right with that, Kevin?"

Matthews: "I'll see how I go."

Duval: "Before I start, I'll advise you that this interview will be video-recorded and I advise you, you do not have to answer any questions if you do not wish to do so. Do you understand?"

Morris: "Why is he being cautioned? Is he a suspect or a witness?"

Duval: "At this time, because he is being cautioned, he is considered a suspect."

Morris: "In that case, can I have a talk with him?"

Duval: "Sure. I'll ensure your conversation is confidential and check that the tapes are not working."

SC Duval left the room and returned after the pair had consulted, knowing full well what the response would be.

Morris: "My client advises me that he has been cautioned in the past. He didn't appreciate until being advised today that he is considered a suspect with respect to the murder of his wife. Given those circumstances, in light of what you said prior to the interview – that he was going to be cautioned – I have advised him of what a caution is and what his rights are. And he wishes to exercise those rights and declines to answer any questions or participate in a video. After he has instructed me, and subject to obtaining a copy of the statements he has given to date, he will reconsider his decision. He is concerned to assist the police in the investigation of the murder of his wife but wants to exercise his own legal rights at the same time."

Interview over; Kevin Matthews would no longer bumble his way through any more police interrogations. At 4.30pm that day, Jason Colenso called Matthews, who dramatically announced he was now a murder suspect and would be going away for a week.

Exactly what occurred on that trip to the APY Lands is unlikely to ever be known. Kevin Matthews has no reason to reveal it, and Peter Campaign – who would eventually accept the awful truth – has said he will never publicly comment on the case. Other surf club members who are close to him say that Matthews's betrayal was one of the most devastating events of Campaign's life. Matthews and Campaign returned to Adelaide on Thursday, September 6 and, the following morning, the Major Crime detectives prepared to make their final arrest. They rang Charlie Tidswell to warn him Kevin's arrest was imminent. Charlie tracked down his nephew Daniel at the Royal Show that day and quietly told him what was happening. In a subdued voice, Daniel replied: "Oh, OK," but didn't seem shocked. He would be going to Yvonne's house in Netley to avoid the media frenzy the family feared would now erupt.

At 9.25am on Friday, September 7, 2001, the Major Crime team arrived at Nambucca Ave. Did they have enough evidence to convict Kevin Matthews of his wife's murder? There was no smoking gun and never would be. But the circumstantial evidence that they had compiled was compelling. There was little chance of gleaning more from the phones and Kevin was sticking by his story; it was time to make their move, before he decided to take any more holidays. Kenny and Shane were also at home with their grandmother, Yvonne. Kevin Matthews greeted the officers at the front door and stepped outside to speak to detectives Keane and Eichner.

Matthews: "How are you?"

Eichner: "How you going, all right?"

Matthews: "What can I do for you, gentlemen?"

Keane: "Firstly, you're aware that we are police officers from the Major Crime Investigation Section."

Matthews: "Yep."

Keane: "My name is Keane." He nodded towards his partner. "Detective Sergeant Eichner. And we've been involved in the investigation into the murder of your wife Carolyn."

Matthews: "Yes."

Keane: "All right, I want you to listen very carefully now Kevin, all right?"

Matthews: "Yes."

Keane: "Because I'm now arresting you on suspicion …"

Matthews: "Are you?"

Keane: "… of being involved in the murder of your wife Carolyn."

Matthews: "That's bullshit."

Keane: "Just listen to me anyway. Now, once you are arrested, you have certain rights. Now if you'll listen to me carefully, I'll give you those rights. Understand that?"

Matthews: "Yep. Can I ring my lawyer?"

Keane: "Yep."

After his rights were fully explained, Matthews went inside the house and brought back a phone to cancel an appointment. He made another call to his friend, private investigator Brett Judd, and informed him he was about to be arrested. He interrupted the call to ask: "What am I getting arrested for?"

Keane: "As I said, you've been arrested on suspicion of being involved in the murder of your wife."

Matthews handed the phone to Keane, who explained to Judd what was happening. Matthews retrieved his cigarettes from his van after Keane gave him permission.

Keane: "All right, what do you want to tell your mother-in-law? Just say that you're coming with us? Or you can tell her what you like but we have to be with you, you see. You're under arrest. We can't just let you wander around and do things, all right?"

Matthews wasn't about to face his sons and mother-in-law. Detectives Kern and Duval, en route with a search warrant, broke the news to them a short time later before they conducted the search. Matthews was also reluctant to allow the search to go ahead, until SC Keane advised him of the warrant.

Matthews: "Yeah? Oh well."

SC Keane recalls: "He was shocked. I think he thought he was untouchable. I think he honestly believed he had nothing to do with it. He didn't want to take responsibility for his actions."

Sgt Eichner says: "I don't think he or Michelle realised the gravity of what they'd done. They were walking around in fairyland. They don't understand the amount of hurt they've caused."

Shane Tidswell says: "Kenny and I were sitting in the lounge room. Two detectives came, but that wasn't unusual, they were there every other day. I remember dad had said to us that he really didn't believe that Michelle Burgess was a part of any of this. (He said:) 'I really don't believe that, but I believe Key was.' Dad just came into the lounge room and said: 'I'll be back later.' I think Kenny and I were almost joking about him getting arrested, which might sound a bit weird. Then someone came in a few minutes later and told us he'd just been arrested. He wasn't actually arrested in front of us. He went with them and he definitely wasn't in cuffs. I don't think we were surprised. I don't remember feeling an element of surprise. It wasn't expected, but not unexpected. That was straight after he'd come back with being in the bush with Peter Campaign. I think the police didn't want him to go anywhere at all, but he did. We thought maybe it was so he didn't run away again."

Detectives Kern and Duval searched the house and seized another key piece of evidence which police were already aware of – a $100,000 insurance policy on the life of Carolyn Matthews. Detectives Eichner and Keane took Matthews to Port Adelaide police station, arriving at 9.46am. He was given permission to phone his sister, Vickie.

Brett Judd called Matthews's mobile phone to let him know that his solicitor, Bill Morris, was en route. At 11.36am, Sgt Eichner, SC Keane, Matthews, Morris and Judd gathered in the police station's video recording room. No one was expecting a lengthy interrogation. SC Keane took Matthews through his rights again. Morris said Matthews had a statement he wished to make.

Keane: "All right then, what's the situation there then, Kevin?"

Matthews: "I'm ... re ... going to take my right up and refrain from answering any ... any questions whatsoever."

Keane: "All right then, so at this stage you don't wish to answer any questions I might ask you?"

Matthews: "I will not be answering any questions."

Keane: "All right then. What I'll do is I'll just put some allegations to you and then I'll invite you to make a comment. Once again, you're not obliged to make a comment. We have received information, and it will be alleged, that you provided David Key and Michelle Burgess a photograph and details of your wife for the purposes of a contract or agreement to kill your wife. Do you wish to make any comment about that?"

Matthews: "No comment."

Keane: "We have received information, and it will also be alleged, that you met with Michelle Burgess and David Key at your place of work shortly before your wife's murder and, in the presence of Key and Burgess, you arranged to have your children taken to the video shop for the purpose of leaving your wife there alone. Do you wish to make any comment on that?"

Matthews: "No comment."

Keane: "All right, Kevin. That's all I need to put to you at this stage. We'll be taking you from here shortly. You'll be taken to the city watch-house where you'll be charged with the murder of your wife. Do you understand that?"

Matthews: "Yes."

Keane: "Is there anything else you wish to ask at this stage?"

Matthews: "No."

Morris advised the detectives that his client did not wish to be interviewed again.

Keane: "I don't envisage any reason why we would speak to Mr Matthews again."

Morris: "No, I can't see it either."

The interview wrapped up at 11.41am. At 12.15pm, Kevin William Matthews was taken to the city watch-house and, at 12.51pm, was charged with the murder of his wife, Carolyn Wendy Matthews. That afternoon, he was taken to Adelaide Magistrates Court for a five-minute appearance in front of a packed courtroom of relatives, media, detectives and curious onlookers. Matthews's arrest was the most extraordinary twist yet in this murder case.

Magistrate Grantley Harris read the murder charge to him: "It is alleged that on the 12th of July, 2001, at West Lakes Shore, you murdered Carolyn Wendy Matthews ... There's no application for bail, you are remanded in custody until (your next appearance)."

"Cool," Matthews replied cheerfully as he was led from the dock and turned to face the detectives who had arrested him six hours earlier. *The Advertiser* court reporter Simonne Reid recalls: "When Matthews said 'cool', there was a murmur that went through the court. No one could believe that he could be so cavalier about a murder charge. He actually strutted into the courtroom quite confidently, like he was walking into the pub. I don't know if that was to cover up his nerves.

"(During subsequent appearances) he always had this bravado about him. You'd imagine that if you were planning on pleading not guilty to murdering your wife, you'd be sobbing or showing some sort of emotion. He was looking at everyone, which he always did in court. I don't think he spoke during the appearance but when the magistrate said 'that's all now, you can be taken back to the cells', that's when he turned around and said 'cool'."

Members of the Semaphore Surf Life Saving Club were appalled to see Matthews in a club polo top – its logo clearly visible – in *The Advertiser*'s front-page picture the next day, which showed him being led away in handcuffs. Crown Prosecutor Kos Lesses requested that Matthews's next court appearance be on September 18, the same date as Michelle Burgess. Before the court appearance, Major Crime chief, Detective Superintendent Paul Schramm, told the media: "We are not expecting to make any further arrests in this matter."

Shane Tidswell says: "(At that stage) we didn't think (Kevin) was involved and we still spoke to him after that. Saw him at the remand centre twice. After the second time, (Kevin's mother) Irene asked us if we wanted to go in again. Kenny and I said no. I don't know what Daniel said, but he continued to see him up until the end of the year. Irene came back and said: 'I want you to write a letter to your old man saying why. You can't just not see him any more.' So we had to write these letters before she saw him the next time.

"I wrote this letter and it was full of hate. It was pretty full-on. I said: 'You had everything and threw it away and now you have nothing. I hope you hang yourself with your shoelaces'. My uncle Geoff said to me: 'The screws read the letter you sent over the phone to me.' He remembers crying, I think it was good for him to know that we were thinking the same things they (the Tidswell family) were thinking. I think he was pretty impressed with the letter, because it put us on the same page that they were."

On September 11, 2001, hours before the planes hit the World Trade Centre in New York, 13-year-old Shane Matthews was interviewed at Port Adelaide police station, with his aunt Lou Tidswell – wife of his mother's brother, Geoffrey – by his side.

Detectives Duval and Kern asked Shane about his knowledge of Michelle Burgess. He knew her as the ex-wife of one of his dad's workmates; he'd seen her at about three Beaurepaires social functions. He also recounted the events of July 12, and the fact that "nothing seemed out of the ordinary" until the boys found their mother slaughtered on the kitchen floor. And with regard to his parents' relationship: "Mum and dad generally didn't argue much at all, sometimes they had disagreements. The last time would have been about two weeks before mum passed away. I don't know what it was about."

Because he was the one who first spotted the knives in the garden, Shane also had to identify them as being from the Matthews's kitchen. An adult Shane Tidswell says: "I don't remember giving that second statement. I've suppressed a lot of my life from before. I guess it's been easier to pretend it never happened. I was still in shock for over a year afterwards. Every single night I was dreaming about mum coming back, or dad would walk into the room and mum would be standing there as well, and he'd say: 'Oh she just went away somewhere for a while.' I was having those dreams every single night for over a year after that. It still wasn't real to me. I didn't go straight into the breakdown stage. It wasn't really happening to me until I realised over a year later."

On September 18, the three accused killers appeared together for the first time in the dock of Adelaide Magistrates Court, whispering among themselves. A smirking Michelle Burgess sat between her two former lovers, surrounded by guards. Magistrate Grantley Harris was told that not all the witness statements had been handed to the trio's lawyers and the matter needed to be adjourned. Forensic evidence, pathology reports, crime scene material and police statements also still needed to be collated. On the same day, Colenso's case was also adjourned to a later date. On both the prosecution and defence sides, there was still much to be done. Ahead of them lay one of the longest and most complex criminal trials in the state's history. But while the accused trio were left to adjust to prison life, Kenny, Shane and Daniel Matthews faced a grim future without parents.

Shane says: "I did realise the first time that our family became segregated. My birthday is September 21. Before my mum's murder, it was both sides of the family, all the uncles and aunties, grandmas, grandpas, would have coffee and cake sort of thing. But then on my birthday that year, we got both sides of the family together and obviously it was after my old man had been arrested. It was very ... awkward to say the least.

"Half the family hates my old man with a passion and the other half's sort of unsure of what's going on, and at the end of the day he's still their brother and son. So it was like, after that night, I think my grandma or nanna or somebody said to me, 'we're not having group family birthdays any more'. It was too much of a big thing. If they got into it in the same room at the same time, it wouldn't have been the best thing. So the last time my whole family was together was on my 14th birthday. It was very quiet. There were a lot of things on a lot of people's minds that weren't being said. Everybody was trying not to say anything and it was just too hard."

On the same day as Shane's tense birthday gathering, Adelaide Remand Centre general manager Derek Taylor read a disturbing "fairytale" that Kevin

Matthews had written to Michelle Burgess. He immediately faxed it to Major Crime. The long, rambling and sometimes incoherent document employs simple pseudonyms. He chose Hansel for himself and Gretel for Michelle, apparently oblivious to the fact that the fairytale characters are brother and sister. SAJ is Jason, Candy is Key; Nadia would appear to be another woman whom Colenso was involved with. The "three pets" are Kevin's sons.

The letter read: "Want to tell you a story from someone who has never lied to you and never will. Once upon a time Gretel met Hansel. It does not matter how but it did happen. Hansel trusted Gretel and gave an oath and devoted his life to Gretel. He loved her beyond his wildest dreams. Gretel made the same oath. Then along came a dark day and shit happened. Gretel was hanging with another named SAJ and Hansel was suspicious but trusted Gretel and was a friend to SAJ. Hansel helped SAJ with support and money. Hansel was being used.

"What was it that SAJ said that made Hansel so angry and cheated that he wants revenge and then go to sleep. SAJ said Gretel was doing candy but candy don't know about Hansel and don't tell candy. Gretel and SAJ have been having fun. Hansel said I don't believe it. Gretel took an oath and talked of dreams. SAJ said Gretel loves it and told SAJ not to tell Hansel. SAJ said forget Gretel, she is cheap and easy. Just a cheap easy ride and loves it. SAJ also said he is also having fun with Nadia but don't tell Gretel. SAJ said he told Gretel he wanted an open relationship but Gretel said no so SAJ cheated on Gretel. SAJ said Gretel approached SAJ and he did not know about Hansel and Gretel.

"Hansel lost it and was distraught and punched the wall again. Hansel has lost all and can't understand why or what he did wrong. SAJ told Hansel that Gretel has no conscience and is not worth it. Gretel is just a good fuck, easy and cheap said SAJ. Then SAJ told Hansel: Don't worry about the cheap slut and if Gretel and candy go down, he don't care. But Hansel you have three pets to look after and you have to so fuck the other two.

"Then SAJ started bragging about how (name removed for legal reasons) gives good head and how much fun Gretel is in a lot of detail to all the other men in the room who are also on holidays. Hansel needing to go home. Hit wall again instead of SAJ. How could Gretel do this to Hansel? Was Hansel just too dumb?

"Why not just end it with Hansel? There were plenty of chances. What happened to the totally honest relationship? Was it just to keep Hansel quiet? The sad part is that Hansel still wants and loves Gretel but can't trust her and the lies. It is obvious Gretel don't want Hansel. I hope Gretel has found what she has been looking for. Once she told Hansel she had but was just using him. Hansel knew nothing of dark day. Gretel said to Hansel she would never do to Hansel what the witch done a long time ago. But this is worse. This scar will take a big Bandaid to hide. Gretel promised to protect Hansel. Another lie. Why did Gretel tell Hansel she loved him before he got into the elevator? When he said thanks, why say yes to February 14? Has Hansel just been a fool and sucked in? He would have given the world.

"Regardless, SAJ is a dog for treating Gretel this way and will sell Gretel out to save himself. Fact: Hansel don't lie to Gretel. Hansel is going to sleep after he gets his three pets set up and wants to know why and no lies before he does. Did Gretel know Hansel wonders did Gretel know SAJ had a friend called Andy and when SAJ went on holidays Andy told Hansel that SAJ told him that Hansel wants to go to sleep. But Andy did not trust SAJ and SAJ wanted Hansel out. But Gretel probably knew this anyway. This story's ending has yet to be finished and Hansel will be home when he hopes and needs to know why before then. Maybe Gretel can finish the story? And send to Hansel.

PS Because Hansel has been threatened he has sent three stamped letters to his solicitor (you can't read them) with instructions to post them:

1. If Hansel goes missing for more than two days.
2. If Hansel has an accident.
3. If Hansel goes to sleep.
4. If three pets get hurt.

Just insurance but won't hurt Gretel. There is still Hansel's oath."

Matthews's childish code seemed to reveal that he had finally accepted the ugly truth – his fantasy bride was actually the town bike. He also seemed intent on convincing Michelle he wanted to commit suicide, and he optimistically believed that he would be released on home detention bail. The Tidswell family were appalled at the thought that Kevin Matthews might not only be allowed to return home, but also take back his sons.

ON SEPTEMBER 26, 2001, the world was only just beginning to grapple with the consequences of September 11, and Australia was dealing with the fallout from the sudden collapse of Ansett Airlines. But in Adelaide at least, both of those stories were pushed to one side for the day when Crown Prosecutor Kos Lesses stood up in the Adelaide Magistrates Court and revealed exactly why freeing Kevin Matthews on bail was simply not an option. The next day, *Advertiser* court reporter Simonne Reid wrote:

> Mother-of-three Carolyn Matthews was murdered by her husband and his lover so they could continue their affair and cash in on her life insurance policy, the Adelaide Magistrates Court was told yesterday.
>
> It was alleged Kevin Matthews and Michelle Burgess were involved in a relationship and hired another man, David Edgar Key, to kill the West Lakes Shore woman. Details of the prosecution case against the three accused were revealed for the first time during a bail application for Mr Matthews.
>
> Opposing bail, Crown Prosecutor Kos Lesses said the murder had been "planned and premeditated" and motivated by "self-gratification and greed". But Bill Morris, for Mr Matthews, 40, said his client was a "five-star candidate for bail" who "has all the trappings of a normal member of our community". He said Mr Matthews needed to be home with his children and earning a wage to pay the mortgage.
>
> Mr Matthews, who was arrested on September 7, smiled and winked at his supporters in the public gallery during the 40-minute hearing. Two bloodied scratches were visible on his forehead and he had a Band-Aid on his left cheek.
>
> Mr Lesses alleged yesterday that Ms Burgess, 28, and Mr Key, 26, had admitted their involvement in the murder to other prisoners. He told the court: "Mr Matthews was having an affair for some time with the accused, Ms Burgess, and the case will be that the two of them conspired to murder the deceased to further their relationship and retain the proceeds of a life insurance policy that existed.
>
> "Mr Key was hired financially by Ms Burgess and Mr Matthews to execute the killing of the deceased," Mr Lesses said.
>
> On the day of Mrs Matthews's murder, the three accused had met at Mr Matthews's work, where they finalised their plan.
>
> "It will also be alleged (Mr Matthews) made a phone call to his home to contact his wife to organise the collection of his children from his home," Mr Lesses said.

Mr Matthews allegedly hired a man named Jason Colenso to "deal with" Ms Burgess's husband, Darren, a potential prosecution witness. Mr Colenso, 31, of Elizabeth West, has been charged with preventing a person from attending as a witness. Mr Lesses told the court yesterday there was forensic evidence placing Mr Key inside the Matthews home. He applied successfully yesterday to have an oral swab taken from Ms Burgess.

Matthews family friend Carolyn Garland recalls: "Burgess had refused to give her DNA and I was in court one day. The (magistrate) was going on and on about how important DNA was and it was not something to be handed over easily and I thought: 'She's not going to make her do it.' And it went on for a while, and then she said: 'You will give up your DNA and if you do not, you will be strapped down and it will be taken from you'. And I thought: 'Yes!' That lady deserves to rot in hell."

The Advertiser report concluded: "DNA from the swab would be compared with blood found on Mr Key's boot and in Ms Burgess's car, the court was told. Mr Morris told Magistrate Sue O'Connor that Mr Matthews would comply with his bail conditions and had friends and family who would act as his guarantor. Ms O'Connor will hear further submissions today on the application."

But Matthews's bail application failed, as did the next, in December. He still had some people in his life convinced he was innocent, including two who continued to offer cash to be bail guarantors. But even they must have started having serious doubts when the police sprung a surprise on Matthews during one of the bail applications.

Sgt Standing recalls: "When he was in jail on remand, Kevin started writing letters to the girls who were in his R&R team. We had them stopped. You should have seen these letters. He was trying to con these girls to visit him. These were young, impressionable girls (in their teens and early twenties). These young ladies were appalled. I pointed out how they were being used and they stopped writing. I think one of them went to see him. Of course he's being the big man in prison and all these pretty girls are coming to visit him with photographs of them in their bathing suits. That's the sort of person he is, he's a user."

"Joanne" – the girl whom Matthews had been texting on the night he was keen for female company – was among a group of three young women from the surf club who visited him while he was on remand and also wrote to him.

On November 8, 2001, he wrote to her: "Hi Dolphin Girl, it's about 5pm and I've been locked up for half an hour or so. I have the radio on and just re-read your three letters …

"Well by now you have heard the latest in the media as no doubt it will be on the news and TV what is said in court. I know I don't have to tell you but I'm innocent and it's frustrating not knowing what they will say tomorrow, so I can't explain anything to you. Wish I could but lawyer won't let me anyway.

"I will never lie to you, you know this and if I'm been (sic) framed I will just have to prove otherwise somehow.

"Well this week past let's see, to start this is my 12th letter to you and the 128th I've written in 62 days. Not bad for someone who never writes …

"I'm going to do my absolute best not to talk or do anything stupid to David in court. I promise. It will be hard standing with the person who killed my wife …

"This time I've requested not to be in the same prisoner transport as David and Jason or not in the same holding cell at court or even facing them. I hate them but I don't want to fight with them. I will stuff up my bail chances and may not be able to stop if I get hold of them, you understand, don't you?"

He repeatedly tells "my little Dolphin Girl" how much he misses her and signs the letter "love Bodgie xxx".

Sgt Standing continues: "(The letters) came up in the bail applications. It took his lawyer completely by surprise – took him by surprise, too. The mother of one of the girls (not Joanne) found the letters and contacted me. The girl wouldn't listen to her and the mother wanted me to support what she was saying. The daughter was 21. She was beautiful. I checked with her that she had written this letter and her mother wasn't very happy. I explained to her what it was all about. And she said: 'The rotten cunt!'

"She suddenly realised how he was using her up and manipulating her. (She said): 'That fucking bastard!'

"Her mother said: 'I've never heard you speak like that!'

"If I'd given this girl a gun, she'd have gone up there and shot him dead.

"In one of the letters, he said: 'When I get out, you can come to my place and we can go and visit Carolyn's grave and read some poetry and come back to my place and perhaps have a few drinks.'"

Standing was incredulous. "A few drinks?"

Kevin Matthews remained in prison. But he remained convinced he could beat the murder charge, stubborn in the belief that because he was not present at his wife's murder, he could not be connected to it. In spite of his initial stupidity in the wake of the murder, he now understood that listening to his lawyer and keeping his mouth shut could still win him back his freedom.

You think I murdered my wife? Go ahead and prove it.

CHAPTER 15

Payback's a bitch
December 7, 2001 – August 10, 2002

TAKING A HUMAN LIFE is generally accepted as the most heinous crime one person can commit against another. When guilt has been established, and the unique circumstances of each crime have been considered, the law dispassionately measures and judges the perpetrator on a sliding scale; at the darkest extremity, among humanity's most depraved specimens, is the contract killer.

Through TV and movies, we know their methods well; their crime begins with a rational, premeditated decision to take the life of another. Motives vary. The person issuing the contract may have a desire to exact revenge; be pursuing material gain; or perceive that in continuing to draw breath, their intended target creates a burden they simply cannot bear.

The next step is to find someone else to do their dirty work. The contract killer wants no connection to the crime, no blood on their hands. They will inevitably be high on a suspect list because, in most cases, they will have an established link to the intended victim and the perception of motive will usually be obvious. Sometimes there is an intermediary, to keep the killer a further step removed, sometimes not. It is at this point that many fail, because their intermediary baulks, goes to the police and the next person the aspiring killer speaks to is an undercover police officer.

Those who do find a genuine potential hitman must then negotiate a fee, with the difficulty of the job often the major factor in the setting of a price. When the deal is sealed, possibly with a down-payment, vital information is divulged, intelligence is gathered and, finally, the hunter begins to stalk their prey. This, typically, is the modus operandi of the contract killer.

Driven by the high media profile of real-life gangland killings –

particularly in the Sydney and Melbourne underworlds – the public perception in Australia is that contract killings are most often committed by organised criminal groups. Consequently, we are fascinated by this category of murder and the people who commit them.

Christopher Dale Flannery was a man who revelled in his nickname of "Mr Rent-a-Kill" and his reputation of having murdered up to a dozen people, many of them during the Sydney gang wars of the mid-1980s. He even tried – and narrowly failed – to execute a Drug Squad officer, Michael Drury, in his own home. Flannery was egotistical, brazen and ultimately doomed. He left his Sydney apartment in May 1985 and was never seen again.

Andrew "Benji" Veniamin played a similar role in the Melbourne gangland war, in which 36 criminal figures or their partners were killed between 1998 and 2010. The former altar boy-turned-Carl Williams hitman was the prime suspect in a handful of the murders. Veniamin was shot dead in the La Porcella restaurant in Carlton in March 2004. Former associate Mick Gatto was charged with his murder but later acquitted on the grounds of self-defence.

On the face of it, Flannery, Veniamin and their underworld employers would seem to be typical hitmen and contract killers; Kevin Matthews, Michelle Burgess and their contract-eating, dim-witted assassin, the rare exceptions. In fact, the reverse is true.

DETECTIVE INSPECTOR John Venditto, who took over as officer in charge of the Major Crime Investigation Section in 2002, was fascinated by the Matthews-Burgess case. So much so, that he embarked on a major study of contract killings, in conjunction with Australian Institute of Criminology senior research analyst Jenny Mouzos, through the institute's National Homicide Monitoring Program.

They set about examining 163 cases – 69 completed contract killings and 94 attempted contract killings – that occurred between 1989 and 2002.

The year-long project was the largest of its kind in the world. Their research concluded "that the incidence of contract killing as a means of finalising disputes is a phenomenon that is occurring in suburban Australia in a context not previously realised or imagined".

The category of "contract killing" made up a small percentage of total homicides in Australia – about two per cent over the 13-year period. The research established nine sub-categories of attempted and completed contract killings, with the most common being "dissolution of a relationship", which involved 19 per cent of the cases. There were 28 targets of attempted contract killings and three completed contract killings involving 45 offenders.

Dividing contract killers into the categories of amateur, semi-professional and professional, it is as if the researchers used David Key as their model in compiling their profile of an amateur hitman: "Their method of killing is poorly planned, often impulsive and disorganised; some physical evidence is left at the crime scene; the typical target is a spouse or business associate; the contractor's motive is mostly personal, and their personality organisation is unstable with marginal adjustment."

The research found that the average payment for an attempted contract was about $16,500. The lowest payment specified in a contract was $500 and the highest payment was Michelle Burgess's and Kevin Matthews's extravagant offer of $25,000 each for the lives of Darren Burgess and Carolyn Matthews.

In any murder case, proof of intent is critical in gaining a conviction. Planning and premeditation is the inherent characteristic of contract killing, but this also makes it the most difficult to prove. The study revealed that only half of completed contract killings were solved, compared to clear-up rates for "traditional homicides" which can be as high as 90 per cent, depending on the jurisdiction. In spite of their mountain of circumstantial evidence, it was this 50/50 statistic that the Major Crime detectives would need to overcome if they were to obtain convictions against all of Carolyn Matthews's killers.

But before the main event started, bit player Jason Colenso needed to be dealt with. He appeared in Adelaide Magistrates Court on December 7, 2001 and pleaded not guilty to attempting to dissuade a witness from attending judicial proceedings. By January 20 the following year – five months after he was taken into custody – he had changed his tune, pleading guilty in the Adelaide District Court.

During sentencing submissions in April, 2002, Darren Burgess was given the opportunity to tell the court the effect Colenso's threats had had on him – bearing in mind that he'd already been the subject of a murder contract. Darren told the court he took tranquillisers and his sleeping and eating patterns had been affected. He'd been forced to move house, his parents were stressed and embarrassed and he had considered changing his identity. "I don't think there's been one night when I have not woken thinking that someone is standing over me," he told the court.

On May 21, 2002, Colenso was sentenced. Judge Jeffrey Anderson noted that he had been diagnosed with attention deficit disorder at the age of four but medication had been stopped early due to side-effects and he was now "barely literate". He sentenced him to 15 months in jail, with an eight-month non-parole period, suspending it on the condition that Colenso, 32, enter into an 18-month, $100 good behaviour bond. After nine months in custody, Colenso finally walked free.

Darren recalls: "They let him out at the sentencing. And he came and sat a couple of rows behind me and Kathy. She was shaking but I said: 'Don't worry about it. Once he knows you're scared, he's got you forever. We're going to walk out and stand out there and let him walk past us'. He was like a kindy kid when he came out, running up and down the stairs, loving it.

"He was also at one of Michelle's hearings at the magistrates court. We had decided to go for some reason. We were talking to (Crown Prosecutor) Kos Lesses. The lift came and Colenso got it. I grabbed Kathy's hand and said: 'Let's go'. And Kos said: 'Oh no, you can't get in there'. But I wasn't going to let him own us. So we got in. He didn't do or say anything. I think he was quite surprised.

"Not long after he got out, he would drive past work and go in and see my mate (at an adjacent business) to get prices and my mate would inflate the prices. So one day I'd had enough so I went over there and said: 'Jason, I don't know if you're fucking stupid or what. If you haven't realised it yet, you can't afford my mate's prices. How about you get in your car and fuck off'. That really set him off and we had a full-on argument. He'd drive past or walk past; he thought he was putting the shits up me. But he was wasting his own time, not mine."

Colenso would later publicly threaten to write a book on the case to help pay for compensation owed to Darren Burgess. But he overlooked two important factors – his kindergarten-level writing skills and proceeds of crime laws. As someone convicted of a crime directly connected to the case, he could never legally make a cent from such a book.

THE MURDER TRIAL would take even longer to make it to court. On March 1, 2002, it had been delayed to allow the prosecution time to obtain full details of the 3000-plus phone intercept records relevant to the case. On

April 5, the trial was again delayed because the 150-plus phone conversations that detectives had decided were relevant to the case had to be typed up and handed over to defence lawyers for review.

In the holding cells of the court that day, David Key handed Michelle Burgess a note through the cell hatch, which gave a concise summary of his changed feelings towards her. He later denied writing it or dictating it, but the prisoner providing his secretarial services did an excellent job, capturing every colourful word and phrase. The note read:

"Michelle, I know you're fucking Jason you filthy slut. You know what happened when I thought you were fucking Kevin. You wait, slut. Your day is coming. I've warned you. Payback's a bitch, Michelle. Everyone is going to believe me, not a lying slut like you. I've got my sister to back me up. You wait cunt. You're going down. 25 bitch. Ha, ha. How's that grab you? Don't even bother talking to me today at court, bitch. I hate even seeing you now Michelle. You fucking whore. You fucked me over for the last time. Do it hard. David."

Kevin Matthews, meanwhile, was intent on improving his public image. He wrote to *The Advertiser* to complain that his four requests to visit Carolyn's Centennial Park memorial plot had been denied. He said he had been told his first request was denied because of "potential media exposure". The second request to see his wife's plot had been made on the couple's 17th wedding anniversary on November 17. "This was also denied," Matthews wrote. "This time they said it does not fit the criteria of compassionate leave while on remand." On December 12, Matthews again requested to visit the plot. Once again, it was denied. Matthews wrote that he had been on a hunger strike to protest against the refusals and had written to the Ombudsman. What he did not mention in his letter was that he was trying to sell his car, his home – the roof over his sons' heads – and anything else he could lay his hands on, in an effort to fund his trial defence. Kevin's sister-in-law, Lou Tidswell, later told police that after his arrest they became aware that Kevin was not keeping up payments on the house and he intended selling it to fund his defence. The family also heard rumours that he intended to keep all the proceeds for his own purposes and the boys wouldn't see a cent. When Kevin's speedboat was sold, the family approached Peter Campaign, who had power of attorney over Kevin's affairs, and he ensured half the proceeds were put into trust for the boys. After Kevin put the house on the market, the family approached lawyer Chris Patterson and had a caveat imposed. And when members of the Tidswell family visited Kevin to discuss why the mortgage was not being paid and rumours of the boys not getting any money, he was furious about their intervention – all he cared about was money for his defence.

Kevin Matthews had greater priorities than providing for his sons. On April 22, 2002, an Adelaide Women's Prison officer opened an envelope addressed to Michelle Burgess. There were no sender's details, but inside was a cheque for $2000, payable to Michelle. Three days later, Michelle received a letter from Matthews, who had drawn no less than 100 love hearts on the envelope. Inside was a typically rambling 22-page letter dated April 19. Matthews seemed to have forgiven and forgotten everything outlined in the Hansel and Gretel fairytale, focusing only on his undying love. Along with the letter was a page containing a dozen treacle-laden rhyming couplets – a sickening wedding fantasy poem titled "I Do". Michelle was given the originals while copies went to Major Crime. In the letter, Matthews wrote:

"My dearest Michelle,

"How are you darling? Me, I'm fine and safe and doing well. I got a third letter from you today. Wow, now I feel special. I think I have sent you a letter every day this week. I also got a postcard of four naked women from behind from brother Steven in NSW. I have to say your letter put a smile on my face and I laughed out loud when I read what you said about me. (boner) You are so ballsy in your writing these days. Good on ya love.

"Your letter was opened. Are they stupid or what? They know we know they read them so do they honestly believe we will incriminate ourselves?

"I got a letter from Sue this morning, she's cool. I've already written to the boys and I've also replied to Sue and co. and sent a card to my mother-in-law but don't expect or want a response there.

"Well, I love you very much Michelle Elizabeth Burgess, so much that I'm willing to sacrifice myself for you. I'm glad your mum and dad seem happier and it sounds like your visit was very positive when discussing the case, that's good to hear. I know what you mean about going to trial, I can't wait either. I am so confident we will go free I can taste it. I also have so much good stuff I want to tell you but I can't, as we are aware. We just get bombarded with negatives all the time but you must not forget this is all circumstantial and their motive is over an alleged affair. Ha!

"Your message saying you love me more than life itself pleased me so much because that's how I feel. Do your mum and dad mention me? What do they say about me? Be honest, I can take it.

"Yes, I heard the message from CC to Dave, it's been going on the radio for four weeks now." (In the lead-up to their trial, Michelle and Matthews used a prison request show on a radio station to send messages of love to each other.)

In reference to the $2000 cheque, he writes: "Use it wisely, no UDLs."

"I was just thinking of last time in the single holding cells outside the courtroom, I was tapping my cuffs on the wall to you. I did get an answer tap, ha ha. It brings a smile to my face. I have to tell you I truly miss just holding your hand Michelle. It always made me feel good."

The final page is messy; he is upset because there has been no message from her on the radio: "Tell me why Michelle. Are we still on track, love? Tell why not love? Are you OK?"

DAVID KEY, meanwhile, was making good on his payback threat, arranging to speak to Detectives Eichner and Keane on June 13, 2002. While there were some elements of truth in what he told them that day, it was also a transparent attempt to shift the majority of blame on to Michelle Burgess and Kevin Matthews. Key and his lawyer sat in front of the expectant detectives in the Major Crime offices.

Eichner: "I understand you're here to speak to us in relation to the murder of Carolyn Matthews and there's some things you want to tell us.

Key: "Yes, uh, Kevin Matthews and Michelle Burgess have been having a three-year relationship and I was brought in on it by my sister to organise something to happen to Carolyn Matthews. But it didn't work out that way. Michelle Burgess got pushy and she did it herself."

Eichner: "Well, I see. And how do you know that?"

Key: "Because I was in the area at the time, I was the one that was driving the car."

Eichner: "Were you present when you say Michelle Burgess murdered Carolyn Matthews?"

Key: "Not exactly, as in, at that vital minute. When I walked through the house, I seen Carolyn Matthews laying there. When I walked back to the car, I did see Michelle Burgess wearing one of my blue jackets and it had blood all over it. And she had blood on her hands and there was blood in the vehicle. That was cleaned up to hide the fact that Carolyn was murdered."

(later)

Eichner: "What sort of relationship did you have with Michelle?"

Key: "Well, we had a sexual relationship. Um, she wanted to marry me and have kids, everything and buy a house and yeah, have a full relationship. But it turned out all she wanted was to find someone to kill Carolyn Matthews and she's trying to pin this on me now. She talked all the time about getting Carolyn murdered. She wanted a decent husband who knows where he's going and what he's doing, having kids, owning a house. She mentioned that to me four or five times while we were laying there on her waterbed in her bedroom."

Addressing the Darren Burgess contract, he said: "I went in to Darren Burgess's office and bought a battery off him just to have a look, see what he looks like, see how he approaches me doing business. The first night I went to the shop, I told Michelle: 'To get him, you've got to be fucking nuts, because he has too many people around him. All right, then you'd have to use a weapon, you'd have to use a gun to get him'.

"She says: 'No, no, no, get him while he's on the road, cut his fucking brakes on his car'. She came up with all these different ideas on how to murder him. I got fed up with it and went back to how she wanted Carolyn Matthews done. So I basically pushed his contract to one side and basically forgot about him. We went back on discussing how she wanted Michelle Burgess murdered."

Keane: "No, no, no – you mean Carolyn Matthews."

Key: "Carolyn Matthews, sorry. I'm starting to stress a little bit."

Keane: "That's all right."

Key explained that on the day of the murder: "Kevin Matthews started stressing out and sending messages saying he was going to knock himself. Being real pathetic and sending stupid messages."

During the meeting at Beaurepaires, "Kevin was standing there like a stuffed (sic) mullet. It felt to me that Michelle was taking control of the entire situation".

When they arrived at Nambucca Ave, Key said he "went off to have a piss" at some nearby flats. He saw an XD Falcon in the car park of the flats and went to have a look at its mags. He walked to the Matthews house and found Carolyn on the floor, conveniently explaining how his bootprint came to be found in her blood. It was an interesting tale, but Key was insulting the detectives if he thought they were going to accept it. If he wanted to win himself any concessions, it would have to be with the truth.

RATHER THAN go straight to trial, the trio of accused killers elected to take the matter to a committal hearing in the Adelaide Magistrates Court. While such hearings are ostensibly to establish whether the prosecution has a prima facie case – sufficient evidence to proceed to trial – for defence lawyers, they are an opportunity to test the prosecution case and seek to establish its strengths and weaknesses. This decision delighted the Adelaide media, who were itching to start unravelling what promised to be one of the most salacious murder trials in many years – and Adelaide is no virgin when it comes to bizarre murders.

Adelaide Magistrates Court is a most aesthetically pleasing location to face justice. The original 1930s heritage-listed art deco building, in the south-east corner of Victoria Square, was linked to a new six-storey building in the mid-1990s, to accommodate the growth business of criminal justice administration. Connecting the old with the new is a curved two-storey stone wall, topped with an ornate parapet. Inside, those visitors not preoccupied with the possible loss of their freedom will also appreciate artistic touches including cast bronze stair balusters, coloured glass fins and special joinery using materials salvaged from the original courts built in the 1800s. Inside the 28 modern courtrooms are contemporary wood panelling and the kind of soft pastel colour schemes often featured in psychiatric wards. In the dock of one of these courts on July 30, 2002, Kevin Matthews, Michelle Burgess and David Key stood to answer the charge of murdering Carolyn Wendy Matthews at West Lakes Shore just over one year earlier. When proceedings began, Key's lawyer conceded that his plea could change. When he was read the charge, Key replied: "Not guilty at the moment." During the 40-minute hearing, Matthews and Michelle smiled and winked at each other and waved to supporters in the public gallery.

Crown Prosecutor Kos Lesses outlined details of the murder contract and the affair, and went on to summarise the events of July 12, 2001. "David Key was hired financially by Burgess to carry out the actual killing of the deceased with the instructions and knowledge of Kevin Matthews," he explained dispassionately to the court. But before the hearing resumed later in the year, Key opted to go straight to trial and lodged a plea of not guilty on September 9, 2002. Key's lawyer decided that before the trial, his client needed his head examined. Forensic psychologist Richard Balfour visited Key at the Adelaide Remand Centre on November 12, 2002 and conducted a two-hour clinical interview and psychological test.

"My understanding is that your client is charged with murder," he wrote in his report. "You have some concerns about his general level of cognitive functioning and how this may impact on his ability to give instructions and fitness to stand trial. Therefore you are seeking a general psychological assessment of your client that addresses these issues."

Key appears to have been open and honest with the doctor, answering all questions about his life from early childhood through to his current predicament. It is a sad indictment of Key's dysfunctional existence that the only unequivocally positive statement in the extensive report states: "Mastered toilet training without difficulties".

When the committal hearing continued in December, the preview of the prosecution's witnesses would have given the defendants' lawyers plenty of cause for concern. Evidence from Key's mate "George", Darren Bland and Kathy Cowled started to build a compelling picture of the affair, the contracts and the murder plots. On December 4, Chief Magistrate Kelvyn Prescott ruled there was enough evidence against Matthews and Michelle to commit them to trial in the Supreme Court.

When the trio appeared in court on January 13, 2001 to be arraigned, a beetroot-faced Kevin Matthews scuffled with two sheriff's officers as he lunged at David Key, who was quickly whisked from court. Exactly why he tried to attack Key is unclear. Was it a genuine display of anger at Key's affair with Michelle, or a feigned outburst at the man he had employed to kill his wife? Either way, it did nothing to help his cause.

David Key felt decidedly uncomfortable when the trial finally began on July 21, 2003. He sat through the opening morning of legal argument, squirming in between Michelle Burgess and Kevin Matthews. He'd been talking to members of his family, who'd been trying to convince him that his only option was to plead guilty and talk to the police. There was simply no other choice – he was going to be found guilty anyway and there was no escaping an automatic life sentence. The lawyers droned on and on. He understood little of what they were arguing about. During an adjournment, he explained his discomfort to his lawyer, Nick Vadasz, who in turn explained the situation to Justice Margaret Nyland:

"The current seating arrangements are causing my client some concern. He is concerned at being surrounded, as it were, by the other two accused. The application is that the seating arrangement be altered so that he could be at the back of the two tiers of seats rather than the front."

Advertiser court reporter Simonne Reid recalls: "I remember all three of them sitting together and Key asking to move. He was moved to the back row and sat there with his arms folded, because I think by that stage it had become obvious to him that Michelle was screwing everyone under the sun."

Just after lunch, during the voir dire hearing to select the jury, the court was told Mr Key was "unwell" and he was excused from the proceedings. He would not return and the trial did not make it to a second day.

Eichner recalls: "Key made approaches to us. He decided to tell us the truth and, through his solicitor, we came to the agreement that he would talk to us and tell us the story. He would plead guilty and give evidence against the other two."

Two days later, Michelle and Matthews both made applications for separate trials, which were refused. David Key returned to the Supreme Court on July 31. Five sheriff's officers separated the three co-accused as they stood, staring straight ahead, while Key was asked how he pleaded. "Guilty, your honour," he told Justice Nyland.

His lawyer, Nick Vadasz, explained: "I can indicate that Mr Key pleads guilty on the basis that he was the person who did the stabbing, notwithstanding his earlier statement to police last year. Mr Key wishes to clear his conscience. I can also indicate that the DPP have stated their intention to call Mr Key as a witness and that Mr Key has indicated he is prepared to give evidence. This development has occurred very much overnight."

Rather than imposing the mandatory life sentence for murder, Justice Nyland decided it would be appropriate if Key were sentenced by another judge and she remanded him in custody until it was decided who that would be. Detectives Eichner and Kern subsequently interviewed Key at Adelaide police station, where he was to deliver his end of the bargain.

Eichner: "Do you agree that yesterday, July 31, you appeared in the Supreme Court with Burgess and Matthews before Justice Nyland and pleaded guilty to the murder of Carolyn Matthews?"

Key: "Yes, I agree."

Eichner: "Do you also agree that you have agreed to provide further information?"

Key: "Yes."

Eichner: "Did you stab Carolyn Matthews on July 12, 2001?"

Key: "Yes I did."

Eichner: "Was there anyone else with you at the time?"

Key: "Yes there was."

Eichner: "Who was that?"

Key: "Michelle Burgess."

Eichner: "Was Kevin Matthews involved in the murder of Carolyn Matthews?"

Key: "No."

This was going to be a long interview.

Eichner: "Did Kevin Matthews have any involvement whatsoever in the murder of Carolyn Matthews?"

Key: "Yes he did."

Eichner: "Just briefly, what do you understand that involvement was?"

Key: "He organised the paperwork."

Eichner: "Can you tell me what happened that day, from the time you got out of bed?"

Over the next two hours, the truth tumbled from David Key's mouth. When he got side-tracked, the detectives guided him back. When he became confused, they were patient. And when he was self-piteous, they were silent. Sgt Eichner also grilled him on Colenso's exact role, ensuring that it was correct that he only entered the picture after the murder.

Key: "We were still buddies. Sit back and have a couple of cones together, run a bit of amok. He didn't know anything about the murder."

Eichner: "It was you who introduced Colenso and Michelle?"

Key: "Jason was told by me and Michelle to go and talk to Darren, to go and threaten Darren. That if he goes to court, he's going to get hurt."

Eichner: "Did you tell Jason to do that?"

Key: "Me and Michelle did."

Eichner: "How did you do that?"

Key: "Michelle and Jason came in on the same visit and we spoke then about it. Cos Michelle and Jason also asked me if I'd say yes to threaten Kevin Matthews with the car. I wanted to know what the fuck they meant. To try and run him off (the road) and make it look like the person who killed Carolyn Matthews is still out there. And that's when I said: 'Are you fucking stupid or what? Do you want to bring more heat down on me?'"

Sgt Eichner queried Key on codes used on the phone by Michelle and Matthews. The detectives wanted to know why the pair made regular references to the initials "M and M".

Key: "M and M is short for Michelle Matthews."

Eichner: "You know that?"

Key: "I put two and two together. You know the games that Michelle and Kevin play with their phone system, kids' games. It's a way to say, fucking, M 'n' M, that's like, Michelle Elizabeth Matthews. You know, it's … they're talking about the future, about once everything's blown over and all the heat's disappeared. The public just forgot about them, too. Then they can get married and live happily ever after."

At the end of the interview, Key agreed that in a previous interview he did not reveal everything he knew and had also made false statements, but everything he had said today was true.

Eichner: "Did you think lying would assist you in any way with these charges?"

Key: "It could have. You know, if I'd told them the full truth in the first place, I wouldn't be sitting in this position now. I would have been on a lesser charge, but at that time I wasn't thinking properly, I wasn't fucking using my head the right way like I am now. I should have told the truth in the beginning instead of sitting around fucking bullshitting and telling fucking stupid lies."

Eichner: "Well then, can you tell me why you've decided to tell the complete story today?"

Key: "Because I can't let this … I won't be able to let this go down until I know that my two co-accused are found guilty for a crime that they set up and used me in part of it."

Eichner: "Was there anything else you wanted to talk to us about, David?"

Key: "There was something, but I've totally forgotten it now."

Eichner: "All right, we'll conclude the interview at this stage. The time is now 6.17pm on Friday, 1st August, 2003."

Key: "Sweet. Toilet time. I've only been sitting here for the last fucking hour-and-a-half. Like, fuckin …"

Mercifully, the tape recording finally ends. Sgt Eichner says he was satisfied with Key's account: "I know that in the first interview John and

I had with David Key, he told lies. I feel that he was completely honest and truthful, and what he told us was a pretty accurate account of what happened. He took the full blame in that interview. He had plenty of opportunity to say she did this and she did that. He took the brunt of it, although he said she egged him on."

SC Keane: "He had the opportunity to lessen his involvement and he didn't."

ON MONDAY, August 10, 2002, David Key faced justice. It had been decided that there was no issue with Justice Nyland imposing Key's sentence and she explained to him that his guilty plea and co-operation with police had saved him from a 30-year non-parole period. Key stared straight ahead and his hand twitched as the judge told him he would instead serve at least 20 years before being considered for parole.

The public gallery, filled with families and detectives, remained sombre. This was justice, but there was little to celebrate. Michelle and Matthews, standing either side of Key again, would return to the same dock the next day.

CHAPTER 16

On trial

August 13, 2003 – October 9, 2003

YVONNE TIDSWELL followed the same physically and emotionally exhausting routine almost every weekday for two months.

She would get Carolyn's boys off to school, prepare herself and then drive to the tram stop to travel to Victoria Square, usually with a friend for much-needed support. Running the gauntlet of the media pack, Yvonne would walk into the Sir Samuel Way building and take a lift up to a courtroom, where her son-in-law and his lover would wink, whisper, giggle, feign boredom or sleep, in a very public display of disdain for the unfolding judicial process.

She recalls: "I could see Kevin from where I sat in court. I couldn't look at him to start with, then I began to stare him out – not that he looked at me that much. At one point he was making out he was asleep, not interested. They never put him on the stand, he would have hung himself."

Every day, in her handbag, or grasped tightly in her hand, would be some small personal item belonging to Carolyn, a symbol of why they were all there. When each day's proceedings were complete, and she had survived more harrowing evidence, Yvonne would again walk with silent dignity past the media pack asking "how she felt", step on to the tram, and return home to cook dinner for her grandsons.

Yvonne recalls: "I sat through all but two weeks of the trial. I went to the doctor and she said stay home for a week and I did and it got to two weeks. That was when Kev was on the stand. The only time I saw him was when he pleaded guilty on the day we went in to start the trial. That stopped the trial for a little while. I went because I had to find out for myself, I had to believe it because I couldn't believe … and I had plenty of support, my neighbour came with me, and my sister-in-law. Same as one of Kevin's friends that had coached, he came in one day to court and he said: 'Yvonne, I had to come and see for myself.'"

THE SUPREME Court in Adelaide, on the south-west fringe of Victoria Square, contains all the facilities required for the trials of people charged with the most serious of criminal offences. All the facilities, that is, except holding cells. Consequently, the trials of accused murderers, rapists and major drug dealers are instead conducted in the nearby Sir Samuel Way building, named after SA's longest-serving Chief Justice and also home to the District Court. It is the biggest and grandest of the court complexes scattered around Victoria Square. Built in 1912, the five-storey building was modelled on Paris's Galeries Lafayette and its first incarnation as a department store lasted until 1980. In 1983, it was remodelled for use by the courts. It is designed around a central atrium, usually as quiet as a library, with an imposing white marble staircase leading off to the 26 civil and criminal courtrooms which serve as the heart of South Australian justice. Atop the atrium is an enormous dome with a leadlight glass window created by South Australian craftsman Ian Mowbray.

From the opening morning of the trial, the public gallery of courtroom No. 8 was full. Evidence at the committal hearing had made it clear that this would be no run-of-the-mill murder trial; a fiction writer would baulk at the kind of twists this case promised to deliver. The true-crime coterie was out in force for every day of proceedings, along with the family and friends of the victim and the accused, for whom the proceedings were anything but entertainment.

Advertiser court reporter Simonne Reid recalls: "The gallery was packed every day. It was because it was the kind of case that had everything. The affairs, the murder contracts, the hitman. It just drew people in. It was packed every day. With other cases, people would pop their heads in but in this case, if there was voir dire or the court was closed for a particular reason, people would wait outside for it to start again, like it was some sort of really interesting movie."

Crown Prosecutor Steven Millsteed, QC, was charged with making sense of the mountain of evidence and presenting it to the jury. His opening address on August 13, 2003, was a compelling summary of the case he was about to present. He opened the case, before Justice Margaret Nyland, by telling the jury:

"It is the prosecution's case that the two accused were having an affair in the months leading up to Thursday, July 12 and that they hired Mr Key to murder Mrs Matthews in order to further their relationship and to be together. Further, there is evidence Ms Burgess despised Mrs Matthews, not only because she wanted to be with her husband but because she believed Mrs Matthews had complained to the welfare authorities that Ms Burgess was neglecting her children. The killing may also be motivated by greed. Mr Matthews stood to gain financially from his wife's death. He insured her life with MLC and under the terms of the policy was entitled to a payment of $100,000 in the event of her death."

Mr Millsteed was a talented, experienced and respected prosecutor, who went on to a long career as a District Court judge. At the time, he was one of the state's top prosecutors and his selection for the trial signalled that the Office of the Director of Public Prosecutions was going all out in their efforts to secure convictions.

That afternoon, after Mr Millsteed's lengthy opening address, the jury was taken on a tour to familiarise them with the case's key locations – Beaurepaires Port Adelaide, the murder scene at Nambucca Ave, the Leg Trap Hotel, the Video Ezy store and Grange Beach, where a police officer in a purple shirt signified the position of the phone box that Michelle used to call Matthews after the murder. Sgt Eichner recalls that the phone box's removal created a major headache for police, who had trouble finding the paperwork from Telstra to prove that it had actually existed.

Witness after witness began building a damning picture of the affair that Michelle and Matthews stubbornly continued to deny. While plenty of the evidence was sordid, it wasn't until Kaylene Kenyon left the witness box that the gallery witnessed some of the courtroom drama they'd been hoping for.

With grim satisfaction, she recalls: "I gave Kevin a parting comment in court and I must say that was the only time I saw a reaction from him in court. And he ended up almost climbing over the plastic thing to get me."

Advertiser photographer Michael Milnes, who was in the public gallery, clearly remembers the moment: "She exited the witness box and strode up to the glass-panelled dock and drew a circle with her finger on the glass and hissed at him: 'What goes around, fucking comes around'."

She used her index finger to punctuate her sentence with a full stop in the middle of the circle.

Advertiser court reporter Simonne Reid says: "That was pretty ballsy, even though he was behind the glass. He launched out of his seat. I think one of the sheriff's officers told him to sit down. Then she legged it out of the court. It was pretty exciting."

DARREN BURGESS took the stand on a Monday morning. He remained there until after lunch on the Friday. Mr Millsteed led him methodically through his evidence. Darren was bemused when he asked him to read Michelle's diary wordplay – Kind, Exciting, Vigorous, Intelligent, Naughty – but did as he was asked.

Both defence lawyers spent hours trying to knock holes in Darren's evidence, claiming he rang FACS to report Michelle and that he was having an affair with Cassandra Hutchinson. Neither claim was true and, in any case, Darren says he was unfazed – he told the truth from start to finish, so he had nothing to worry about.

He remembers: "It was pretty hard, walking past them (Kevin and Michelle) all the time. They looked at me, I looked back – I wasn't scared."

Kathy Morton, who was also due to give evidence and wasn't allowed to enter the court, sat outside for the entire week, wanting to ensure that the first face Darren saw when he emerged from court was a friendly one.

Simonne Reid recalls: "When Darren Burgess gave evidence, I remember thinking he looked like a very normal man who was completely bewildered by what he was caught up in. Sometimes he'd just look down and shake his head and his expression was saying: 'How the hell did I get involved with all these misfits, how did I become a piece in this puzzle?' He was actually a lovely man. He looked absolutely disgusted that the person he'd chosen as his life partner turned out to be evil personified."

David Key was a Crown witness, but that made Mr Millsteed's task no less easier as he led him slowly through his evidence.

Reid recalls: "Key was stone-cold in parts of his evidence. His anger at Michelle was palpable but his evidence was precise and deadpan."

On cross-examination, Gordon Barrett, QC, for Michelle, asked Key about what happened to the murder contract that listed Mrs Matthews's details.

Key: "I put it in a sandwich and ate it."
Barrett: "That's true is it, you ate it?"
Key: "Yes it's true."
Barrett: "You put it in a sandwich and ate it?"

Key: "Michelle made me a sandwich and I put it in there and ate it. Quite tasty, actually."

Barrett: "Did you eat the photograph too?"

Key: "Yes."

Barrett: "And the sticky tape?"

Key: "I ate everything. It was in the sandwich. I'm not going to waste a nice sandwich."

Barrett: "Are you just being trivial?"

Key: "No I'm telling you the facts."

Reid recalls: "When Key said he'd eaten the contract, no one in court could believe it. I think Justice Nyland asked him to repeat it. People were shocked and there were even some giggles in the gallery. He was very composed. You knew he wanted to burn Michelle and he used all the damning things he knew to do that. You don't get TV shows or movies as good as what this guy was on the stand."

Challenged on the veracity of his first interview with police, Key explained: "What's written in that statement is all fabricated. You are going over information that is just full of shit. I might not be able to read and write, I might not be the sharpest tool in the shed, but I can make up a good fucking yarn." Key told the court he had warned Michelle that if he was charged with murder, she would go down with him. "She was warned before this murder that if I went down for it, everyone went down for it," he said. He also described Michelle as someone he wanted to punch in the head and who "whinges more than my mum's dog".

For Carolyn Matthews's friends and family, the evidence ranged from infuriating to heartbreaking on a daily basis. But Simonne Reid says: "There were some comical moments even though it was a very serious trial."

When Mr Millsteed questioned Key's friend, George, over his attempt to buy a gun, he enquired: "Is it true that you don't have a very high IQ?"

Incensed, George replied: "I'm very offenced by that," prompting mirth throughout the court.

And while she never gave evidence or moved from the dock, it was Michelle Burgess's behaviour which attracted the most attention.

Reid recalls: "Burgess would sit there in court with this flirtatious, smug look on her face all the time, giving coquettish glances. Whenever Millsteed mentioned sex, she'd giggle then cover up her mouth and then look around – 'whoops, I shouldn't be doing that'. Then have a sip of water and try and compose herself. She and Kevin would whisper to each other; I can't actually believe that they didn't have sheriff's officers in between them or have them separated further apart in the dock.

"Michelle would target men in the gallery and give them the eye. Milnesy sat in the front row with me and she would do it to him and I would nudge him and say: 'It's your turn today'. There was the looking up and down and the batting of the eyelids and the little half-smiles, playing with her hair. It was very flirtatious. At one stage, I thought she was trying to do it with the detectives behind us. It was like she had no understanding of how serious the situation was. I think she has the ability to make men who aren't overtly attractive feel attractive. She certainly cast a spell."

Night after night on the TV news, day after day in *The Advertiser*, the extraordinary story played out, witness by witness, headline by headline:

The laughing murderer: Court told of mother's final moments; Matthews murder trial told of "cuddle" – They acted like young couple; "She's dead. You're dead. That's a promise, not a threat." Husband tells: my wife had contract out on me; Court hears of $50,000 "double-hit" – Two mums hatched contract murder plans at school; I planned to tie her up, put her in a van and stage a crash, says killer; Burgess forced me into murder, court hears – Kill her, be a man, show you love me; I ate the murder contract – and it was tasty.

STEVEN MILLSTEED rose on September 30, 2003 to give his closing address. By the time his measured, eloquent and thoroughly convincing performance was over, the defence lawyers must have felt despair. How could they possibly talk their way out of this?

Reid recalls: "Millsteed was incredible, I was not at all surprised when he was later called to the bench to be a District Court judge. He would set the scene and create the story and then tie everything up but he never missed a beat, either. I think, to be a really good lawyer, you need that element of being an actor; knowing when to use the flourish of the hand or turn to the jury. He did do that but it wasn't over-the-top, it was all very controlled. He was a thorough gentleman throughout it. It would have been easy for him to take the piss as well. But he had the knack of making some of the witnesses look silly by themselves, without him having to help."

Mr Millsteed opened his summary of the case: "It is difficult to think of a more outrageously brutal and callous crime than the one which brought an end to Carolyn Matthews's life. And if you, the members of the jury, are satisfied that the prosecution has proved its case beyond a reasonable doubt, then the need for you to say so is obvious and needs no elaboration by me."

He proceeded to condense the case built by the prosecution's 70 witnesses and almost 100 exhibits across the six weeks of evidence, into a compelling portrait of the bizarre murder conspiracy that the two accused killers had hatched. It was the Perry Mason performance David Key had dreamed of, but on the wrong side of the court.

MICHELLE BURGESS called only her parents in her defence. On the witness stand, Angela Goldup admitted to Mr Millsteed that she would do "a lot" to protect her children and grandchildren. Her evidence was focused on the evening of July 12, 2001 and, specifically, her phone conversations with Michelle and the exact time she arrived at her Holden Hill home to pick up her children. In line with Michelle's alibi, she told the court she was looking after her grandchildren while her daughter had new tyres fitted to her car at Port Adelaide.

There was a call at 6pm which Mr Millsteed said was Angela ringing to find out where Michelle was. Mrs Goldup insisted she was just asking Michelle if she would like her to buy tea for the children, but that Michelle said: "No, I am on my way," and that she arrived soon after.

Mrs Goldup said Michelle returned to collect the children from her Holden Hill home about 6.30pm – Carolyn Matthews was stabbed to death about 5.45pm. The 20km journey could be completed in around 43 minutes, meaning it would have been possible – just – for Michelle to have made it back to her mother's home if her mother's story was to be believed. Mrs Goldup repeatedly denied suggestions by Mr Millsteed that Michelle had arrived closer to 7pm.

She also denied Mr Millsteed's suggestion that a call she made to her daughter's mobile at 6.37pm was a hurry-up call and, in any case, "I don't think she was capable of doing it (the murder) anyway," she told the court. Keith Goldup backed his wife's testimony, telling the court his daughter was leaving his home when he arrived at 6.30pm.

Under questioning from Mr Millsteed, Mrs Goldup admitted that she could have said to police in her first interview that she didn't know what time Michelle had picked up the kids. And the jury had also previously heard the phone conversation between Keith Goldup and his daughter on August 3, 2001, in which he mentioned her arriving at his house at 7pm on the night of the murder. It was a long way from being a rock-solid alibi, and Mr Millsteed had little trouble highlighting the doubts over the veracity of the Goldups' stories.

Sgt Eichner recalls: "Her parents were particularly supportive of her and did the right thing right throughout, as far as she was concerned."

SC Keane says: "Her mum was prepared to go along with what she said. She was happy to twist things around to suit her daughter. But dad was pretty up-front. He was prepared to support her but I think he knew from day one that she'd got herself involved in something very bad."

Kevin Matthews's lawyer, Stephen McEwen, had even less available to him in his bid to mount a defence. Putting Kevin on the stand was out of the question. So who else would be willing to take the stand and give evidence that not only was Kevin not involved in his wife's murder, he was also telling the truth when he said he was not having an affair with Michelle Burgess? Clearly, there was no one. In his closing statement, Mr McEwen was reduced to insulting the intelligence of his own client to support his case:

"This is the man that, after Michelle Burgess was arrested and went to court, he turned up at court in front of all the media with that hat on. Yet this is supposed to be a man who has managed to scrupulously keep himself at arm's length from evidence. I don't want to be disparaging but that is how much of a mastermind we are talking about here."

He said Matthews's train of thought would need to have been: "Everyone knows I'm having an affair, or there is rumour and suggestion I'm having an affair with this woman; I'll go and murder my wife and take up with her (Michelle)".

He said this would have been "certainly pretty brazen, extraordinarily stupid and just incredible to even contemplate". "Is someone really going to be, on the Crown's scenario, both very clever and a mastermind and keep it at arm's length then, when it comes to the murder, the conspiracy about the murder, do it in that very public, obvious way?" Mr McEwen said.

"You may as well get a big white sign and texta and write on it 'We are about to commit a murder, come back here tomorrow when the investigation begins'."

AS THE final week of the trial began, Kevin Matthews and Michelle Burgess publicly reaffirmed their love for each other. Kevin, it seemed, was now content to ignore all the evidence of Michelle's extra-curricular activities with Key and Colenso. His one true love could never do such things.

Their declarations of love were broadcast on *The Prison Show*, on Adelaide FM station Three D Radio. Using only their first names, or middle names William and Elizabeth as aliases, the duo sent letters to the station which were read out on air. The messages included: "Dear William, never forget that I'm standing by you no matter what. Good luck for this week, darling. You're my destiny. I love you with all my heart. All my love, from Elizabeth."

"Dearest Michelle, chin up, darling. No matter what, we'll always be one. My love for you will never die. You are my soulmate and my best friend. Eternal love from Kevin."

"Dear William, just remember together forever, no matter what happens," Michelle wrote. "Please keep your chin up. My love for you will never change. I'm so much in love with you. Good night and sweet dreams and I'll see you Tuesday. All my love, Elizabeth." And: "Dear William, I've never loved another like I love you. Only you've left footprints in my heart. Only you are my constant thought. All my love, Elizabeth."

Matthews couldn't let the opportunity pass, penning yet another love poem:

> Dearest Elizabeth, darling, close your eyes and I'll kiss you,
> Open your heart and I'll miss you,
> You gave me a rose,
> I gave you diamonds
> Our love continues to shine on.
> My thoughts and dreams are with you 24/7
> With eternal love from your Kevin.

As the trial approached its final hours, Justice Nyland asked Mr Millsteed to list off the 18 separate pieces of corroborative evidence that had been presented against the accused pair. The long list of circumstantial evidence told its own story – and that would appear to be why Justice Nyland had it repeated to the jury before she began her own summing up. Her most memorable statement concerned the prosecution's star witness:

"Ladies and gentlemen, let us not beat about the bush about David Key. It is pretty difficult, I think, to envisage a more unpleasant and unattractive individual than him. Some of the terms used by counsel to describe him were vile, repulsive, vindictive, erratic, controlling, manipulative and vicious. We know he is a drug taker and an admitted liar. There is no doubt he is all that and there is probably more. Key is a man with a violent and aggressive personality. He has demonstrated little compunction in brutally killing a decent, hard-working mother of three, a woman who he has never met. He is, however, a critical witness for the prosecution and it is your task to examine his evidence to determine whether he has told you the truth as to the essential matters that arise for your determination in this case."

The case would be won or lost on whether the jury believed David Key. The corroborating evidence the prosecution had produced was, surely, enough to convince even the most sceptical observer. Yvonne Tidswell, who had endured another difficult day, was not so sure.

She recalls: "Shane was in court to hear the verdict and he was sitting alongside of me and I could feel him shaking. I was hoping for guilty verdicts but at one stage I came out and I was in tears and John Keane said: 'What's wrong?' I said: 'He's going to get away with it.' Because I'd been talking to his mother, and she suffered too – she had two breasts removed during the trial because of cancer. The stress of the trial made it worse. Kevin's step-sister was there in court supporting him. His mum brought up six kids, she was a real Briton and she hasn't had the support I had. His step-sister said: 'I hope he's got a jacket' – because every day in court he only had a shirt and tie on – 'because it's going to be cold when he gets outside'. I said to John Keane: 'He'll walk out of here tonight and take those three boys and Max and that's it, and take his hundred thousand'. He said: 'He won't get that'. I said: 'Why not?' He said: 'Because he's been involved, he'll never get it'."

The jury's six men and five women (one had dropped out mid-trial, unable to cope with the evidence) deliberated for 17 hours and returned at 6pm on Thursday, October 9, 2003. The packed courtroom tensed as Matthews and Michelle were ordered to stand and face their fates.

Kevin Matthews, Simonne Reid observed, looked like a "raging bull". His chest heaved in and out, his nostrils flared and his temples moved from the grinding of his teeth. Michelle stared ahead, unblinking and stoic, as the jury foreman read out the two guilty verdicts.

Justice Nyland set the mandatory life sentences, with the non-parole periods to be decided at a later date. As they were led from the dock,

Matthews turned to talk to Michelle, but she glared fiercely at him, storming into the holding cells without a word. A fool to the end, he winked and blew a kiss, dramatically turning to his few supporters in the gallery and saying "bye" to his mother and sister. Neither replied.

CHAPTER 17
Screwing the screws
2003 – 2004

THERE WAS AN inherent flaw in locking up Michelle Burgess in a women's prison – the presence of male prison officers. Denied her freedom, she retained what she believed were her two most valuable weapons – her seductive charm and raw sexuality. Michelle would not tolerate being treated as just another prisoner. She was special. And she would find someone to treat her that way. A prison source who observed her closely during her early years in custody says:

"Michelle kept a fairly low profile for a while. There were officers that we know about that she was involved with. One was a bloke we used to call (name withheld for legal reasons). He was a blowhard and ladies' man. There was a complaint made that he was fraternising with Michelle Burgess too often. Those sorts of things, male officers and female prisoners, people take notice of.

"There was an issue with (this prison officer) where a number of prisoners complained that he was walking around the kitchen with his shirt off, flexing his muscles. He denied it and said he spilt something on his shirt, took it off to clean it and then put it back on. Prisoners lie but sometimes they tell the truth. (The officer) was moved back to Yatala as a result. I was getting told that there was a lot more going on between Burgess and (this prison officer) and there was no doubt she was doing a bit of business with him and fixing him up with hand jobs and head jobs but we could never prove it. The thing with this was that a couple of the women who made the reports were not the sort to dob in screws or make complaints about other women. And we think there was another one (relationship with a prison officer) before him but we couldn't prove it."

A second prison source says: "I've interviewed Michelle many times. She's a very strange lady. She's got tickets on herself. She will bad-mouth staff on the phone, and then hide from the staff involved. It's a bit strange. She's described herself as a Queen Bee in there. She's not."

(Although, there is no doubting her resemblance to Bea Smith, the notorious character from the TV drama series, *Prisoner*.)

"She wasn't one of the heavies in there, but that's what she would tell people. I don't think she was involved in the drug scene. A lot of the heavies are involved in moving drugs around and I don't think she was involved in that. I always found she'd talk to me, but I never spoke to her alone. I was always wary of that. She doesn't seem to have a conscience. I've heard her talk on the phone system. She makes every post a winner.

"When I've spoken to her, I sat there and looked at her and I've thought: 'I can't see anything special about her'. I looked at her and thought: 'I don't see what the attraction is. She's just a Plain Jane'.

"A lot of our staff talk too much about their lives and she would home in on that and make a move on the appropriate people. She seems to pick a certain type of man. Male, middle-aged, having trouble at home, not happy with his wife, a bit lonely. And she leans on that kind of person."

A third prison guard who we'll call Alan – to protect his innocent wife and children – fitted the profile perfectly.

The first prison source recalls: "The women said there was something going on with Burgess. If I remember rightly, Alan was assigned to the male pre-release centre and he got himself assigned to the kitchen on the women's side. We hadn't even opened an official file on it, we'd just heard rumours. I think we lined up a couple of the women and spoke to them and they confirmed there was definitely something going on between Alan and Burgess.

"Shortly after this, the manager's called and said: 'You're not going to believe this, Alan's walked in and said: 'I heard questions are being asked about me, here's my resignation.' The resignation was accepted. He complained because he was banned from visiting her. His big story was: 'I'm in love with this woman, I want to spend the rest of my life with her.' Well, it's going to be a long life mate because she's here for the rest of hers. He left his family for her, went nuts.

"They brought in a rule that male officers were never to speak to Burgess alone. It was always to be in pairs, and preferably one of them a female officer. We used to joke that she was a black widow. She was an absolute predator. Some of these screws are stupid. Alan was having problems at home and they talk about their private life at work. It's not like she's drop-dead gorgeous. She's nothing special to look at, she's a plump bushpig, but she thinks she's a goddess. She thinks men are always perving at her.

"She had an ability to exploit people's vulnerabilities. She knew a hell of a lot about the prison and how it operated. She cultivates people and also has the ability to be divisive. She put herself at risk on occasion by putting one group against another and then she'd have to keep a low profile. She has shown not one shred of remorse. And neither is that arsehole boyfriend of hers (Matthews) up at Port Augusta (Prison). He still reckons he's innocent. They had a big falling out. They were writing love-dovey letters. Then he wrote a letter demanding the engagement ring back and the shit hit the fan and they hated each other. She wouldn't give it to him."

A candid police source says: "He found out she was rooting another prisoner. She was in the infirmary and she was rooting a bloke who was in for armed robbery, and she started writing to him and Matthews found out. You often hear about blokes who have a network of sheilas, she's a sheila who has a network of blokes."

Michelle's relationship with Alan became public on November 26, 2003, when *The Advertiser*'s Nigel Hunt reported:

> A prison officer who works at the Northfield Women's Complex has quit because of his sexual relationship with convicted killer Michelle Burgess. The officer resigned last week and revealed his relationship with Burgess, described during her murder trial as a sexual predator. The development follows two earlier investigations by Department for Corrections investigators into other prison officers linked to Burgess.

Three weeks later, the *Sunday Mail* reported that:

> Male prison officers at Northfield Women's Complex are refusing to deal in person with convicted killer Michelle Burgess. One prison officer quit his job last month after forming a relationship with Burgess and his colleagues are concerned about the potential for being compromised when alone with Burgess.
>
> More than one officer will deal with Burgess when she is alone,

such as in her cell and being escorted around the prison to the recreation area and kitchen. "People are concerned enough by a potential flirting situation," Public Service Association chief industrial officer Peter Christopher said.

"The male officers are not dealing with her one-to-one. They are trying to avoid a one-on-one situation. I understand that's quite an informal arrangement put in place in recognition of potential risks to themselves."

Mr Christopher said it was important prison officers had a safe workplace. "How one defines safe varies considerably," he said. "The individual cell visit would always be a situation where no individual officers would go in."

This story prompted an angry response from the deluded Kevin Matthews, because it also referred to him as "Burgess's lover". He wrote:

"The story was on Michelle and her ways, so why was a photo of me put in the story? We were not proven to have had an affair. We were convicted of murder, not adultery. My innocence is still maintained, this Michelle and I are not lovers and were not lovers.

"If you must write this tripe please use the word alleged. Your story ... does not help my case when you print 'Kevin Matthews, Michelle's Lover'. We are not lovers now and Michelle is in a relationship with the ex-screw from (Northfield)."

ALAN'S ENDURING "LOVE" for Michelle Burgess infuriated his scorned wife, who we'll call Jane. Finally, she could hold her tongue no longer and told her story exclusively to Nigel Hunt. In *The Advertiser* on August 14, 2004, in "Killer's lust tears a family apart", he reported:

> Jane said her husband had told his family he and Burgess "have a special bond and chemistry" and he planned to wait for her while she served her non-parole period.
>
> Banned from visiting Burgess until May this year, he now visits her every weekend, which causes angst among staff at the Northfield complex. After living with Burgess's mother for a period after leaving Jane, he now lives in a unit at Elizabeth, complete with Burgess's furniture.

Jane says that Burgess has destroyed her marriage and left her life in tatters. "To be dumped after 30 years of marriage for a cold-blooded murderer is very hard to take," she said. "I could maybe come to terms with this if he was in a normal relationship, but I can't understand how a man could destroy his own family for a killer who is behind bars."

Jane has nothing but contempt for Burgess, whom she says is a "cold and calculating" predator. "She goes for the weak and just grabs what she can to service her own sexual purposes," she said. "She is good at her job, she does it very well. My husband became a convenience to her, someone on the outside that could bring her things and do things for her. He never should have stepped over that line."

Jane cannot come to terms with what happened and believes the Correctional Services Department should shoulder part of the blame because it allowed Burgess to continue contact with male prison officers after the first two incidents were discovered and dealt with. She believes the department failed in its duty of care towards her husband by not taking action to prevent this type of situation arising again once it became known there was a problem. "They let it happen," she said. "There were two other officers involved with this woman before she got hold of my husband. They knew she was a risk and what she was capable of doing. I believe that people out there knew and just turned a blind eyeto it."

Jane says that despite repeated requests for more information from Custodial Services Director Eva Les, she has been told nothing. "I have phoned Eva Les many times, but she refuses to tell me anything on the grounds of confidentiality so I am still looking for answers," she said.

Jane has written to Family First MP Andrew Evans, who has in turn written to Correctional Services Minister Terry Roberts, but to no avail. She is now planning to write to Premier Mike Rann to demand an inquiry into the matter.

"I am not going to stop; there has to be an investigation into this," she said. "Other families have also been destroyed by this woman and I will not ever see another family ruined the way they let my family be destroyed."

Alan eventually came to his senses. When approached for an interview for this book, he would not comment on the relationship, but his wife said that he ended it about three years after it began and returned to the marital home. His affair shattered the lives of his wife and children, but they have slowly rebuilt their relationships with him.

Jane is unequivocal in her attitude to Michelle Burgess: "They need to watch her, every single minute. She just has this way of winning men over. She can't be trusted; she is a black widow."

CHAPTER 18

Justice

CAROLYN MATTHEWS never had the chance to confront her cowardly killers. But the modern justice system recognises that victims deserve their day in court – and Carolyn's family embraced that right. Before the judge announced their non-parole periods, Kevin Matthews and Michelle Burgess were brought to court to face the family's grief, fury and anguish. When they killed Carolyn, they scarred many people for life – her grandmother, mother, sons, their extended families and Carolyn's many friends.

Sgt Standing says: "Murder has more than one victim to it. Murder has victims who are victims for life. And they can never, ever walk away from it. It's with them every day of their lives. In this case, it has been particularly devastating for some of the people involved."

The victim impact statements gave the court and the public insight into the horrific toll of Carolyn Matthews's murder.

Yvonne Tidswell to her son-in-law: "If you wanted to leave your marriage, why didn't you do that? The boys would have still had their father and their mother. Now they have nothing. You were part of our family for 23 years. I hate you for what you have done to my grandchildren. I want you to be punished for this but I can't honestly say how I feel about you. I don't know what to think about you. One of your favourite sayings to Doug and I was 'trust me' and we did, with our only daughter and grandsons."

Yvonne Tidswell to Michelle Burgess: "What was your motive? Jealousy of a loving, caring, hard-working businesswoman and mother? Carolyn was happy caring for her family and their future as well as spending thousands of hours assisting others in the community through life saving. She was working towards her sons' future but you put a stop to all that. You took her life, her future, and all that she was and will ever be. You took the future from her children, you took their mother from them. You have destroyed so much. You are completely opposite to her. She wasn't self-centred and selfish like you obviously are to do what you have done."

Peter and Sarah Tidswell to their brother-in-law: "What sort of person can plan to murder a human being, even worse, his wife, and then let his children, his own flesh and blood, discover the gruesome sight of their mother, brutally stabbed? You took the life of a beautiful person. You betrayed your family, you lied and you have scarred three innocent boys for life. All we can do is hope that justice is served and you pay the maximum penalty. That way we will never see your face again. Nothing will bring Carolyn back but knowing you will never see the outside world again will be one good thought."

Kenny Matthews to his father: "I have been alone for two years. Losing my mum was hard. No parents to talk to, no one to believe, no one to trust. I will have to grow up through the rest of my life with no parents. No one to share my accomplishments with, no one to whinge to when I'm upset, no one to share my good times with. To this day, I am still shocked and can't believe this has happened to me. I have lost my mother and father. There is nothing worse. I have had to give up my West Lakes Shore life and I am forced to live here with my grandmother at Netley, away from my friends and lifestyle. My whole life has been ruined from that day. My mother was taken from me. I will never get to grow up sharing my life with her. You had a great life with the surf club, great friends, nice house, a family that loved you and you threw all that away for one stupid woman, one stupid mistake which ruined the lives of everyone around you. Your family, friends and especially the lives of your three sons. We will have to go through the rest of our lives thinking: 'Why, how could this happen to us?' It's obvious you didn't think of anyone else but yourself. You didn't think about the lives this has affected around you. How three boys will grow up the rest of our lives without parent guidance to help us through our toughest times. You will never be forgiven for this. How could anyone forgive you?"

Kaylene Kenyon to her best friend's husband: "I came to realise what a callous, conniving and totally selfish man you really are, Kevin. Not one thought for anyone else. During the trial, it came out that Michelle and David would like to pay me a visit and this has affected our teenage daughter. As the newspaper stories came daily, she started reading them and cutting them out at school for me. She became wary of anyone approaching us when we're out. Two years and a guilty verdict down the track, I still have days where I cry for hours over the senselessness of this crime. Twice in my life, I have felt a stabbing physical pain in my heart that cannot be consoled. Once when our son Shane passed over – you even named your son after him, such was the bond – the second was Carolyn's passing. You, Kevin, knew without a doubt when you picked up the boys what was about to happen and you knew what they would find on their return. They will see and pay forever. The only thought you had was for yourself. Why couldn't you just walk away? You have betrayed us, taken away our trust, taken my friend from me, her children from their mum. How dare you? Our lives are changed forever. We will never forgive you."

A statement written on behalf of Carolyn's grandmother Iris Baldock, to her granddaughter's husband: "Carolyn was her first granddaughter. The loss of Carolyn has caused so much grief and trauma at the age of 86; it has become very difficult for her to cope with all the stress. Until Carolyn's death, Iris's life was like any happy, bright independent 85-year-old, but now her life is full of pain and turmoil."

Charlie Tidswell to Michelle Burgess: "What on God's Earth were you thinking when you hatched such an evil and stupid plan? Did you really think you would live a long and happy life with Kevin by killing Carolyn? You have destroyed the rest of your life. Your children's, your parents' and maybe some of your so-called friends' lives. Was this relationship worth the long-term consequences and heartache? My questions will probably never be answered but I hope you will reflect on them while you spend the best part of your life in jail without the freedom to enjoy the relationships you long for."

Many of these statements, and others, were read in court on February 26, 2004. Kevin Matthews remained unmoved and emotionless through all of them. But when Mr Millsteed rejected a suggestion that Matthews had been manipulated by Michelle Burgess into arranging his wife's murder, Matthews's apathy turned to anger. "That's bullshit ... more guesses," he cried before slumping in the Supreme Court dock with his head in his hands.

The court was also told about a rambling, abusive letter Kevin had written to Darren Burgess dated September 27, 2003 – after the trial verdict.

Part of it read: "Well Darren, all I can say is I hope you are proud of yourself. You and your northern suburbs ferral (sic) friends caused the death of Carolyn by putting your noses in where it was not wanted.

"You set off a chain of events that has seen my children lose their mother to another northern suburbs feral dog and scumbag in David Key. Surely you are not naïve enough to believe you are blameless in my wife's death.

"Now that the trial is over I can confirm to you that your jealous, immature perverted mind got it wrong. You mistook friendship to be an affair. How feeble-minded can you be? Your jealousy was the seed planted that resulted in the death of my wife by another jealous cocksucker in Key.

"You are and have been blind to the fact that all I ever done was encourage Michelle to fight to get you back, if not for love but for financial reasons and the benefit of your kids.

"The trial is over so they can't touch me. I'm quite happy where I am. No people or things to fuck me off or hide from. No responsibilities, no pain and plenty of laughs.

"Just wanted you to know I hold you responsible for interfering with my marriage and causing a chain of events that led to Carolyn being stabbed to death. Hope your thoughts of the total fear she must have gone through all in the name of your jealous pride.

"You once thanked me for taking Michelle from you. Well you were wrong and you got it wrong. But given what has happened to us both, you can be proud of the fact that your old man pushed us together. So it's I who thank you.

"Well, as long as you are happy at my children's expense. As long as you are proud to be a dog. Nice to be all buddy buddy with the dog coppers but you'll now realise they used you. I love it here so fuck you!!!!

"PS give my future stepchildren a big sloppy kiss from me. Regards, Kevin."

If Matthews wanted the court to show some mercy when he was sentenced, his idiotic behaviour was doing him no favours.

On Friday, April 2, 2004, Justice Nyland delivered the non-parole period requested by Steven Millsteed: 30 years, which was 10 years more than Key. Although some murderers had received longer non-parole periods in South Australia, they were all prior to Truth in Sentencing laws and therefore automatically entitled to one-third off their sentence. That meant that Matthews's and Michelle's sentences were effectively the longest non-parole periods for a single murder in the state's history. Michelle's sentence was unmatched by any woman in South Australia – and possibly the nation – until 2011, when Acting Chief Justice Nyland would sentence 36-year-old mother Angelika Gavare for another crime that seemingly could only have occurred in Adelaide. She murdered and dismembered her 82-year-old neighbour Vonne McGlynn with the aim of selling the pensioner's possessions and home for her own benefit, then lied through her teeth in a failed bid to cover up the horrendous crime.

When Justice Nyland announced Michelle's sentence, the public gallery broke into spontaneous applause. Matthews briefly waved to his mother and sister, while Michelle remained impassive.

Kaylene Kenyon recalls: "I started the applause in court when they were sentenced. Carolyn is gone, but they are going to pay. That's very important to me. Carolyn's kids lost their mum and Darren's kids lost their mum. They all suffered terribly. I can't believe they're still breathing. I think capital punishment is the best punishment for people like that. They're never going to change. Carolyn was a good person. She was a Leo – she was loyal. She was my friend."

Justice Nyland said the killers' determination to continue their affair at any cost "provided the motive for this terrible crime". She said neither defendant had shown any remorse for the "premeditated, heartless and brutal crime". The judge said Mrs Matthews was a decent, hard-working woman and a loving mother.

"Although Key was the person who actually killed Mrs Matthews, I am satisfied that he was only the instrument for the execution of plans made by the two of you to get rid of Mrs Matthews," Justice Nyland said. "I consider your criminality, in fact, to be greater than that of Key. This was a crime which, in my opinion, was committed out of lust and greed. In my view, that places it in the most serious category of crimes of murder. Addressing Matthews, she said: "A particularly callous aspect of your conduct was allowing your sons to find their mother's bloodied body."

Shane Tidswell recalls: "I went to dad's sentencing. I didn't want to look at my old man, I was full of hate. But then, I would look up when he wasn't looking at us. I almost felt a little bit of pity, but then, not. After all, he had been our dad. I think that was the most hurtful thing."

After sentencing had concluded, *Advertiser* reporter Simonne Reid and photographer Michael Milnes followed Matthews to the court's underground car park, seeking a final photograph. Matthews obliged, providing a front-page picture.

Reid recalls: "We were right up at the window and he had his cuffs on and he turned and blew us a kiss." While Kevin headed back to Yatala, and Michelle to Northfield, Carolyn's family and friends gathered at a Central Market bar with the prosecution team and detectives, who had worked so hard to deliver the bittersweet victory. Together, they raised their glasses to justice – and to Carolyn.

NO CHARGES were ever laid over the murder contract on Darren Burgess's life – although, in the event of not guilty verdicts in the murder trial, it is likely that police would have pursued every last avenue available to them to gain convictions. But since this did not happen, Darren, Kathy and the four children they jointly parent, were not considered victims of crime, at least in the eyes of the law. For the next decade, newspaper and magazine journalists, documentary makers and writers pursued Darren, wanting him to reveal the details of his relationship with Michelle and the events of 2000 and 2001.

Before agreeing to cooperate with this book, his only public statements were the intense grilling he faced on the witness stand in 2003 and, at the request of police, he agreed to a brief interview for the *PASA* in 2010, focused on the impact of crime on victims. He was determined to put Michelle behind him and rebuild his life and the lives of his children. In the immediate aftermath of Michelle's arrest, Darren had hoped that he and the children would be able to start a new life, free of her dangerous manipulation. When she was found guilty, he dared to believe it. But even behind bars, Michelle Burgess retained enough power to cause heartache and havoc.

After her arrest, the courts had immediately granted Darren day-to-day care of his children. On December 18, 2001, the Goldups were granted monthly visits with their grandchildren. In January 2002, a year after Darren left his wife, and while she was still on remand for murder, their divorce was finalised. In March 2002, after extensive interviews with the family, a psychologist recommended that the children be allowed to visit their mother in prison.

Darren recalls: "It was March 2002 before Michelle saw the kids again. I didn't want them going to a jail. But she was presumed innocent and the courts said she should have the same rights as any other parent. Obviously there were restrictions because of where she was, but fortnightly visits were approved. They would be climbing the walls when they came home. Kathy bore the brunt of it. They would be fine at home and then go on a visit, and I don't know what was said to them, but they would take it out on Kathy, call her names. After sentencing, they returned to the psychologist who recommended that the visits be reduced to once a month and that I not take them. My lawyer said I could fight it, but they said it was likely that the court would go with what the psychologist recommended. Michelle insisted she wanted them every second week.

"We hired a barrister who said we could take the matter to trial but it would cost us $2500 a day and it would take five days or longer. It got to a pre-trial hearing. And Michelle was getting legal aid, not paying a cent. The situation had already cost me thousands, so I had no choice but to drop the matter.

"My daughter has maintained fortnightly visits but my son's visits ceased when he was 12 or 13. He didn't explain why, but I got the feeling he didn't want to see her anymore because of what she'd done. But I believe he has a bit to do with her now. When he was about 16, he got his licence. He wanted to buy a car. He was staying at Michelle's parents' home, I think on school holidays. His grandmother rang me and said: 'He's getting a car and that's it. He's bought a V8 Holden'. I said: 'He's not getting a V8 Holden'. She said: 'He's already paid a deposit'. I said: 'I don't care, he can lose the deposit. You try to get a V8 insured with a teenage driver.' That fell through. But he bought another car and hid it from us for two weeks. We went to parent-teacher night and they said he was causing grief at the school. There were some other issues too and he called up his grandmother one night and she raced over here and got him and said he could live with her. It's not perfect but at least he's not couch surfing. He's got no rules, does what he likes and goes where he wants. Within a week of him moving out, I had the police on my doorstep complaining about his driving.

"With regard to my daughter, I honestly think that she can't move on with her life, nor can my son, until Michelle admits what she's done. She's still telling them she didn't do it. In the heat of the moment, I've told my daughter I don't want her to end up like her mother, and she'll say: 'But she hasn't done anything'. Because that's what she's being told. I think if she could accept what her mother has done, she could move on with her life. She loves her mother and I'm not stopping her from seeing her. But she's living in this grey area because of this element of doubt.

"There is not a day in my life that goes by that I don't think about everything that's happened. Kathy's been there with me all the way through it. She pulls me in line when I need to, helps me stop dwelling on things. There are a lot of people worse off in life than us.

"I was previously a bit softer, a bit of a push-over. Now, I don't take shit. I'm a stronger person. Even at work, as a manager, I have no trouble voicing my authority. (If I could have done anything differently) I would have walked away after the first affair. I would never have gone back. Michelle realised she could do whatever she liked. I have a much better life now. I'm a happy man.

"I hope that later in life, my daughter will choose to read this book. But she might not want to know about it. There is a lot in this book I didn't know about. It infuriates me that so many other people knew what was going on but never said anything."

In his victim impact statement, which was only considered in relation to Jason Colenso's crime, Darren Burgess wrote:

"I believe we will not know the full impact this will have on our children's lives until they are much older. I know that they are in a much better place now than they were when all this happened. Michelle, I believe, could not have given them any thought whatsoever, as anybody in that position, separating with a young family, would have put them first and foremost. To do what she has done is unspeakable. That she could have done this to her children. The kids are well looked after by my fiancée Katherine Morton and by myself, with help from my parents. I couldn't ask for any better people for my children to be around as they are doing well with the current situation, no thanks to Michelle.

"After the murder, my son also said he overheard David and Michelle organising the murder. I thought that maybe it was a little boy fantasising and making up stories until the murder trial, when I heard the evidence and this is when it hit home that my son must have overheard conversations. Our phones were tapped because we kept receiving menacing phone calls. We were constantly feeling like we were being watched and followed. This was no way to live. This has cost us, both Kathy and I, some close friendships with family and friends. They don't want to be associated with us because of some silly belief that we are mixed up in the case. I guess in one way this is a good thing because we have learnt who our good friends and close family are. They are the ones who have stuck by us and supported us."

Darren Burgess and Kathy Morton married in December, 2012.

KEVIN MATTHEWS lodged an appeal against his sentence on October 30, 2003. He listed three grounds for appeal:

1. That Justice Nyland erred by not ordering separate trials for he and Michelle.
2. That the verdict was "unsafe and unsatisfactory" and "contrary to the evidence".
3. That Justice Nyland should have ordered a retrial when one juror withdrew from the case, saying they were "unable to continue".

When he made a court appearance for the appeal on June 21, 2004, he was smiling, happily chatting to a sheriff's officer and pointing out people in the gallery. But he was visibly stunned when he heard that Michelle had also appealed and wanted it heard at the same time as his appeal.

On July 12, 2004, the third anniversary of the murder, Matthews again faced court. Supreme Court Justice Ted Mullighan asked him if he wanted to sit next to his former lover, for the first time since their trial had ended. Matthews responded with a slow and solemn shake of his head. As a result, he and Michelle appeared in court one after the other. Her grounds of appeal were that Justice Nyland:

1. Did not leave it open for the jury to find her guilty of an alternative crime, such as impeding an investigation or assisting an offender.
2. Did not allow into evidence materials relating to her estranged husband and to Kathleen Cowled, the woman who introduced her to Key.
3. Allowed into evidence records of mobile phone messages between her and Matthews.
4. Commented to the jury about witness accounts of Michelle visiting Matthews at his work while accompanied by Key.

Both asked for their respective appeals against their convictions to be adjourned. Matthews's appeal had already been given the go-ahead to proceed and, on November 5, 2004, the Supreme Court also granted Michelle leave to appeal. Her list of grounds had grown to 17, and the court approved 12 of them.

Their court victories were incomprehensible to the Tidswell family. Was it possible, after all that the court had heard and accepted as the truth, that these two killers could win a retrial or even walk free? It was a long and agonising wait. Finally, on July 29, 2005, Justices Kevin Duggan, Bruce Debelle and Robyn Layton delivered their unanimous decision in the Court of Criminal Appeal. At the end of 20,000 words of mind-numbing legalese came the long-awaited decision – appeals dismissed. The judges found that none of the evidence presented amounted to a miscarriage of justice, and that Michelle and Matthews were not prejudiced by having a joint trial.

Outside court, Yvonne Tidswell said: "I'm relieved, very, very much so, that it's all over ... I did not want to go through it all again."

THE FORMER family home was sold in April 2002 after the Matthews boys made the difficult decision to sell it. In reality, they had little choice, since all of them were school age and in no position to pay the mortgage.

Shane Tidswell says: "(After the murder) we had moved back into West Lakes, because in the aftermath we got the ultimatum to move. Yvonne was staying with us at West Lakes and then we got the ultimatum to move to my nanna's (Irene Matthews's) place or to move up to my grandma's (Yvonne's) place. They asked us what we wanted to do to the house and told us, the longer we hold on to the house, the more expensive it's going to get for us because nobody can actually pay for it.

"We were like, just sell the house, because it came down to our decision, I guess. Financially it was probably a good thing at the time but if we'd held on to that house for five more years and sold it, oh my god, the amount we would have got for it."

After the sale, an application was lodged with the Lands Titles Office for the large block to be subdivided. Approval was granted for two smaller homes to be built and demolition of the home began on April 6, 2004, four days after the killers were sentenced. As it was reduced to rubble, the kitchen walls were one of the last parts of the house to fall.

Every cent Kevin Matthews could lay his hands on went towards his legal bills. His sons were not only left without parents, they were also left penniless. In line with standard practice, the boys and three other family members sued the State of South Australia and the three killers for compensation. In their statements of claim, the boys sought the maximum $50,000 for psychological injury and financial loss. Each received a payout in a confidential settlement. Because of Kevin's murder conviction, the $100,000 insurance policy on Carolyn's life was never paid out.

Shane says: "It was a little bit weird getting victims of crime money. Because the only thing we ever inherited from our parents was the victims of crime money, I guess. My auntie sold everything my dad had so he could continue paying his lawyer. By the end of it, we didn't inherit anything from them, maybe a couple of grand. But the victims of crime money came in handy. Kenny owns two units now and I own a house. And we wouldn't have been able to do that without that money there. And Daniel's going to buy a house when he's finished his apprenticeship.

"I became independent at the age of 13. I worked at Hungry Jack's when I was younger. I had to pay for my own school uniforms. I was thrust into maturity a lot younger than I should have been. Which was probably why I rebelled a lot when I was 16."

In the wake of their father's arrest, the three boys made the practical decision to live with Kevin's mother, Irene Matthews, because Kenny and Shane's school was a short distance from her Semaphore home. When Kenny finished school, he moved in with Yvonne and Shane later did the same. When Kenny bought a unit, Shane moved in with him. Later, when Irene moved into a retirement village, Shane bought her home with her blessing and moved back in with Daniel.

Shane says: "We are probably closer now than we have ever been in our lives. There was a period afterwards where I didn't even speak to either of my brothers for about a year. Just because, I think, I was going in a different direction."

Explaining why he changed his name from Matthews to Tidswell, Shane says: "I did that before I turned 18. I wanted to do it because I figured that at the time it happened, I was 13 and the two most important people in my life were my mum and my dad. My dad did something wrong and my mum didn't. I think I did it half just to piss my old man off. And half as a memorial to my mum. I did the paperwork a month before my birthday. I remember going into the Births, Deaths and Marriages and I said I wanted to change my name, so they gave me the form, said: 'Fill this out and we'll have an interview with you and talk about why'. I remember I filled out the form and it says 'reason' at the bottom. I wrote 'because my father murdered my mother I am changing my name from my old man's name to my mum's name'. I am assuming that when they have the interview with you they're supposed to dwell on why, but when they read that, they didn't say a thing, they just said: 'Yep, no worries, sign here'. Done.

"I've got birth certificates saying what my last name was on the back. I don't think my brothers would (do it), purely out of respect to my dad's family. I did it because I just really wanted to piss my old man off, I guess. It was the only thing I could do that would really get to him. It was one of the main reasons. I sent him a copy of my new birth certificate and he wasn't too happy. That was the effect I was going for.

"It's so difficult to comprehend (what he did). He was just a down-to-earth, head-screwed-on sort of bloke. But I guess that's what happens when … well, the way Michelle is and the way she can manipulate people. And that's what she did to my old man. But I don't want anything to do with my old man, ever. As far as I'm concerned, it was a lifetime ago. I wouldn't be the person I am now without it happening. I'm not saying it should have happened or anything, but I am probably a better person than if it didn't happen. Then again, I would never want it to happen to anyone's family for any reason. It has affected me a great deal. I was diagnosed with post-traumatic stress disorder, went through depression, anxiety and stress, all at the same time and a sort of breakdown a few years ago. But I'm over that as well and getting on with my life."

Shane says he's happy to talk about his mother, but when asked about his memories of her, there is a 10-second pause.

"I don't know really. To be quite honest, I've blocked out as much as I can from before that time. It feels like it happened a lifetime before. And I guess I never really think about it. It just happened and that was it. I just put everything out of my mind … I don't know how to say it. I'm not one to dwell on things, so I haven't let myself think about mum too much at all. Just trying to think now, I can't think of any moments that stand out. It's what happened before she died and what happened after. I know that she was always there for us and always did everything for us. I know she was a bit of a hard arse because I'd been sent home sick (from school) more than mum had actually let me stay home sick. I guess both of my parents worked a lot. It was hard for us to be home sick. We only stayed home if we were really sick.

"I got a tattoo a few years ago when I was 18. It's got my mum's birth and death date on it as well. It was my first tattoo when I was younger. I just thought something simple like the footy black armband. It means more to me than anything."

In *Contract Killers: Who Killed Carolyn Matthews?* – a documentary which screened on Foxtel's Crime & Investigation channel in 2011 – Shane said: "It upsets me a lot these days that my brothers and I never had the chance to be friends with our mum. I've seen all my mates and their parents getting along and going down to the pub and have a beer with their old man. It's not so much like a mother-father-child role. They've created that friendship. I feel something that I've missed out on – and I'm sure she would feel the same – is having that friendship. And not having to scream at us because we've been naughty all the time; to be able to appreciate our company."

Each of the boys has struggled in their own way to cope with the unfathomable losses they have endured. They were robbed of their parents, their home and the lives they had before July 12, 2001. But, surrounded by a loving and protective extended family and the fiercely protective members of the Semaphore Surf Life Saving Club, they have survived and, against the odds, flourished. Their family unanimously agrees that Carolyn would be proud of each of the strong, independent young men they have become.

WHILE MICHELLE BURGESS had sought "love" with prison guards, Kevin Matthews embarked on his own search for romance. In August 2009, it emerged that he had placed two entries on the American-based lonely hearts website LostVault.com. He provided his personal details, an obligatory poem and also wrote:

"Smile, my name is Kevin and I am seeking female pen friends of any age. Life in jail can be very lonely and I love receiving letters, it makes all the difference. I am very respectful and an honest person. I'm a good listener and friend. If you write me I will definitely reply. Please ask any questions you like of me, my interests are poetry and making people happy. Give me a chance, you won't regret it."

On another page he protests his innocence:

"I was arrested on 7th October 2001 and convicted of a crime I maintain I am innocent of. Never the less I received a life sentence with a 30 year non-parole period. I've not given up on proving my innocence in the future. I have three young adult sons and I am a widower, I love to write to female pen friends only and I also love to write poetry to which I've been published in USA more than once. You can ask me any questions and I'll answer. If you write I will definitely write back. You will find me honest, caring, genuine and a good friend, I am kind and life in jail is lonely so please give me a go and you will not regret your friend in me."

The entry also included a picture of a mournful-looking Matthews, now sporting a long, grey beard. Correctional Services Minister Tom Koutsantonis told the *Sunday Mail*'s Nigel Hunt that it was inappropriate for prisoners to have access to such websites and called on their operators to act more responsibly.

"I was disgusted that a website would deem it appropriate to humiliate the memory of the victim and to antagonise the victims' families that are left behind, given the brutal nature of this murder and his conviction," he said. "I immediately wrote to the website ... given how inappropriate and disturbing it is to the victims.

"This is completely abhorrent and unfair to the victims that are left behind. Our major concern has always been that we put the interests of the victims first and we do not want in any way victims having to re-live what happened to them over and over again by prisoners resuming a normal life behind bars. That will not be happening."

It emerged that Matthews had given the details and the photograph to a friend, who sent it to the website. Both pages were removed after Mr Koutsantonis complained to the website's operators.

Sgt Mick Standing smiles with grim satisfaction when recalling the final result of the case: "Kevin's conviction was the cream on the cake. With the evidence that was available against Kevin, I thought it might be a bit thin. We certainly had sufficient to charge him. But I think the jury ... understood that he sent those boys in after he got that phone call. Once they accepted that had happened and we could prove that had happened, that was a huge strong point in convicting him.

"I think Kevin is a sleazebag. If you go down to the Semaphore Surf Life Saving Club and look for his name on the boards, you won't find it. They have removed everything. I don't think they even refer to him down there anymore. But everyone thought he was a great bloke. There were other things that Kevin Matthews did – things that I can't talk about – that suggest that he was not the up-front guy he wanted everyone to believe he was. (For legal reasons, these allegations cannot be revealed.)

"We'll never know what other women he had affairs with. He was a big man. He had it all before him. But I think he thought he was a bigger man than he really was. He was a louse for what he did, not only to his wife, but to his boys. Sending them in the house when he knew what they were going to find. What sort of a man would do that?"

SC Keane says: "I've heard that to this day Kevin doesn't think he's done anything wrong and he doesn't understand why he's in jail. But that's the sort of person he is. He's convinced himself he's done nothing wrong."

Sgt Eichner says: "If you believe what everyone's said, he's a totally different person to what he was when he first got married. He's got very good children, they've come through this remarkably well. Yvonne Tidswell has done everything for those kids."

Detective Inspector John Venditto says: "The results reflected the quality and integrity of the police investigation. It is rare to catch both the instigator and the hitman and even rarer to obtain a successful prosecution against all of those involved in the contract."

THERE IS deep sadness in Yvonne Tidswell's eyes. But she is also a woman of remarkable strength, and she shares it with people who need it most. After her daughter's death, she became an integral part of the Homicide Victim Support Group, founded in 1994 by Lynette Nitschke, whose daughter Allison, 18, was murdered by a fellow boarder at St Mark's College in North Adelaide.

Of the group's 15 regular members, Yvonne is one of only two who has seen a killer brought to justice. She says: "I feel that with other people now, I can help because I've been there, done that, in court and you can help others in that way. You go around the table there, and there's the two killed overseas and nothing's been done about it, (another victim's mother) and they know who's done it, and they can't prove he's done it. I'm one of the few that's got justice."

When Carolyn's dog Max died in November 2008, Yvonne was shattered. He had been her constant companion and was always by her side whenever she visited Carolyn's memorial plaque.

"I couldn't replace Max. I miss him when we go to the cemetery. He'd roll around there in the bark, as if he knew. I tell the boys (her sons) I miss Max more than I miss them," she laughs.

"I paid for her funeral and the headstone; he never paid me back, of course. But it was the least I could do. I tried to get it changed (the plaque includes the line: 'Adored wife of Kevin') but he'd signed for it. The only way would be for him to sign it over to Kenny, the eldest. I put tape over it; when the weather gets to it and it peels off, I put another bit round. I did put a bit of elastic around it once, but it didn't stay. The boys said you could always angle-grind it off, but that's defacing other people's property – you'd be in big strife."

There are many photographs in Yvonne and Doug Tidswell's lounge room, a place which has seen their family grow and prosper. In one picture, Kenny, Shane and Daniel are all smiling, the happiest of families. Their proud mum is also in the picture, but their father has been digitally removed. For this family, he has gone forever.

MICHELLE BURGESS remains in Adelaide Women's Prison at Northfield and maintains her innocence. She receives regular visits from her parents and her daughter. Male prison guards ensure they are never left alone with her.

DAVID KEY, who was warned as a teenager by his sisters that "one day you'll get locked up for murder and no one will come and see you", was transferred to a Perth prison on July 13, 2010 to be closer to his parents. They had left South Australia in the wake of their son's brutal crime. Before his transfer, there was an 18-month period in which he had no visitors.

KEVIN MATTHEWS remains a high-security prisoner at Port Augusta Prison and is scheduled to be transferred to Mt Gambier Prison in 2018. He continues to maintain that he did not have an affair with Michelle Burgess and did not kill his wife. He still writes nauseating poetry.

SOMEWHERE, in an alternative universe, Carolyn Matthews is a happily divorced mother-of-three whose life is flourishing after she found the courage to walk away from her selfish, cowardly, cheating husband. Like her mother, she will become a proud, doting grandmother, a powerful gravitational force who holds her family in a safe and loving orbit. Carolyn remains utterly committed to the Semaphore Surf Life Saving Club, and to her business, but these pursuits always take a back seat to her precious boys and their lives.

Her inexhaustible energy, her genuine love for life and all its joys and tragedies, has grown stronger, no longer suffocated by a man who was never worthy of all she had to give. The bitter truth, though, is that Carolyn is gone, robbed of the chance to live the fruitful and happy life she worked so hard for and deserved. But in the hearts and minds of her mother, her sons and the rest of her beloved family, Missy's mischievous smile lives forever.

CHAPTER 19

Profile of a killer

WHAT MOTIVATED Michelle Burgess's malevolence? Of all the questions that her bizarre actions have raised, this, ultimately, is the one that has never adequately been answered.

Was she really driven by lust and greed? Or was it much more complicated? After compiling a forensic profile of Michelle, Dr Jack White believes the latter. He is an Adelaide psychologist who has been in practice since 1986 and has specialised in Forensic Psychology since 1990. He is a former National Chair of the Australian Psychological Society College of Forensic Psychologists (1996–2000) who combines clinical work with teaching Forensic Psychology in the Masters program at the University of South Australia.

Dr White was also one of the experts to whom David Key's lawyers turned when they were trying to establish their client's competence. With Key's co-operation, Dr White was able to produce a thorough profile detailing not only who he was, but also how he came to be a dysfunctional, drug-addled criminal of low intelligence with limited prospects.

No such analysis had ever been conducted of Michelle Burgess and Dr White says he would usually interview a subject before drawing detailed conclusions. But with Michelle unavailable for interview, he agreed that the research for this book contained sufficient information for him to form a speculative forensic profile of her. After completing it, even he was surprised by its findings, commenting: "I must say that my conclusion was something I did not see coming and it may raise some interesting legal questions." In the context of the murder case, the assertions he makes are nothing short of extraordinary; but they carry no legal weight because all appeals in the case have been finalised; any chance Michelle had to change her fate is long gone.

A Psychological Profile of Michelle Burgess
Dr Jack White

Writing psychological reports for court matters involves evaluating offenders who come from varied backgrounds and who commit the most notorious crimes.

Robert Joe Wagner, a hardened killer associated with 10 of the Snowtown murders, was a victim of extreme childhood sexual abuse. He told his story of sexual abuse to his parents and the police, but reported being disbelieved by the authority figures.

Michael Barry Fyfe, the Birdman of Yatala, murdered former policeman Joe Tilley in the prison kitchen. Fyfe refused to offer any explanation as to why he committed the murder and has remained in solitary confinement continuously since 1996. As a child, Fyfe was repeatedly sexually abused by his father and forced to have sex with his sister until the age of 14 years.

Such cases illustrate extremes of human behaviour and expose critical elements that influence response patterns. As a psychologist, it is remarkable to observe how predictable human behaviour can be, especially in the context of criminal behaviour. While media and politicians often advance the proposition that certain humans are "evil", when all the data is taken into account, such a concept is rarely accurate and most often simplistic and misleading.

Work done by a forensic psychologist is akin to solving a complex jigsaw puzzle. The assessment process begins with determining the critical pieces of the puzzle and then putting them together in a logical manner. The jigsaw pieces include information from a variety of sources: client history, psychometric testing and collateral data. The critical jigsaw pieces are defined by empirical and theoretical criteria and putting the pieces together utilises an overall assessment model where the relationship between the components is logically connected. The model predicts psychological output in terms of mental health dysfunction, addictive and dysfunctional behaviours. So what are the core elements (or pieces of the jigsaw puzzle) needed to profile an individual in order to make predictions of subsequent behaviour?

From a personal history perspective, important information includes family background (for example, the individual's relationship with parents, siblings, grandparents); exposure to trauma (emotional, physical, sexual); education (relationship with peers, scholastic achievement); relationship history; childhood behavioural problems; health and mental health history and exposure to substance abuse.

From an individual difference perspective, genetics and environment play an important role in determining the individual's "psychological strength".

The person's intelligence is the first genetic/environmental element that defines an individual's psychological strength and reflects the person's capacity to solve life problems. An "above average" intelligent individual may have the resources to solve problems more easily than the "below average" intelligent individual, who will be more inclined to making poorer decisions that are often impulsive. Individuals with limited cognitive skills are challenged in their capacity to think through solutions to problems, and this in turn may lead to further psychological impairment (frustration, aggression and low self-image).

By contrast, individuals capable of solving problems are more likely to obtain practical solutions to life's stressors. An individual's personality is the second genetic/environmental measure of psychological strength. It relates to the person's capacity to cope with the stresses of life. The neuroticism component of personality defines the individual's intrinsic psychological strength for coping, such that low neuroticism reflects qualities of emotional stability and resilience, while high neuroticism reflects vulnerability and the likelihood of psychological impairment when the individual is subjected to stress.

The next component of the model involves external supports. This will include the support the person has from family, friends and professional supports. Without adequate supports, the individual is more vulnerable to psychological problems.

Next, the assessment model critically examines the impact and strength of a person's life stressors that include: family trauma (the death of a spouse, child, parent or friend); relationship changes (divorce, partner separation); family changes (marriage, pregnancy, birth); education (school failure, school changes, bullying); employment issues (workload excesses, conflict, dismissal, retirement); health and mental health issues (injury or illness); victim of abuse (physical, sexual or emotional); traumatic events (for example, flood, fire disasters, victim of crime, motor vehicle accident etc.); financial issues (loss of housing, foreclosure on a mortgage or loan); financial debts (drugs, gambling, legal costs); substance use (excessive alcohol and drug issues) and legal issues (court trial, incarceration).

Finally, the model requires a measure of client motivation, which reflects the individual's desire to provide a functional response. In situations where dysfunction offers benefits (for example, compensation payment or avoidance of criminal responsibility) this measure can be an important component in determining functional output.

Thus, the assessment model predicts psychological dysfunction when there is an imbalance between the protective forces. The system is vulnerable to collapse, when the person's internal resources (personality and intelligence) are weak; and/or when the individual has inadequate supports; and/or when the stressors are too great; and/or when the motivation to protect the system from collapse is impaired.

So how can this model be applied to understanding the profile of Michelle Burgess?

Because Michelle Burgess was unwilling to provide information about herself or to undertake any psychometric assessment, details associated with her history and psychological make-up have been constructed around the "collateral" information and, when no data was available, a best estimate was determined relevant to known criteria.

The first important component in understanding Ms Burgess relates to her parents and her relationship with them.

From a psychological perspective, children typically model their behaviour on a parent with whom they identify closely, and this modelling may reflect both positive and negative attributes. Ms Burgess's flirtatious nature was likely a key attribute she learnt from her father.

The impact of parental separation varies considerably between individuals, and can often have a significant influence in the person's development depending upon their age at the time and the circumstances of the marital breakdown. Children who are very young may not always appreciate the consequences of their parents separating. Older children may also be less affected as their development is largely completed. Most often, children in their adolescence have difficulty coping with the consequences of parental separation. As a rule of thumb, adverse outcomes are roughly twice as prevalent among children of divorced families compared with children from intact families.

Such negative outcomes include: greater financial hardship; less socio-economic achievement; increased risk of behavioural problems (including withdrawn behaviour, aggression, delinquency and other antisocial behaviour); poorer academic achievement; greater sexual activity (earlier cohabitation, higher likelihood of pregnancy and parenthood); more depressive symptoms and greater alcohol and substance use.

In Ms Burgess's case, it was apparent that she became pregnant and cohabitated early (aged 18 years), had poor academic achievement (not completing beyond Year 9 level), exhibited behavioural problems (high truancy at school) and engaged in significant alcohol abuse.

As the youngest of five children (two brothers and two sisters), this may have had an important influence on Ms Burgess's development. Typically, youngest children may develop good social skills, fostered by constant peer interaction, but may have difficulty establishing autonomy in adulthood, frequently feeling inferior to others. This is likely to be compounded by the realisation that throughout childhood, everyone else was stronger, older and more competent and they were never able to compete on an equal footing.

While Ms Burgess appeared competent socially, she lacked confidence to establish her independence and as an adult was constantly seeking the company of others (usually males). She had a skill in manipulating others for her own benefit and targeted the weaknesses of others in order to charm and exploit their personal vulnerabilities. This control contrasted with her own weakness of needing to be wanted and desired by others.

A core feature of her psychological make-up was her insatiable sexual appetite. Ms Burgess was focused on having many sexual conquests as a feature of her psychological make-up. At least 11 sexual partners were identified between 1990 and 2004. David Key described her as having sex, "throughout the house or in the car – sometimes twice a day". While she was frequently described as being a "plain Jane" she was generally perceived by others as being promiscuous and seductive with irresistible sexual charm.

Sexual promiscuity and hyper-sexuality can be a symptom of bipolar disorder, especially associated with the manic phase of the condition. Sexual predatory behaviour may also reflect a person's immature understanding of intimacy. The person really wants closeness, but lacks the emotional elements of satisfaction and trust. Typical characteristics of sexual predators include: a sense of entitlement, low self-esteem, a need for power and control, lack of empathy and an inability to form intimate relationships. Ms Burgess exhibited characteristics of manic hyper-sexuality, immaturity and a need for control.

The Psychometric Profile
In order to construct a psychometric profile of Ms Burgess, standard personality and clinical psychometric tools were adapted utilising estimates of Ms Burgess's responses based on her background history and details provided by the individuals who knew her best.

Intellectual Profile
Estimating a person's level of intelligence can often be misleading by basing the estimate solely around the "clinical interview" because this can create a bias where people with more verbal and social skills are perceived to be more intelligent, when in fact this is only one aspect of intellectual ability. Best estimates of intellectual ability are made with standardised instruments. In the absence of being able to formally assess Ms Burgess, the next best estimate was likely based around her schooling achievements.

In this context, it was indicated that Ms Burgess did not progress in her schooling beyond Year 9 level and dropped out during Year 10. Further, it was indicated that Ms Burgess tended to be a truant student and was not motivated for scholastic success. Similarly, Ms Burgess's work history did not indicate that she was particularly endowed with intellectual prowess; her talents did not progress her beyond working as a checkout operator in a supermarket. On the basis of such data, it was likely that Ms Burgess was intellectually in the "low average" range of intelligence. As such, her general problem-solving skills were likely to be limited and she was more likely to be impulsive with her decision-making.

Personality Profile
The NEO Personality Inventory-Revised was used to measure Ms Burgess's personality using a dimensional approach. The instrument is a standardised self-report measure, which includes 240 items. It is a sophisticated psychometric tool that allows the clinician to measure personality traits, which characterise the individual and provide information, which can

assist the assessment of likely responsiveness to treatment, and prognosis prediction. The instrument generates a personality profile that includes five factors:

1. Neuroticism (emotionally stable vs unstable).
2. Extraversion (outgoing/energetic vs solitary/reserved).
3. Openness (inventive/curious vs consistent/cautious).
4. Agreeableness (friendly/compassionate vs cold/unkind).
5. Conscientiousness (efficient/organised vs easy-going/careless).

The Big Five model is a comprehensive, empirical factor analytically derived model that defines human personality. Ms Burgess's profile indicated that she perceived herself to be a relatively emotionally stable individual who was able to deal effectively with stress and she did not perceive herself as having problems in relation to anxiety, anger-hostility, self-consciousness or vulnerability to stress. She recognised that at times she was inclined to act impulsively. Ms Burgess was superficially a warm and friendly person who was assertive, readily attracted to excitement-seeking activity and was inclined to praise others. She was open about her feelings but conservative with her ideas. She had limited trust in other people and tended to be very stubborn and set in her ways. She was neither altruistic nor straightforward. She lacked tender-mindedness. Ms Burgess perceived herself as being competent, but also indicated that she lacked logical organisation, did not have clear goals, was not very deliberate in following through tasks and lacked dutifulness and deliberation.

Clinical Profile

The Personality Assessment Inventory (PAI) was used to objectively assess aspects of Ms Burgess's clinical profile. The PAI is a standardised self-report questionnaire of 344 items that provides a profile of a person based on his or her responses to items that examine aspects of a person's behaviour and thinking.

The measure includes four primary sets of scales: validity scales, clinical scales, treatment scales, and interpersonal scales. The instrument has been normed with a census-matched standardisation sample (N=1000), college sample (N=1051), clinical sample (N=1,246) and public safety sample group (N=17,757). The following report was based around a computer-generated PAI profile and, as such, was intended to provide a description of Ms Burgess's clinical profile with minimal interpretive bias.

Ms Burgess's PAI clinical profile was marked by significant elevations across a number of different scales, indicating a broad range of clinical features and the likelihood of multiple diagnoses.

The configuration of the clinical scales suggested that she was a person who was impulsive, hostile, bitter and lacked empathy. Her interpersonal relationships were characterised by marked conflict and even those close relationships that were maintained had suffered strain from her hostile and self-centred style. The combination of impulsivity, egocentricity and anger may cause her to lash out impulsively at those whom she felt had slighted her in some way. These same traits also place her at increased risk for acting-out behaviours and it was likely that these behaviours had led to impairment in her ability to maintain her social role expectations.

Ms Burgess had a personality make-up that incorporated numerous antisocial character features. She was unreliable and irresponsible and was unlikely to have success in either the social or occupational realm.

She had a history of antisocial behaviour, which manifested from adolescence and involved illegal acts such as theft, destruction of property, and physical aggression toward others. She was egocentric and showed little regard for others or the opinions of the society around her. In her desire to satisfy her own impulses, she would take advantage of others and had little sense of loyalty, even to those who were closest to her.

While she may report feelings of guilt over past transgressions, she was unlikely to feel remorse of any lasting nature. She placed little importance on her social role responsibilities. Her behaviour was generally reckless and she enjoyed risk-taking behaviour, despite the likely dangers to herself and to those around her. Ms Burgess was suspicious and mistrusted others. Such a pattern is often associated with prominent hostility and paranoia. She was hyper-vigilant and questioned and mistrusted the motives of those around her. She was sensitive in her interactions with others and was likely to harbour strong feelings of resentment as a result of perceived slights and insults. She was quick to feel that she was being treated inequitably and often held grudges against others, even if the perceived affront was unintentional.

Consistent with the constellation of hyper-vigilance, suspiciousness and resentment, she was seen by others as being quite hostile. Working relationships with others were likely to be strained, despite efforts by others to demonstrate support and assistance.

Ms Burgess experienced significant manic problems. She was impulsive and unusually energetic. Her level of activity was high and she was involved in such activities in an overcommitted and disorganised manner.

She experienced accelerated thought processes and the content of her thoughts was marked by inflated self-esteem and grandiosity. Her relationships with others were affected by her frustration that others were unable or unwilling to keep up with her plans and ideas. At its extreme, her irritability resulted in accusations that significant others were attempting to thwart her plans for success and achievement.

Ms Burgess had a history of involvement in intense and volatile relationships and tended to be preoccupied with constant fears of being abandoned or rejected by those around her. She was also impulsive and prone to behaviours likely to be self-harmful or self-destructive, such as in spending, sex and substance abuse. This pattern of impulsivity and volatile relationships may place her at increased risk for self-mutilation or suicidal behaviour, particularly during times of marked conflict in relationships.

Ms Burgess had no significant problems in the areas of unusual thoughts or peculiar experiences, drug abuse or dependence, unhappiness and depression, marked anxiety, problematic behaviours used to manage anxiety, or difficulties with health or physical functioning.

Her self-concept was generally positive, and was indicative of an uncritical self-evaluation. Given her own perceived stable sense of self-worth, the responsibility for any failings in her life were more likely to be attributed to others than to herself.

Ms Burgess's interpersonal style was best characterised as involving a very strong need for attention and affiliation. Such needs may result in her being perceived by others as controlling, which may take the form of interfering with others' social interactions in order to meet her needs. Her need for attention may be sufficiently strong that she will seek any opportunity to interact with others, as long as the interaction permits her to maintain some control over the relationship. This control, perhaps intended as helpful by Ms Burgess, was likely to be viewed less positively by those around her.

Conclusion

Diagnosis

Ms Burgess was given many descriptions: flirtatious, manipulative, promiscuous, seductive, vindictive, impulsive, self-infatuated, narcissistic, dominant, emotionally cold, smug, exploitative, divisive and remorseless. For some she was "a high-class sheila" and the "Queen Bee". For others she was a "Plain Jane" and "Black Widow". The psychological profile indicated that she was a person of limited intellectual ability. Her personality profile indicated that she was low on neuroticism and inclined to act impulsively. She was superficially friendly towards others, assertive and readily attracted to excitement-seeking activities. She was open about her feelings but conservative with her ideas. She had limited trust in other people and tended to be stubborn and set in her ways. She lacked tender-mindedness.

Ms Burgess perceived herself to be competent, yet highly disorganised. Her clinical profile indicated that she was strongly elevated on measures of antisocial behaviour, mania, paranoia and certain elements of borderline personality features. The treatment profile indicated that Ms Burgess was elevated on aggression and stress. The interpersonal profile indicated she was highly dominant and friendly towards others. From a diagnostic perspective, Ms Burgess was likely to satisfy DSM-IV diagnostic criteria for Bipolar I Disorder, Manic (Axis I) and Antisocial Personality Disorder, Narcissistic Personality Disorder and Borderline Personality Disorder (Axis II).

What was the relationship between Ms Burgess's crime and her psychological condition?

On October 9, 2003, a Supreme Court jury in Adelaide found Michelle Burgess and Kevin Matthews guilty of murdering Carolyn Matthews.

David Key was earlier sentenced for his role in the killing. In many respects the murder was impulsive, chaotic and extremely violent. Although it was likely that Ms Burgess had limited direct involvement with the stabbing itself, she was at the scene and was directing and provoking Key to mutilate the victim. Her motive appeared to be more than just pure jealous vengeance in killing her lover's wife. It also appeared to fulfil a wild and crazy fantasy that had been her focus for several weeks prior to the killing. The plan of hiring a moronic, drug-crazed fool as the "hitman" to carry out the murder defied logic, even for a person of low intelligence. The most extremely disturbed psychopathic killers were better organised in the planning of their crimes.

The only "rational" explanation for the bizarre events at West Lakes Shore on July 12, 2001 is that her actions were driven by an acute manic episode (mental illness) where she had lost touch with reality and was manic and delusional.

Mania is characterised by the person having an elevated mood, which can take the form of euphoria. People with mania commonly experience an increase in energy and a decreased need for sleep. A manic person may exhibit pressured speech and racing thoughts. In a manic state, the person may be easily distracted and experience significantly impaired judgment. Typically, those experiencing a manic episode may go on a spending spree or engage in behaviour that is quite abnormal for them. They may indulge in substance abuse, particularly alcohol. Their behaviour may become aggressive, intolerant or intrusive. A manic person may feel out of control or unstoppable, and be "on a special mission" or have other grandiose or delusional ideas. Sexual drive may also increase. At more extreme phases of Bipolar I, a person in a manic state can begin to experience psychosis, or a break with reality, where their thinking is affected along with mood.

Interestingly, the hypothesis that Ms Burgess's behaviour was driven by elements of "mental illness" raises the question of mental impairment, and a possible legal defence. A person can be found "not guilty" by reason of mental impairment (formerly "insanity") if it can be proved (on the balance of probabilities) that as a consequence of the person having a mental illness, the person commits a crime and either does not know what they are doing, or does not know that what they are doing is wrong, or are unable to control their conduct.

Whether Ms Burgess's barrister Gordon Barrett, QC, considered this option can only be speculated upon. Suffice to say, she received the mandatory life sentence with a 30-year non-parole period associated with that sentence.

Wakefield Press is an independent publishing and
distribution company based in Adelaide, South Australia.
We love good stories and publish beautiful books.
To see our full range of books, please visit our website at
www.wakefieldpress.com.au
where all titles are available for purchase.
To keep up with our latest releases, news and events,
subscribe to our monthly newsletter.

Find us!

Facebook: www.facebook.com/wakefield.press
Twitter: www.twitter.com/wakefieldpress
Instagram: www.instagram.com/wakefieldpress

www.ingramcontent.com/pod-product-compliance
Lightning Source LLC
Chambersburg PA
CBHW021804220426

43662CB00006B/169